What others are saying about The Pearson Girls

"*The Pearson Girls* welcomes you into the rich lives of an unforgettable family. The writing is ginger-quick, the tales as clear and focused as Ansel Adams photos, sharply detailing life on the Dakota plains more than half a century ago. The "Girls" were clearly women of the 90s — ahead of their time, yet emerge as timeless personalities. Family values in this absorbing account come back to life as we remember it and as we wish it could be again."

> — Ann Compton, ABC News White House Correspondent

"This memoir captures the spirit of a time, a place and a collection of fascinating people. It's a loving portrait of the hinterland that would have tempted H.L. Mencken to take a side trip."

> — Bob Fishburn, Book Reviewer, *Roanoke* (VA) *Times*

"The heart of a remarkable prairie family has been perfectly captured here."

> — The Rev. Theodore Stoneberg, Professor of Pastoral Care & Counseling, School of Theology, Anderson (IN) University.

"A wonderful cake of zest, charm, and humor, with the photos a glorious icing."

> — Jeanie Neyer, Artist and Author (*A Holocaust Portfolio*), New City, NY

"*The Girls* brought back fond memories of my own childhood and the farms I knew in Ireland."
> — Renee Doolan, Assistant to Ambassador John L. Loeb, Jr. (Retired), New York City

"*The Pearson Girls* is not just about North Dakota; it's what North Dakota is about."
> — Allan Burke, Editor/publisher, *Emmons County Record*

"Set in what Eric Sevareid referred to as 'a large, rectangular blank spot in the nation's mind,' *The Pearson Girls* fills in the blanks and adds all the colors of the prairie rose and the Great Plains sunsets as it tells the story of five delightful aunts and the niece who lived 'amang [them], taking notes' (Robert Burns)."
> — Chandice Johnson, Director, NDSU Center for Writers

The Pearson Girls

by

Kathy L. Plotkin

The Pearson Girls

A Family Memoir of the Dakota Plains

by

Kathy L. Plotkin

Institute for Regional Studies,
North Dakota State University

Published by the Institute for Regional Studies,
North Dakota State University,
Fargo, North Dakota 58105

Manufactured in the United States of America.

International Standard Book Number (ISBN):
0-911042-51-2

Library of Congress Catalog Card Number 98-66956.

Cover: From left to right, Agnes (squinting), Elsie (standing),
Lucille (in profile), 1914.

Cover design: Ann Seibel, North Dakota State University Office
of Publication Services.

Acknowledgements

A long, long time ago I once knit a sock. One yellow wool sock. Turning the heel of the first proved to be so large a challenge I never had the heart to start the second.

The years have passed, and I have found myself once more, knitting. This time, though, I have worked with words — more suited to my nature. Using the sharp, prodding needles of my own memories this book has been created from the colorful yarns spun from letters and reminiscences of my aunts, Flora Pearson Johnson and Charline Pearson Falconer, as well as many letters from my grandfather, Charlie Pearson. Others in the family have joined me in my knitting and purling, most especially my first cousins, offspring of the Pearson sisters.

The end result is dedicated of course, to The Girls: Lucille, Elsie, Agnes, Flora and Charline, though only Flora remains on "this side of the veil," and to my cousins — Agnes's children Greg and Gwen Meyer (who died at 22 in 1963), Flora's daughters, Carla Stoneberg and Connie Salmela, and Charline's children Tom, Paul and Anne Falconer.

Special acknowledgements are due to Flora, who is, as the editor of the *Emmons County Record* recognized on her visit to Linton in 1996, the "ranking member" of our remaining family, and without whose remarkably vivid memory, as well as her "advice and consent," there would have been no book.

A special recognition is also due to my beloved husband, Shepsel Plotkin, who has been magically transmogrified by my loving cousins into a Pearson. When I told him some of the stories now included here, he like the angel in Revelation, commanded in tones that brooked no caviling, *Write,* and then hovered solicitously until the book was finished.

May the memories of the Pearson clan warm the hearts of other American homesteaders' descendants, and may they join me in a salute to our hardy heritage.

klp, 1998

Contents

Photo gallery: pp. 78-92 and pp. 159-175.

Foreword

The Pearson Girls is a book about North Dakota and how it once was — a simple story of a Swedish immigrant's family, who homesteaded a farm in Emmons County and raised five daughters in the early part of the 20th century. Their tale is filled with wisdom, a great deal of humor and a measure of pathos. These are memorable people blessed with ample hearts, and their share of human frailties.

The life-lessons of the Pearsons are a gift from our past to us today. Sad to say, word-of-mouth and letter histories, the shared memories of previous generations may soon be lost in the hurly-burly of modern day living. Tomorrow's generation may yearn for stories such as this, hoping to better understand their past, their people and hopefully, themselves.

The author is doubly blessed with a poet's vision and a realist's eye. She shows, not tells, the lessons about the courage and vitality of the homesteading spirit, the webs and tangles that bind families, about piety and activism, loyalty, faith and love.

This book is a keeper.

—Allan Burke, editor/publisher, *Emmons County Record*, Linton, North Dakota

Preface

All of the Pearson girls were beautiful. Smart, too. Everyone in Emmons County said so. Family lore has it that a debate still surfaces there now and again about which of the five was the most beautiful — a debate argued heatedly back in the twenties by an enviable number of would-be swains who swarmed to my maternal grandparents' farm in our part of the south central North Dakota plains.

This frequent swarming was much disapproved by my very particular grandfather. Ultimately he admired all of his sons-in-law, but no male while still in wooing posture could ever quite pass Grandpa's muster. What green and callow boy could be good enough for a Pearson girl?

As for my pick, whichever girl I was with was always the most beautiful. I must tell you, though, that my godmother Aunt Flora, seems in memory now to have been awarded my personal blue ribbon most of the time — and not just because in 1930, as a nursing student in Bismarck's St. Alexius Hospital, she was allowed in the delivery room for my debut, and was thus the first person to welcome wailing, scrawny me into this world some 20 seconds before my mother saw me.

Flora might have suspected my early assessment of her beauty was somewhat skewed in her favor because all day long on the Sundays when she and the rest of the girls made the sixty-mile car trip from Bismarck back home to the Pearson farm, she let me wear her nurse's Bulova wristwatch with the big sweep hand.

Or perhaps it really was the soft little blond peach-fuzz above her upper lip that I found so compellingly beautiful. She still loves to tell the story about the day I sat beside her in the car, riding along with the sun highlighting her face in a crosslight. I patted the fuzz and assured her that I loved ladies with whiskers.

In order of birth, the five Pearson girls were first my mother, Laura Lucille in 1903, who for reasons family lore has not recorded, was the only one christened with a middle name until the last baby.

Next after my mother was Elsie in 1907. At some point in time she elected to be Elsie Jean; Agnes put in her appearance in 1909, and after reaching the age of reason chose to be Agnes Josephine; Flora, born in 1912, first opted for Flora Margit, but later waffled between Flora Caryl, Flora Willow, and Flora Conner at various ages, but finally, after she married my Uncle Jake, settled permanently on Flora Pearson Johnson.

How people acquire middle names in later life has always been of more than casual interest to me; the story of my Uncle Jake's experience is one shared by many immigrants to this country. Jake's parents, like the Pearsons, had neglected to provide him with a middle name, and he (unlike the Pearson girls) neglected to give himself one. He always wrote "nmi" on any paper requiring such. Thus as he was being inducted into the military to participate in World War I — after he had convinced the military authorities that the leg he'd almost lost in a threshing machine accident was perfectly war-worthy — the officer in charge asked him for his FULL name.

"What? No middle name?" he thundered. The man behind the desk was appalled at Jake's parental omission and promptly took it upon himself to fill that intolerable oversight.

He announced grimly, "Well now you have a middle initial. It is F. and it stands for Fritz." Not a Swedish name, nor one that Jake would have chosen, but it stuck. That is how Flora became Mrs. Hjalmer F. (as in Fritz) Johnson. But that's ahead of our story.

The last Pearson baby, Ardis Charline, came in 1917 and was always called Charline, not Ardis. Her name was pronounced CHARleen, not SHARleen because Grandpa's name was Charlie, and my grandmother, after producing four girls and not one boy, wisely gave up trying to provide a male namesake for my grandfather. Complications following this fifth baby's birth had almost caused her own demise.

My memory of "The Girls" begins to grind with some precision somewhere along the years of 1934 and '35, the only full years I spent with my grandparents on the farm.

How I *longed* to be one of the girls. How I yearned for

them to be still living with Grandpa and Grandma and me on the farm. They could never come back for visits long enough or often enough to suit me.

It was not sufficient glory to be the first and so far, only grandchild. I did not, or so I thought then, need aunts. I needed to be a bonafide Pearson girl with all the magical properties I attributed to these luminous creatures; perhaps equally important — and striking to the root of motivation — I ached to share the wonderful secrets that made them laugh so hard and happily behind closed doors. How I burned to be part of whatever it was they shared.

My mother sent me to the farm and the care of my grandparents at an early age, (around four) while she sought to wrest a single-parent living from the Depression economy in Bismarck, the state capital which then boasted a big city population of 15,141.

She must also have been healing from the private sorrows of her divorce (oh shameful, shocking word) from my father. I don't really know; she never wept in front of me. At any rate, for some little while I saw as little of her as I saw the rest of the girls. That made her as elusively magical as my aunts.

I knew that Laura Lucille was beautiful because everyone in my young life told me so. Looking at her pictures today, I can judge for myself that she was extraordinarily good to look at. Her classic beauty was captured frequently by box-cameras and miniature folding bellows cameras of the twenties, all of which the girls called generically "Kodaks."

Like Garbo's looks, my mother's hold up even by today's standards. Not that she looked like Garbo, of course, even though she was half Swedish. Lucille had thick waves of dark brown hair, sometimes cropped in a bob, sometimes piled high in a "beehive," a coiffure achieved by a significant amount of what she called "ratting" or what I call today, "back-combing." Chestnut she liked to call the color, and I suspect it was secretly augmented with henna rinses, although my Aunt Flora vigorously pooh poohs this. Both color and waves were inherited from Grandpa — no blond Scandinavian, he.

Her sensually full lips and truly green eyes, slender figure, shapely calves and well-turned ankles made her a "looker." Always she kept something veiled, gravely withholding some private secret that no one could or should know. Perhaps that was why, in most of the pictures I have left today, she stands diffidently, eyes cast down, refusing to meet the rude stare of a prying camera.

Elsie had almost amber colored eyes, slim legs, trim ankles and a Gibson-girl shape. To her great chagrin, she was endowed with a glorious bosom, the kind not in vogue in the thirties, and of the amplitude that put Jane Russell on the map twenty plus years later.

Elsie's generous smile revealed deep flirtatious dimples and perfect, not just near perfect, flashing white teeth. The makers of Ipana — that famous old brand of toothpaste, now a page in history — might well have loved to claim credit, but salt and baking soda served as toothpaste at the farm. Elsie and my grandmother Inda both swore to the younger sisters that unusually beautiful teeth were the result of eating raw potatoes as a regular regimen. But then, my grandmother also swore that eating carrots would make hair naturally curly, and except for Agnes and my mother, the rest of the girls proved her wrong on that score.

I think Elsie was most likely the shyest of the quintet, but her soft throaty laugh belied her reticence. Like the synoptic gospels, the girls agree about the main elements of the story: they remember that even in the Depression, Elsie could always be counted on to somehow have a dollar in her pocketbook — and was always willing to lend it. No small matter in those days. Always a perfect lady with a supremely erect carriage, she was nonetheless addicted to one particular four-letter word. When agitated beyond controlling her tongue, she could be heard to blurt softly but passionately one word: *RATS*, then revert to her ladylike self. She was the most like my grandmother of all the girls, and according to her sisters, her mother's favorite.

Elsie was a Campfire Girls leader while still very young (the CG's were a precursor, no doubt, of the Girl Scouts), and it is thought in our family that it was Elsie and not the Boy Scouts who originated the phrase, "Be Prepared." Long years later when she visited Charline in her dry-to-the-point-of-arid Southern California home, Elsie brought an umbrella with her. "And do you know," Charline says, "it actually rained while she was here!"

Agnes was next. Agnes with the pretty, piquant, perky face, roguish brown eyes, irrepressibly bouncy black-brown hair, and the impish gaze of a merry minx. I was too young then to know about such things as coquettes, but I at least recognized that she, too, was endowed with the Pearson alchemy. Agnes radiated energy and spunk, again according to her sisters, their father's favorite, perhaps because she was so much like him from curly hair to competitive spirit.

In 1932 she married my Uncle Oscar, memorable to me as the wearer of a handsome blue sweater with a big L on the front, won in his football days at Luther College in Decorah, Iowa. He was an enormous man, and the most jocular of all my uncles.

I saw Agnes less at the farm than the other girls, for after her marriage she quickly fell into the social life of a new young matron befitting her role as wife of the town of Wishek's school superintendent, so her 80-mile trips to the farm were less frequent than the other girls.

I was occasionally shuttled to visit "Anks" and "Oksher" as they say I called them, in their small white frame house in Wishek, though the mode of transport escapes me now. Images of Agnes's spanking clean kitchen with a color scheme of red and white are with me still. To this day, any red and white-checked tablecloth will start a Pavlovian salivation for her tantalizing prune custard coffee küchen.

Many years later when I was a young bride myself, she presented me with that treasured recipe as a particular favor. My efforts never turned out well — my bread dough not springy enough, though I never suspected her of doing what she told, with meaningfully arched brows, that most good cooks in her sewing circle did. Rather than refuse a request for a recipe in which they took special pride, they gave it willingly, even graciously, but omitted a key ingredient.

Flora came next, the only towhead in the brood, with shy, sky-blue eyes that later turned more gray. She was always the smallest, the dainty one with as sweet and innocent a face as any you will ever come upon this side of the Rockies, though she avows a naughty streak a mile wide, or maybe only as wide as the big white stripe down the back of my pet baby skunk, Bennie Blue. Her estimate, not mine!

Finally Charline put in an appearance, the baby sister of

zaftig form and velvet voice. I remember her voice most of all, full and throaty, like Elsie's, but lower in register. When she laughed I always wanted to laugh too, even when I didn't get the joke — which at pre-school age was most of the time. Her dark brows framed gray-green eyes; like Elsie, she was genetically favored with a generous mouth, beautiful teeth, full bosom, and shapely legs. She was closest to my own age, so I could pretend with some sense of reality that she indeed was really my sister, not my aunt.

These five prairie roses, redolent of femininity, were the object of my adoration. Only later did I learn that they had also been my grandparents' chief farmhands, the sturdy boys my grandfather never sired. From the time they were little girls until they went away to high school and college in Ellendale or Wahpeton, or Bismarck, they worked, — and I mean *worked* — shoulder to shoulder with my Swedish immigrant grandfather and his beloved Hoosier schoolmarm wife. The old saying, "A man works from sun to sun, but a woman's work is never done" not only held more than true in that household, the wry wisdom of one oldtimer was also true: they all worked from *"can* see 'til *can't* see."

Together the little family braved the challenges of North Dakota blizzards, droughts, grasshopper plagues, twisters, sheep and cow herd epidemics, dust storms, prairie fires, wolves and crop failures. They were North Dakota homesteaders, a hardy breed America will not see again.

The girls were also, by their own accounts, a pentagram of holy terrors.

1

When Johnny comes marching home again,
Hurrah! Hurrah!
Civil War Song

Genealogy has never interested me much. Like Emily Dickinson, as a child I found the Bible an "arid book," especially when the begats set in. Dakota people, it seemed to me — and I, for sure, was one — should rely on their own individual merits, their own successes, their own pluck, for a sense of mental and spiritual self-worth, not on ancestor worship.

My youthful prejudice was further fanned when I was transplanted to very close to the part of Virginia whence the Pearson girls' Confederate great-grandmother, Delilah Smith Wingfield had fled to Indiana after the Civil War, taking along her four remaining sons and three daughters — ranging in age from seven to twenty-one. Her second to youngest child, the girls' grandmother Susan Charlotte, would have been about eleven years old when the Widow Wingfield moved from Boone's Mill, Virginia to Hoover Station, near Logansport, Indiana.

The year of Delilah's migration north is recorded as 1870, five years after the end of the War Between the States, as I was cautioned to call the Civil War by my well-meaning southern neighbors. Her husband Oliver, and eldest son William had both been "murdered by the Yankees" in 1862. Oliver fell in battle serving under Stonewall Jackson (immediate commander, Jubal Early); William died of a gangrenous wound received at Cedar Mountain shortly thereafter. These double tragedies were anti-climactically exacerbated by the mysterious disappearance one starless night almost immediately after the end of the War, of all the lumber she and Oliver had managed to accumulate. The couple had planned to build a new home for their burgeoning family on their Boones Mill property when he returned triumphantly home, for they expected the war to be a very short, victorious skirmish.

My fanciful interpretation of our ancestress Delilah Wingfield's exodus from Virginia was that with vision and fearlessness (she had been known to behead a venomous snake in her backyard with a kitchen knife, indicating a certain bravado) she decided that if the carpetbaggers and other riff-raffy thieves were going to take over the south like the proverbial ten-year locusts, she and her fatherless brood would go *north* to make a new life.

The actual facts are, that in emotional devastation and without anybody's sound advice, she sold her valuable farm land and naively accepted Confederate dollars in payment. Penniless, she fled to Indiana and the mercy of relatives, where she literally wept away the rest of her life. The care and bringing up of her children, including the Pearson girls' grandmother Susan Charlotte, were left to her kin.

Four generations later, here I was, almost lemming-like, having made the circle back down south, alternately amused and appalled by the amount of time the good matrons of the small Virginia town I landed in could spend tracing lineage.

"Oh yes. Um-hum. And *her* mother was kin to the Tyler Whiteheads of Fredericksburg. Now Mary Wade Tyler Whitehead was kin to the Hamilton Todds on her father's side, and his people were originally the Richmond Todds, my dear."

A pause. Then, talking about a newcomer not present, another biddy would peer over her half-glasses and ask, "Uh-hum, and just who are her *people*?" About then I was looking for an escape hatch.

The idea of letting these dear old souls know that thanks to Wingfield ancestors, I was eligible to join the United Daughters of the Confederacy (as well as the DAR!) was an unthinkable option suggested to me by two of the girls, Elsie and Agnes. Both of them had been climbing about a bit in our family tree and become intrigued with my return to the south.

To poke into the recesses of times gone by, I huffed, was not my style. This Yankee had no interest in clinging to the tatters of past enmities or wartime glories of the South, even if it meant a step up in the social register. Besides, hadn't I heard tales of renegades in our family to make me think there might even be a pirate back there somewhere? Better to let sleeping ancestors lie.

Actually, the story of one particular ancestral curmud-geon delights me enormously. Flora, too. She wrote once that she had no interest in proving her descent from several Greats (gr.-gr.-gr.-gr.-gr. ad infinitum) to William the Conqueror or 27 Knights of the Bath. She and I prefer rascally gr.-gr.-gr.-gr. (or so) Grandpa Jackie Conner, late (very late) of Indiana.

Just before dying he requested that his coffin be filled with pitch, thus sealing him in. Then the coffin was to be laid on top of the ground and covered with stones. This was to prevent the devil from reaching up and dragging him down to where he knew he deserved to go. His instructions were carried out to the letter.

No one is quite sure what the venal things he did were, but it is suspected that in his career as a trader with the Indi-ans, he may have been less than honest. It is also more than suspected that he had an Indian wife or two in addition to the Elizabeth whose bones lie not far from his in the Indiana grave-yard. It is also thought that one of his 14 sons, Elijah Conner, (the father of my Great Grandpa Conner) had a second wife who was Indian. The younger generation in our clan loves to specu-late that the high cheekbones that run in our family could well come from Indian genes. A Pocahontas or a Sacajawea in our background would be quite welcome, especially to me.

In later years the Jackie Conner cairn mausoleum succumbed to forces of nature. It is told that curious ones and vandals invaded his privacy, and that callous youths had been seen using his skull for a football.

I once suspected that Agnes, who told the story with dramatic flair, might have made up that last part. After all, she wasn't Lucille's sister for nothing, and Lucille's imagination leaned to the noir side. But on further investigation, I learned the tale is even told by a tour guide in Conners Prairie, Indiana, near where the would-be devil escapee lived out his disreputable life.

Now, having firmly disavowed the worth of genealogy except for renegades, I find myself hoisted on a dilemma. How to spin the tale of the Pearson girls without delving into at least some of the family lore — lore that includes how the Olaf Pehrsons (who became Pearsons) emigrated to North Dakota from Sweden, and how fate led the granddaughter of that erstwhile Southern lady Delilah Wingfield, namely my grandmother Inda Conner, from Indiana to Dakota to meet her future husband in the Dakota plains.

If it is true, as the saying goes, that the apple falls close to the tree, the answer is, it isn't possible to avoid the issue of heritage, so here I go, swinging sheepishly from branch to branch in at least a generation or two of the Pearson girls' family tree.

2

Carry me back to Old Virginny
James A. Bland
Weep No More, My Lady
Stephen Foster

In the first chapter we left Delilah Wingfield weeping inconsolably in Indiana while relatives cared for her seven youngsters. Who the relatives were, as well as how the fledgling Wingfields coped with their new life is not known, although Wingfield family archives observe that another branch of the family left Virginia for Indiana in 1867, three years before Delilah moved there; the bereaved and penniless widow may have found a haven with them.

What we know for sure is that a very young Susan Charlotte Wingfield, Delilah's second-to-youngest child, married a William Henry Harrison Tipton Denboe Conner on September 18, 1875, in Logansport, Indiana. At the age of 19 she gave birth to the first of their seven children: the Pearson girls' mother, Inda Conner, born August 31 in 1876, less than a year after Karl Pehrson — known to us as Charlie Pearson — was born in Sweden.

Inda's father, William (H.H.T.D.) Conner was a member of an impressively large clan of Hoosier Conners; there is even an Indiana town called Connersville. What other claim to fame he might have had besides his extraordinary number of middle names, has not been noted anywhere.

William and Susan Conner produced the girls' Uncle Charley in 1877, Uncle Tom in 1879, Aunt Laura in 1882 and Uncle Arthur in 1895. During this fecund period, William Conner found one vocation after another either unfruitful or unsuited to his talents.

The Dakota Territory was divided into two states in November of 1889. That same year Charlie Pearson's family

moved to Emmons County, and William Conner received an
invitation from a pharmacist friend who had migrated from the
Hoosier state a few years earlier to what had just become *North
Dakota*. Would William H.H.T.D. Conner like to run the farm
Mr. Brinkhurst now owned, located just outside the town of
Braddock near Horsehead Valley?

Yes indeed! Grandpa Conner could see that this venture
was just the ticket to save his floundering career. With high
hopes he betook himself north; six weeks later his family joined
him.

Thus it was in 1889 when my grandmother Inda was 13
years old that she, her mother and four younger siblings left
Indiana, taking their first train trip north by way of Chicago.
They arrived in North Dakota at a town named Sterling in
Burleigh County, only one county and 12 miles away from
Emmons County. They were met by their still optimistic and
happy father, driving a team of horses and a wagon to bring
them to a new home and a new life.

It was during the years on the Brinkhurst "place" that
Inda undoubtedly began to hone the skills so necessary to a
successful life on a farm. She also learned to play the piano —
thanks to a tiny but effective local piano teacher named Mrs.
Thistlethwaite — and spent enough well-applied time in high
school to be in great demand by various North Dakota county
school superintendents as a contract school teacher, her vocation from the time she was 16 years old until she married at the
age of 25.

Why, or exactly when her father's budding farm career
took a nosedive we don't know, but he is quoted as saying more
than a few times in the course of his long life, "I seed I couldn't
do it, so I give it up."

Whatever the reason, in 1896 the Conner family left the
Brinkhurst farm and ultimately wound up in Bismarck where
they lived in a white frame house boasting a capacious front
veranda, a house worthy of the fictional Bobbsey Twins. How
the Conners could afford it is a mystery, although by that time
Inda was 20 years old and had been teaching for more than
three years; it is possible that she contributed to the family
coffers.

We learn through a 1913 clipping from the *Bismarck
Tribune* that Grandpa Conner eventually parlayed a horse and

buggy into a new career: the town's cab service. *Mr. Conner has become a familiar figure to every resident of the city while engaged as a hack driver.* But his horse-drawn operation was never more than modestly profitable.

Fortunately not afflicted with her mother Delilah's southern vapors brought on by the ugly face of adversity, Susan Charlotte (better known in the family as Lottie) set about to boost the family's minimal finances by making and selling jelly from door to door, jelly she made from the wild chokecherries and bullberries (sometimes called buffalo berries) that still grow in abundance outside the city limits. Nonetheless, she found time to give birth to Uncle Marshall in 1889 and to Aunt Faye ten years later at the age of forty-three. Grandpa Conner evidently had at least one memorable talent.

By the time I came along in 1930, Inda would have been an ideal model for a Norman Rockwell grandmother, with her comfortably plump lap and brindle-going-white hair kept in a grandmotherly pug at the nape of her neck, stray tendrils wisping about her ears.

In 1893 however, at seventeen she was a formidably handsome young woman: slim but buxom, and graced with high cheekbones (that stray Indian gene?), clear complexion, dark brows, heavy black lashes, full lips, generous mouth and blue-to-green eyes. More than that, she emanated dignity, authority and intelligence in her young girl photographs. From stem to stern she was a lady, a lady to be reckoned with, judging by her steady, serene gaze and ramrod posture.

After the move to Bismarck, her younger brothers regularly rode out with her on horseback a partial way to her destination as she began each of her school-teaching sessions. She was heading to towns such as Dawson, Barlow, Carrington or — most fatefully — Williamsport in the Tell District.

Her contracts could be as short as one month, or as long as nine; her monthly salary ranged from $30.00 a month all the way up to a munificent $35.00. Contracts were always skewed in favor of the school boards, some stating that "school may be terminated at any time, with no compensation to the teacher." Translated, that meant if the school board ran out of money, the teacher had to leave, though Inda never ran into that particular problem.

She always rode sidesaddle on her buckskin horse, Dolly, though sometimes she hitched Dolly to a little cart as transport to her next contractual assignment. Dolly, by the way, was a true buckskin: cream colored with a black mane and tail. Dolly lived to a ripe old age, and is remembered well as a horse with pluck and personality.

Her brothers' concern for Inda's safety was not misplaced. For example, one time she and Dolly were trailed for miles of desolate prairie by a pack of wolves, though they reached their destination without being attacked.

More angst was caused, though, by the not unwarranted fear of Indians. After all, this was Custer country. All during the 1880s and 1890s throughout the whole territory, but especially in places close to reservations, there was fear of an Indian outbreak, though little was heard of it in the towns. With the settlers in the rural areas fear was everywhere, and an accompanying state-wide hostility to the Indian populace. A massacre of an entire family named Spicer at a farm in the Williamsport area had brought the settlers' anger to a ferocious boil.

It was the custom in those days for a schoolmarm to board with one of the families in her school district, an honor almost always vied over jealously; to have the schoolmarm live with you was a signal honor, not to speak of the added income from her room and board.

Being the star boarder was not always a pleasant experience. One place Inda stayed the family themselves did not use butter, but they knew Inda did. Though cash was in short supply, they valued Inda so much they bought a pound of butter, just for her. Every day they set her private butter on the table, unaware that the unrefrigerated butter had grown rancid quickly. Each day they offered the same butter, and Inda bravely tried to eat it, but never could make a dent in that seemingly unending supply of rancid butter. At another home where she once boarded, there was a family of ten, and never enough to eat; her wasp waist became even waspier that year. One very poor family who opened their home to her had only one pot (no plates) for all to eat from. Fastidious Inda ate from it with great difficulty.

She was in the habit of staying after school for an hour or so, preparing lessons for the next day, and sweeping up the little schoolhouse so lonesomely set in the middle of the prairie, no house around for miles. One evening as she swept busily she felt another presence. Out of the corner of her eye she could see a man she didn't recognize start to enter the schoolroom. He didn't speak, but kept slowly inching his way until he was well within the room, though not coming towards her. Who was he? Someone homeless? A drunken Indian? She didn't know — but memories of the Spicer murders raised the hairs on the back of her head.

She pretended to be oblivious of the silent interloper, swept ever more briskly, circling toward the front door, with her back always to the intruder. When she reached the door, she dropped the broom, dashed for Dolly and the two of them galloped home.

Charline, who told me the story in a letter says, "She forgot her lunch pail and her hat." Flora demurs. She says, "She didn't forget her hat, she wisely abandoned it!" Well I should think so! Charline adds, "She never stayed late after school again." The unidentified visitor remains unidentified to this day.

Elsie spent the most time with Inda, preferring household tasks to field work, and thus was the sister who heard Inda's stories more than once while they shared kitchen chores. It was Elsie who was asked for a contribution to an Emmons County historical booklet published sometime after World War II, and there she related Inda's experience vis a vis the Spicer family murders.

In November 1897, one family Inda stayed with in the Williamsport area needed their spare bedroom for an unexpected visit of a relative; Inda was shuttled off for a few days to stay in the only hotel in the community. She returned to her make-do housing after dark on the night of November 14 and prepared for bed as usual. When she rose the next morning she glanced out her window at the rear of the hotel. Her horrified eyes fell on three Indians dangling by their necks at the end of nooses, hanging from a beef windlass (a butcher's pole, from which slaughtered animals were hung). She knew immediately what had happened.

Earlier that year — February 17 — six members of a family named Spicer, well known in the community, had been viciously massacred in their own home near the town of Winona, not far from Williamsport. The murderers were believed to be five Indians, (one a half-breed French-Indian, and one a half-breed Negro-Indian) on a drunken rampage. They had been looking for more "Red Water" (liquor) and were enraged to find none, having been misled by a local prankster who had told them to search for it at the home of the Spicers, whom he knew to be aggressively vocal teetotalers.

Local legend later had it that the only family member who escaped the massacre was a sleeping baby, unnoticed by the murderers, though this was not so. Every member of the household who had been on the premises was bludgeoned, axed and/or stabbed to death with a pitchfork: Mr. and Mrs. Spicer, their daughter, Lillian Spicer Rowse (who was visiting her parents, awaiting the return of her traveling husband Billie), her twin infant sons, and Mrs. Spicer's mother, a Mrs. Waldron.

The five accused villains were quickly caught. The French-Indian half-breed named Coudotte, was tried in a district court at Williamsport and found guilty, but the conviction was appealed to the North Dakota Supreme Court and a new trial scheduled. He and two of the other confessed murderers — Holy Track and Standing Bear, awaiting their first trial — were held with him in the Williamsport jail. The other two, Blackhawk and Defender, were being held in a Burleigh County jail, and thus escaped the vigilantes.

According to the *Emmons County Republican* of October 4, 1934 in a latter day account of the event, when news of the decision of a new trial for Coudotte reached the residents of Emmons County, about forty enraged friends of the Spicer family went to Williamsport late one night and forced the sheriff to hand over his three Indian inmates — Coudotte, Standing Bear and Holy Track. This was obviously to be a vigilante lynching, prairie style. Sadly, Standing Bear and Holy Track were mere boys of 18 or 19.

Although all of the forty masked lynchers were later identified, they were never prosecuted. Their version of justice was the sight my grandmother had wakened to. The horror of the entire episode stayed with Inda all of her life.

According to Charlie, who also regaled the family with this story, the remaining two miscreants who had been charged and held in the Burleigh County jail, were released for lack of sufficient evidence. Defender died soon after of consumption, while Black Hawk disappeared onto the close-by reservation,

Standing Rock, near Fort Yates, and was reputed to have been shot not too much later, assailant unknown.

Charlie was also deeply affected by the event. He wrote in one of his letters late in life that he had actually talked to two of the Indians (probably Standing Bear and Holy Track) before the lynching, in which he took no part. "It was whiskey that did it," he said. I think he was referring to the murderers, though he might well have also meant the posse. Looking for some "Scotch courage" prior to the lynching, a portion of the group may have paid a call to one of the well-known "blind pigs," the illegal sources of booze. The once popular saloons (9 in the the small town of Winona when Dakota was still a territory) had disappeared after North Dakota entered the Union as a Prohibition State.

Inda's baby brother Marshall, who was not only a professional historian for the State of North Dakota in his retirement years, but an obsessive raconteur all his life, preferred his own, more colorful version of the story: that *Inda* was the only one to be saved from the Indians because she (according to him) was boarding there, and slept in a side-wing off the regular house of the Spicers and was thus overlooked in the massacre.

The truth is as I have written it, which leaves the rest of Uncle Marshall's colorful stories in varying shades of doubt!

3

"Scandinavian immigrants take more readily to farming, become quicker Americanized, and possess a better education and have proportionately more money at the time of their arrival, than any other immigrants, and it is no wonder that the Northmen are considered to be the best immigrants which the United States receives."
History of Scandinavian Immigration,
Edited by N. Nelson, 1893

The five girls loved to hear about when "Papa" was a little boy coming across the ocean from Sweden, or about the trolls that folks in his homeland believed lived under bridges. One of their favorite stories was the great mystery of the woodmill factory. When all the workers had gone home, so the tale goes, the building suddenly lit up, all the machinery started to moil and toil at full speed. But there were no people there. The trolls at work, of course. Who else?

A story that precurses Charlie's life-long love of music took place just before the Pehrsons left their homeland. As he told it to the girls, his mother was moved one mid-morning to send the little under-school-age boy to have at least a glimpse of a Swedish school room, for in all likelihood, he would never return to Sweden.

He was to walk to the school where older brothers John and Andrew were in class and have a short visit. Little Karl (for he was still Karl then) walked a path down a long wooded slope to the bridge crossing a small stream. There he stopped, looked upward toward the tree-covered heights and listened to the silence, which was suddenly a-trill with the song of an unseen bird. It was the sweetest sound he had ever heard; he stood still, trembling from the beauty of it. The sound stopped. He waited, but now there was only silence.

He was so moved by this experience that he forgot all about the school room, turned and hurried home to tell his mother about the joyous song he had heard.

"I never did see the inside of a Swedish school — but I saw and heard something so beautiful that I will never forget that in my whole life."

In telling the story in later years, Charlie recalled the bird was a nightingale, which seems unlikely, for the nightingale is a bird which sings amorously almost exclusively at night. More likely the bird Charlie heard so early in the morning those many years ago was one of the numerous North American thrushes to be found in Sweden, not unlike the meadowlark, the golden-voiced songster dear to the heart of Dakotans.

A latter-day Pearson girl, his granddaughter (my cousin Connie Johnson Salmela) shared her meadowlark experience in the heart of the Dakota Badlands in a recent letter...

I listened. Every meadowlark there was singing his or her heart out with pure joy for the perfection and grandeur of that particular morning. The meadowlarks were everywhere and didn't mind lighting close to me on the sturdier weeds and fence posts nearby, singing just for me. He is a work of art, the meadowlark, with his brilliant yellow chest topped by a dark brown, almost black, collar. As I listened, I was quite sure no symphony has ever attained the sweet, joyous songs and trills of these feathered musicians.

In all events, Charlie's anecdote of his nightingale tells how much his mother Karna, who had only three weeks of school her entire life, valued the idea of education; and how, even with his later practicality and unquenchable thirst for book-learning, it was Charlie's love affair with music and the outdoors that gave peace to his soul. Connie's more recent paean of praise to the meadowlark tells the story of how that love was passed to his heirs.

The girls would sit for as long as Charlie would stay after supper, coaxing him to tell "just one more story." They lingered over their own dinners as long as possible to stave off doing the dishes, or even more worthy of postponement, bedtime with the chickens.

As Inda and the older girls cleared the dishes Charlie

would turn the kerosene lamp down low and in the flickering light reflected from its freshly scrubbed chimney, tilt his ladder-back wooden chair on its hind two feet — to his and its peril — lean back from the yellow-flowered oilcloth covered square table and begin to embroider his tales.

Many years later he acquired an early Oliver typewriter. He took to it like the telegrapher he had once studied to become, so when pressed by far-flung grandchildren for "his story," he sat right down and with typical efficiency and cryptic observations packed 80-plus years of living into a page and a half — single-space, all one paragraph. He typed with two forefingers, all caps, no periods, rarely taking a comma's breath. I have the girls to thank for filling in the ellipses of many years omitted in his abbreviated life story.

He titled his tome *The Autobiography of a Little Sweed American*. He always spelled Sweden "Sweeden" and nothing any of his schoolmarm daughters said ever changed that. He typed....

My parents were born and raised in Skone, the bread basket of Sweeden and there I was born near a town by the name of Stor Herrestad, Large Herrestad English spelling.

His father, Olaf Pehrson and mother, Karna Swenson, worked at the "same place" (meaning farm) as young people; she was a housemaid and he, the foreman. They married on December 24, 1871 when he was 25 and she was 28.

There were three boys and two girls in our family while we lived at that place, Andrew Richard, the oldest, John Frederick, second oldest, then myself, Charles Henry, the runt of the family, then my sisters Caroline Ellen (Carrie) and Louisa Agnes," (Lizzie.)

Charlie later told his siblings that he remembered the day that Louisa was born.

I was sent out to pick plums. When I came home, there was Lizzie.

Oscar William, Edward George and Anna Marie were born later in Bismarck and Sims, then still Dakota Territory.

It was Carrie's daughter, Ida Esther Hoover, a first cousin of the girls, who related the story of how their grandparents met, as it was told to her as a child, by Olaf. As a young man, while changing jobs, he was walking to his new employer's farm. He came across a fortune teller in some village along the way, who told him that he was very soon to meet his future wife, that they would work together for some time but would become dissatisfied with working conditions, and emigrate to a foreign country. They would live on the land, have about eight children, and enjoy prosperity.

The gypsy proved to be right, for as Olaf continued his journey he rested overnight at a wayside cottage and met Karna, whether at her own home or at a place she worked is unclear. They were attracted to each other, and she either accompanied or followed him to his new employment where she also obtained employment.

The young couple was betrothed "for some time," says Esther Hoover. It is worth noting here that long betrothals were an established custom in Sweden, as a "wholesome check on hasty unions," according to the Lutheran Church, the Swedish state religion until 1995. Betrothal was considered a "half-marriage" and there was usually cohabitation prior to the formal wedding, which explains the arrival of Uncle Andrew only three months after the marriage of Olaf and Karna. Children born of a betrothal were legitimized by the actual wedding, which was always a public affair followed by a huge gala afterwards — paid for, no doubt, from the savings of the couple during the long betrothal. This system was much preferred by the Church, for failure of a marriage was considered a far greater evil than the early arrival of betrothal babies.

Charlie doesn't note it in his autobiography, but all the Pehrson boys were named for kings, no matter that they weren't Swedish kings. My generation of Charlie's female descendants, none of whom can be reckoned as flaming feminists, nevertheless pointedly note that the Pehrson *girls* were not favored with queens' names. No one has ever explained why not.

Charlie's autobiography continues...

I was born on the 12th of October, 1875 at 8 o'clock in the morning my father told me and I was babtised (his spelling) *when I was 5 days old, a blacksmith's wife, Mrs. Elna Anderson held me.*

Karna's mother advised her daughter to "be good to him; he won't last long." Fortunately for my story, time proved her wrong.

When Charlie was a year-and-a-half old, the little family moved to a place seven miles east of Goteborg called Molnycke in his autobiography, but spelled Mölndal in today's Atlas. Here his father became overseer of a large estate with a "good salary." But Olaf Pehrson was ambitious. He wanted land of his own, which he couldn't get in Sweden, for all the good farmland was owned by the nobility. There was another reason for him to be restless. He didn't want his young sons conscripted, as they surely would be if they stayed in Sweden, for the military conscription laws put into effect following the Franco-Prussian war of 1870 were onerous. At the age of 35 he eagerly started making plans to leave for "the U.S. of A."

The January, 1930 *North Dakota Historical Quarterly* notes that in 1875 the United States government created an Immigration Board for the Dakota Territory, the express purpose being to attract settlers to the empty plains. Pamphlets, maps and newspaper articles were distributed throughout Europe and it is probable that one of them fell into Olaf's receptive hands. Other entities were equally active — some would say aggressive — in efforts to attract immigrants: railroad corporations, steamship lines, land and townsite companies all could smell profit coming in from overseas newcomers, both as laborers and consumers.

Whatever his source of information, Olaf was impatient to set out. Land! Not only available, but *free*! What more could a man with his drive, his ability, his determination want from life?

Karna was not so eager. Olaf had just received a handsome raise, she had five youngsters to handle, one of them a toddler and one an infant in arms. Besides, as she told Olaf, she wasn't comfortable with moving to a country that had so recently been through a civil war. But Olaf had already made up his mind. "That war ended seventeen years ago," he reassured her.

I can well remember what my mother said when my father, resting on the sofa after dinner reading from a Sweedish and

*English dictionary, the sentence I will do the best I can to have it
done in time. You would laugh if you heard it then. Mother said
to him you will never learn it, but he did.*

Karna never learned to speak English, but "she understood it first rate," Charlie comments.

He was going on six years old when the family left
Sweden on June 15, 1882. The trip across the ocean seems to
have been the most memorable event of his entire life — at
least one would believe so, for of the page and a half of the
Little Sweed's Autobiography, almost two-thirds is about the
voyage. On the other hand, like many writers, he may just have
gotten bored and decided to wrap up the rest of the 80 years
with his customary dispatch.

They left Sweden at Goteborg sailing for Hull, England,
which took three days, followed by a ride across England in a
"poor old train" to Liverpool which had no toilet facilities so the
train would just stop periodically somewhere in the countryside.
The passengers were required to get off and manage the delicate
maneuver however they could. Six-year old Charlie was more
than a little fascinated by "so many tails exposed to the sun."

At Liverpool the children were left in the station while
their parents "took a look at the city." Presumably, they all
seven spent the night in the station, as there is no mention of a
hotel.

*I was asleep so I do not remember when they came back.
The next day we boarded a steamer for Boston, USA.*

The three-week trip across the sea was not uneventful.
Olaf had originally booked on a "fairly decent vessel," but it was
unexpectedly delayed from leaving port, requiring three days for
repairs. Olaf did not wait. He was either too impatient to begin
their life in the new country to be held up any longer, or just
refused to waste money putting up a family of seven for three
nights in Liverpool.

He might well have regretted his decision to sail on a
lesser boat. During a heavy fog about halfway across the ocean,
a sailing vessel ran into their little ship with its 1,140 frightened passengers. The impact was so forceful that its mast fell
onto their deck, and Charlie was knocked breathless, falling

against a wall. Fortunately, he was more scared than hurt, but their own ship was damaged and needed repair.

The now mastless boat was tied to the back of their own and "we fixed it up again," Charlie notes. "We" might well have included his father and two older brothers, all expert carpenters. There is a reason for their proficiency. Olaf had been hustled off as an apprentice to a master carpenter at the age of eight, a craft he learned well, and passed on to his sons. Olaf, by the way, never went home again after his apprenticeship.

The unfortunate vessel soon took off on its own, but ...our boat went quite a little lower after that...I could stand looking over the side of the ship and see its bottom as it plowed from wave into another wave.

For a few hours after the misadventure the captain of the vessel kept the travelers locked in their steerage quarters, lest they do again what they had done during the mishap: everyone ran to see what was happening, the result predictable. With all the passenger weight on one side their own boat tilted steeply and almost capsized.

Evidently the captain relented a little later, for Charlie writes that since there was never a calm day during the crossing, his oldest brother Andrew frequently took him up from the steerage quarters to a higher deck, to help offset the waves of seasickness they all felt. They quickly learned not to look out at the waves, for the movement of the sea made them dreadfully nauseated. Charlie looked only at the deck, and inhaled fresh salt air.

Mother Karna had made rye bread for the journey, and Charlie reports that he ate his share, plus all the crusts anyone else left, commenting that rye was their usual fare at home. Wheat bread was only for holidays. But there was also white bread provided on board, and he ate so much he didn't ever want to see any more. That revulsion was short-lived. The girls recall that no one was a bigger fan of their own mother Inda's big, golden-crusted loaves of fat white bread than he. It seems unbelievable, but to him "store bought'n" white bread was an even bigger treat.

They landed at last at the Boston Immigration Center, with tiny Charlie holding on to his father's extraordinarily large index finger until the very last moment when he had to walk alone through the small passage, wide enough for only one person at a time to be inspected. He bravely let the officer in charge roll up his sleeve to see his vaccination. Miraculously the ordeal was finally over, and with the rest of the family he was safely on his way to becoming an American.

Soon boarding a train, their first stop was Buffalo, New York, where a Mr. Swanson, a friend and former neighbor, was to meet them. Sharp-eyed Charlie was the first to spot him at the crowded train station, teeming with masses of other anxious, tired steerage passengers. But his father "ssshed" him sternly when he squealed, "There he is! There he is!" Who could believe that the "little runt" was right? But right he was, and the weary group breathed a collective sigh of relief as they hooked up with Gus Swenson, their only contact in the new world.

Mr. Swanson was a veteran of one year in the States, and knew about a large coal mine in Sims, North Dakota, where he'd heard they were hiring men to make coal cars. It was said they paid $5.00 per car. With one of his sons to "bolt" for him (inserting the bolts that held the sides of the cars together) Olaf Pehrson was sure he could build a car a day. $5.00 a day! A king's ransom.

4

Work for the night is coming
When man works no more
Hymn by Lowell Mason/Annie L. Walker Coghill

It is not certain why the Pehrsons didn't go first to Sims,
a thriving metropolis of 2,500 souls at the time — today only a
ghost town not even on the map. It may have been that the
offer Olaf received almost immediately from the Northern
Pacific to supervise a bridge project was more lucrative than
building railroad cars for them. The fact is the Pehrsons spent
at least a year in Bismarck, 67 miles east of Sims.

Here Olaf supervised a crew of men commissioned to
dismantle the wooden Northern Pacific Railroad bridge across
the Missouri River outside the city, the trick being not to disrupt
train service while they replaced the wood, section by section,
with steel and iron. They worked through one entire winter in
the bitterly frigid Dakota cold. His crew marveled that Olaf,
whose hands were so large there were no gloves big enough to fit
him, handled the freezing steel barehanded day after day with
no complaint, nor apparent discomfort.

Charlie skips a good bit from here on in his attenuated
autobiography, but the girls say Olaf and Karna "filed on" a
homestead just outside Sims in 1883, close to their original
destination, only a year after their immigration. While once-
again pregnant Karna and their youngsters managed the farm
outside Sims, Olaf would spend two more years working for the
Northern Pacific, sometimes as a pile driver out of Bismarck
and sometimes making railroad cars in Sims. (Piles are vertical,
tall beams of hardwood frequently tipped with metal at the
base, driven into the ground to reinforce structures.)

Charlie's tales to the girls include the first night the
Pehrsons all traveled from Bismarck to their new homestead

outside Sims. The entire family hunkered down in a small
coulee (a very narrow, steep-sided ditch) adjoining their property
with just a few boards over their heads for protection. They
slept that night sheltered only by the Dakota stars. Apparently
Olaf had already accumulated lumber and supplies and stored
them previously on the property, for Charlie relates that the
very next day Olaf and the boys started to build their first new
home.

Interestingly enough, the Custer Trail passed right by
their house in Sims, as well as by the Sims schoolhouse. (It was
along this trail that George Armstrong Custer had led his troops
in 1876 as they wended their way to the infamous Little Big
Horn Battlefield in Montana.) Charlie, and later his daughter
Agnes, had a lifelong fascination with the Custer story.

Charlie had stories of how "us kids" yearned for sweets,
which were non-existent in their small home at Sims. After a
particularly grueling summer, his oldest brother, Andrew,
persuaded mother Karna to let him take a load of the summer's
hay they had just finished harvesting to town to sell, and to
keep to spend however he chose whatever money he could get
for it.

Amazingly, Karna agreed. Andrew made a successful
sale and returned home weary but happy five days later, the
entire $5.00 garnered from the hay sale all spent. Charlie
doesn't say what his brother bought, except for one item: a big
tin bucket filled with jelly, which he brought home with him.

Charlie and the other kids spotted Andrew almost a mile
away, driving the two-horse team and the empty hayrack. With
yelps of glee they ran the distance to meet him. The delighted
children devoured the entire bucket of jelly before reaching
home, "and never even got a stomach ache."

Tiny Karna, who looks in pictures to have been half the
size of Olaf, was no slouch as a farm manager. She may not
have been able to speak English, but she knew how to sharpen
her pencil when keeping the books. Other than the one aberration when she allowed Andrew to spend the money from one
load of hay on a frivolity like a pail of grape jelly, there seems to
have been no nonsense tolerated under her frugal hand. That
grape jelly incident must have been a notable rarity because this
story has survived in the family more than 100 years.

Karna's father had been a butcher in Sweden, so when it

came time to render and dress the slaughtered lambs or pigs, Karna knew how to make use of every whit of the carcass, right down to the intestines. Pickled pigs feet were considered a particular delicacy, as was head cheese.

Her thrift served the family well, and through Charlie, who learned early never to throw anything out because "you might need it some day" the trait was passed on to the girls. Elsie seems to have been the one with whom it took seed most fruitfully but it totally bypassed my profligate mother Lucille and me. Though Mother read me the Aesop fable about the grasshopper and the ant many times, (the point not entirely lost on me) both she and I remained grasshoppers all our lives. As far as we were concerned, a penny earned is a penny to be spent.

Elsie, on the other hand, in whose care I was entrusted for great spans of time in the 40's, frequently chanted that World War II slogan:

> *Eat it up,*
> *Wear it out,*
> *Make it do*
> *Or do without.*

I may remember that annoying little ditty, but still avoid its philosophy. Not without guilt, of course.

It was at Sims where eight-year old Charlie began the first of his approximately six years of formal schooling, though his real education was acquired largely through omniverous reading and acute observation of whatever was going on around him.

Since the Pehrsons had acquired several cows, he first peddled milk in town at dawn, then dashed to school in time to set the fire in the stove so the room would have the frigid winter chill removed when the rest of the class arrived. Presumably he was paid a small stipend for this extra chore.

The three months of school each year were held in the winter. Historically, the reason schools were let out for the summer was that farming parents desperately needed their offspring to help out at home, a concept few youngsters today would consider the *real* world. In the summer Charlie herded neighbor's cows as well as the Pehrson's, and as he grew sturdier, worked with threshing crews and haying crews.

By 1888, the same year the William Conners moved to Dakota from Indiana, the Pehrson family realized two things: there wasn't enough hay growing on their property at Sims for their burgeoning herd of livestock; secondly, Northern Pacific was replacing North Dakota lignite coal as fuel for its locomotives in favor of bituminous coal to be found in Billings, Montana. Olaf's work with the NP would be ending soon.

It behooved the Pehrsons to think about moving, although at some unrecorded point in time Karna's brother, Nels Svenson, had also emigrated from Sweden to North Dakota and was living in Sims. Karna might have had more than a pang of regret at leaving her only close-by relative for yet another new home. What *is* recorded is that one winter while they were still in Sims, one of Karna's nephews walked the sixty-seven miles to Bismarck and on his back carried home a 100-pound sack of flour for the Pehrsons. This deed certainly indicates a closeness between Karna's family and that of her brother Nels.

Not too much later they decided to trade their first homestead in Sims for one in Emmons County, some 60 miles southeast of Bismarck and six miles south, one and one-half miles west of Kintyre. Later (the claims couldn't be made simultaneously) they would be able add to the acreage of their homestead property by staking a "tree claim." This amounted to an agreement to plant 10 acres of trees on their farm. If, after eight years, a homesteader could prove that 675 of these trees were alive and well, an additional 160 free acres of land would be his, as per the Timber Culture Act of 1873. The fee for filing a tree claim was an affordable $14.00.

It was Karna who effected the trade of their first homestead filing for the second, with young Charlie serving as her translator. It was she who pointed out to the government's homestead officials that the family had not yet "proved up" (or finalized) on their first homestead, and thus were entitled to file for property more suited to their needs. Karna knew how to negotiate and Charlie had quickly picked up the English language, so with him at her side, she faced the officials fearlessly. They agreed without a quibble to allow the Pehrsons to relinquish the claim on the first property and re-file on the second.

Olaf and Karna's new property was located in what was called "The Tell District," not exactly a town, but an area in Emmons County named for Swiss hero William Tell by earlier

settlers from Switzerland, their new neighbors, the
Grunefelders, although by the time the Pehrsons came, the area
was considered to be a Swedish community.

Olaf and Karna quickly settled into the local ways, Olaf
becoming a highly visible and dominant figure. Karna, too,
earned her niche in the little community, though not so visible
or political. Olaf built a loom for her and she became noted for
her weaving, though it was her skill with hooking rag rugs that
that brought in her "pin" money. Neighbors would come by with
bags of rags all cut up in one-quarter inch strips for her to make
into rugs or carpets for which she charged 25 cents a yard. For
a long time she enjoyed it — or perhaps more candidly, the pin
money — but eventually she stopped her little business and
gave what time she had for crafts to her spinning wheel.

Their youngest daughter, Annie, wrote in a short memoir about her parents...

*I like to think of her humming and singing "In the Sweet By
and By," and "Shall We Meet?" as she worked at carding and
spinning wool. Perhaps as she sang she was thinking of the
mother she had left in Sweden whom she was never to see again.*

Olaf and Karna had a "fair-sized" house Annie says in
her notes about her memories on their farm...

*We were often hosts to travelers and peddlers. An Arab
peddler, (Alexander by name) used to come and stay with us
every now and then, and he and Dad would talk for a long time
at night. It would be interesting to know what they discussed, he
being a descendant of Esau.*

One might assume correctly that there still aren't too
many "descendants of Esau" in North Dakota even today.

In 1893 Olaf renounced his allegiance to the Swedish
king and became a full fledged citizen of the U.S. of A. the same
day. Somewhere in this period of time, the Pehrsons anglicized
the spelling of their name to Pearson, but in my memory, Olaf
and Karna are forever "Pehrson."

On April 23, 1894 Olaf was appointed postmaster of
Tell, an operation he ran from their home, an assignment in
which he took great pride and pleasure. The handsome desk he

crafted for the post office is still in existence at the Emmons County Museum in Linton, thanks to the foresight and generosity of a neighbor, Carl Pearson (not a relative), whose parents had bought it at a farm sale.

Combining the careers of postmaster, carpenter and farmer was sometimes tricky, however. To the great amusement of the younger Pehrson offspring, one day Olaf was on the roof making repairs of some kind. It was a terribly hot day and he had been peeling off outer garments one by one until he had nothing on but his underwear, when he spotted someone riding up the driveway to pick up his mail. To see dignified Olaf scramble to get his clothes on tickled the kids no end. Not a one offered to play postmaster and provide the visitor with his mail — it was too much fun watching Olaf fling on his clothes and dive down the ladder to greet the visitor.

Olaf and his sons helped build the Maria Lutheran Church, the local Swedish Lutheran Church which he and Karna helped to found. It was located on the west shores of Goose Lake, a little east and south of Braddock. The family burial plot is still there, as well as those of many other families of that era, but the church building is long gone. The homesteaders' bones would be left to the care of granite gravestones, winter snows, and hot summer winds, were it not for the vigilant Maria Lutheran Cemetery Association which has loyally mowed and trimmed the lonely graveyard all these many years.

The Pehrson clan also built the Tell School in the early 1890s. It still stands — serving now only as a center for local elections. Olaf and his boys contributed the carpentry for the school on condition that the building never be moved, a strategy of enlightened self-interest. Schoolhouses were small and could easily be moved — and frequently were — from one area to another, depending upon the political influence of a particular constituent, or more likely, a school board member. Olaf made sure school would always be within walking distance for his own children, and he also saw to it that the agreement could not be easily broken. (Nevertheless it was, eventually!)

He could also be generous without thought of return. One particularly bitter cold January a neighbor named Andrew Hanson braved 9-foot snow drifts to walk two and a half miles in 40 below temperature to reach Olaf's farm. My memory of this kind of cold is that even to breathe is painful, the slightest intake of the frigid air cuts to the lungs like a knife. Two layers of woolen scarves are as nothing between you and the elements.

"My father has died," Andrew Hanson announced simply after entering the warmth of the Pehrson home.

Olaf knew what was not spoken. There was no way for his neighbor to get to Bismarck to buy a coffin, no way for a proper burial.

"I will make a coffin. The boys and I will bring it to you." Olaf said it matter-of-factly. The two men looked at each other in Scandinavian taciturnity; nothing more was said. Andrew nodded, grasped both of Olaf's big hands and departed.

The trouble was that Olaf had no wood on the premises with which to make the coffin, and no way to buy any until there was a thaw. So he did what was necessary. He pulled enough planks out of his own barn to construct a casket, then painted it with a concoction of lampblack and kerosene. Charlie told the girls, "It looked like one of the new-fangled steel coffins, if you didn't look too close. Didn't have handles, of course."

How the grave was dug in that frozen earth, I have no idea. But there was a proper funeral. Olaf officiated and gave a eulogy, because there wasn't a real minister around within miles. Itinerant preachers rode around the territory on horseback, but not in weather like that bitterly cold January.

Annie notes that Olaf's favorite hymn was called *The Security Hymn.* I like to think they sang it at that wintry funeral.

> *Gläd dig då du lilla skara*
> *Jakobs Gud skall dig bevara*
> *För hans vilja måste all*
> *Fiender till jorden fall.*

> *(Little flock, to joy then yield thee —*
> *Jacob's God will ever shield thee;*
> *Rest secure with this defender,*
> *At his will all foes surrender.)*

Flora wrote a letter once in which she confided...

Papa once said that Olaf was a stern, patriarchal father and he never welcomed his children up onto his knee. Whereas Inda called her parents "Ma" and "Pa," Charlie addressed his as

"Mother" and "Father."

    *Grandpa Olaf would come over from his place to our
farm sometimes. I remember his white hair, black bushy eyebrows and his brown snappy eyes. His demeanor was equally
snappy and we learned to stay away from him after accepting his
customary gift of a jar of colored stick candy. He believed that
children should be seen and not heard. Of course, if he had ever
talked to our other grandfather, he would have known for sure
that these particular children were not to be trusted!*

    I never met Olaf. The girls say he was a formidable
figure, not given to dandling granddaughters on his knee. But I
think Olaf had the Right Stuff. Just to be around a man so
large, so determined, so sure he could handle the challenges of
homesteading must have provided the girls with a sense of
security, if not engaging their youthful affection.
    It was in those early years in Emmons County that
Charlie and his brothers spent countless lonely hours herding
the stock from early morning until late evening. To pass the
time they looked for Indian relics — finding arrowheads for the
most part — and studied cloud formations. They learned to
predict weather conditions, and almost always got the stock
home to shelter before the storms hit. The older boys cut and
hauled the family's winter supply of firewood from the Missouri
River area; fetching a wagon load meant a two-day trip with a
team of oxen. Other winter supplies, which included a large
order of white muslin for shrouds in case someone died, meant a
week's trip to Bismarck with horse and wagon.
    Charlie was 14 years old and working as Karna and
Olaf's chief cattle herder when he started the more lucrative
challenge of sheep shearing. He would let the cattle run while
he was practice-shearing sheep for neighbors, then go round up
his cows for the night after he'd finished shearing. Within a
year he had become expert.
    He always moved quickly at whatever he did, but at
sheep shearing he vied with the speed of light. His record (pre-
electric shears) was 163 head in one day. Still in his early teens,
Charlie exhibited a talent for negotiating favorable deals. He
contracted with a farmer in the nearby town of Edmunds to
shear a herd of 7,500 at 7 cents a head, turned around and sub-
contracted to some other shearers for 5 cents a head, took a 2

cent over-ride on their work, and sheared an average of 138 sheep a day himself. That meant he was averaging $9.66 a day from his own work, not counting his sub-contracted over-ride — totaling more than double what his father made at railroad car building! He wasn't boasting, just stating a fact when he said...

I have shorn over 40,000 sheep in my day. I made good money at it.

With the very first of that "good money" he bought all the volumes of *Ridpath's History of the World*, a popular reference of the time, and read them all.

During the years between 1888 and 1897 Charlie was studying new ways to farm. At first the Pehrsons raised very few crops for a good reason: drought. Additionally, much of the land around them was still unclaimed, so they could enlarge their cow herd and let the cows graze on the vast prairie surrounding their place. Gradually more and more homesteaders began to file claims and settle; the Pehrsons realized they would have to change their modus operandi.

It was then they turned to farming grain. Olaf had always broadcast grain by hand in Sweden, walking the plowed fields with a large leather shoulder bag from which he strewed seeds carefully as he went. He could manage about 15 acres by himself, but even if he had one person to "walk for him," meaning follow along and show him where he'd already sown, Olaf could only manage about 25 acres a season. He harvested the ripe grain with a scythe, with help from the older boys. The younger boys, and their sisters too, helped with gathering the grain and tying it into bundles.

Charlie's aptitude for things mechanical was already blossoming, and he persuaded Olaf to invest in drills and plows — in a word, to venture into "modern" farming. Father Olaf and his middle son took to the new methods with enthusiasm and profit. Charlie was the only Pehrson son who embraced the homesteaded land for a lifetime; his younger brother Edward also homesteaded nearby, and he farmed off and on over the years, but Uncle Ed's first love and primary career was carpentry. The other brothers were already gone or leaving soon, the three girls married; Carrie moved to Bismarck, and Annie and Louise farther north to Canada with their young husbands.

It was payment for the work he did for his father over these years before he reached the ripe age of 25 that ultimately enabled Charlie to buy the richest hayland from Olaf, (80 acres over and above his own homestead acreage). Olaf had purchased it from the government for $1.75 per acre ($140) shortly after he first homesteaded in Emmons County. Charlie paid his father $15.00 per acre ($1,200) for the hay meadow and still thought he had a bargain! In his lifestory of the little Sweed, Charlie says proudly....

I would get 130 tons of hay per year from that land regardless of what kind of a season it was. Father had the finest hayland that lies outdoors and I bought that from him when he quit the farm.

But he is jumping ahead of the story, for Olaf didn't "quit the farm" to retire in Bismarck until 1909, a year after Karna died of an intestinal problem (which Charlie, with his unique medical theories, always thought resulted from eating unpeeled summer pears.) He had by that time been a homesteader in his own right for seven years.

The girls say Charlie was right about one thing: that haymeadow which he ultimately acquired was the one crop they could always count on, no matter how severe a drought, for it was fed by several springs that never dried out, and water tables very close to the surface.

My farm was just one mile from his (Olaf's), and I think it was the finest farm in North Dakota.

Charlie may even have been right about that, though he did have a tendency to think that whatever he had was *The Best*. Many times it was, for he was canny in his business dealings, and had a good sense of the real value of a thing, never mistaking high price for quality. In some cases he was so shrewd, he was thought to be either Scottish or Jewish, or possibly a combination of both.

In his one-and-a-half autobiographical pages Charlie skips over the early years spent on Olaf's and Karna's homestead, and with his penchant to cut to the chase, gets quickly to the main story of his own life:

A lady came to teach our school who later became my wife...I had her to file a homestead alongside of mine, then we bought another quarter which made 480 acres in the farm. While living on this farm five daughters came to live with us.

How adroitly he phrases this last, as though he had nothing to do with the five daughters' arrival! Which brings us to the subject of how Charlie Pearson met Inda Conner.

5

It won't be a stylish marriage;
I can't afford a carriage,
But you'll look sweet
Upon the seat
Of a bicycle built for two.
Popular song of 1800s

Inda was originally named "India," a name for girls favored in the south in those days. Remember India of *Gone with the Wind*? Somewhere early in life my grandmother decided to call herself "Inda," but if it was before she came to Dakota, no one knows. It was the only name any of us ever heard her use.

In the fall of 1897 Inda was assigned a school in the county seat of Williamsport in the Tell District. One day soon after her arrival, she and Dolly, her faithful buckskin whom she always rode side-saddle, trotted onto the Olaf Pehrson farm to collect her mail at the Tell Post Office, since Rural Free Delivery was a luxury not yet conceived by the U.S. Postal Service.

As fate would have it, young Charlie was out in the barn shearing sheep, but Olaf was busy too, and instructed his son to stop shearing long enough to go give the new schoolmarm her packet of mail. A thunderous bolt of North Dakota lightning would not have been noisier than Charlie's fall into the arms of Amor as he handed Inda the letters she had come to collect. Beautiful Inda represented everything Charlie admired most: education and "get-up and go." Good looks didn't hurt, either.

For her part, Inda was looking at a very handsome and muscular young man with a long silky black mustache and roguish brown eyes, albeit slightly sweaty at that particular moment of meeting. Whether she, too, was immediately smitten I cannot attest. I do know that a five-year courtship began that

day, though Charlie's intent to marry Inda was palpable early
on.   He was not a man to dally about making decisions, and it
was his boast that he always "knew a good thing when he saw
it."

Any intention he may have harbored to propose marriage had to be delayed because of Charlie's promise to his
parents to stay with them and help them homestead until he
was 25, a promise he would never break. He believed in the 4th
Commandment quite literally, and felt that if he stayed home to
help his parents, his life would be blessed. He never had reason
to doubt he was right.

Both his older brothers, Andrew (he of the grape jelly
incident) and John left the family homestead early. Andrew was
17 and John only 14 when they ran away to find their fortunes.
John worked for a while in mines at Butte, Montana, then
joined the Army to fight in the Spanish American War. Stationed in the Philippines, he won a place in the army band —
reputedly playing a mean cornet, and later suffered a leg wound
which did not prove to be fatal. Karna proudly displayed all the
photos he sent her of his commanders on the walls of her
prairie home so many, many miles away, most especially one
Richmond Pearson Hobson, who seemed to capture the family's
imagination because he was quite handsome, and more important, he had Pearson in his name.

Charline writes of his return to Dakota 40 years later:

Aunt Mabel and Uncle Oscar (Charlie's youngest brother,
then living in Mandan) *brought him to the farm one night about
9:00 and Papa had gone to bed. We got him up and told him a
man wanted to see him about a job and he came out all frowzily,
trying to wake up and mumbling that he had no job to offer.
Uncle John burst out crying, "Don't you know me, Charlie?" And
Papa said, "Should I?" Of course, here was a 54-year-old gray-
haired mustached plump man in place of the slim, 14-year-old
boy. We all cried.*

Andrew, the victim of gold fever, never settled down.
Leaving in 1900 for the far west and Alaska, admitting selfish-
ness in doing so, he promised that when he made his big gold
strike "all will receive a share," but there was never a payoff for
high-spirited Andrew. When he died of a heart attack at around

50 years of age somewhere in the remote far west, (one report is that it was in Shasta, Washington; another, at Sisson, California, working at odd jobs for a millionaire) authorities found only Charlie's name and address on him, so Charlie once more paid for his brother's trip home, the last of eight trips, as well as the funeral and burial in Maria Lutheran Cemetery, near Braddock, where Olaf and Karna were buried.

The second reason for delaying the marriage was more practical than idealistic. Charlie cannily reasoned that if both he and Inda homesteaded on property side by each as unmarried individuals, they would have double the acreage when they married. The homesteading process took five years to "prove up" before the land could become legally theirs. Inda continued to teach all around southeast North Dakota and Charlie continued to help farm his parents' land.

He kept the romance flourishing by commissioning his baby sister Annie, then about twelve or thirteen years old, to take his notes in her school lunch pail to her teacher Inda, which he admonished Annie firmly not to let the other kids see. He needn't have worried, if the only note extant that he wrote her during this period is any example: he chatters on a bit about some photographs he has enclosed, and then signs it passionately, "Your friend, Chas. H. Pearson."

Later, after that particular contract with the Tell school had ended and she was traveling north to her Dawson assignment, at least once Charlie rode with her on the train, their companion bicycles in tow. The conductor of that little Soo train obligingly made an unscheduled stop right by her school out in the middle of nowhere and deposited the young lovers and their bicycles by the railroad track. Surely Charlie must have kissed her then as they stood alone in the sight of no one but the retreating locomotive.

The day finally came when Inda arrived at one of her classes with a handsome engagement ring — a gold embossed band — on her left hand.

"Hey teacher," one unscrubbed young urchin asked curiously, "Where'd you get that goddam beautiful thimble?"

A well-worn 5 x 7 photograph, circa 1902, of Charles Henry Pearson and Inda (nee Conner) Pearson sits across from me in a plain walnut frame in my bookcase as I write. The two look back at me in unblinking solemnity. It is my favorite picture of my mother's parents.

Charlie sports a dapper black derby and the full droopy brown-black walrus mustache he favored in his twenties. Inda wears an ankle length skirt, high-necked white shirtwaist, and a wide ribbon-banded straw sailor hat perched atop her loosely knotted bun hairdo. They stand beside a handsome bicycle built for two in the middle of a narrow, wooded lane. It is summertime, probably late June because the tree leaves are out full and lush. Their faces are so grave and dignified, I cannot help but wonder how such serious people could have engaged in the kind of wanton acts usually required to produce five daughters.

In my imagination they are on their honeymoon and have just pedaled down from Bismarck where Inda has spent the summer at home before the wedding. Now they are to look at their adjoining Emmons County homesteads. They will farm this entitlement as a couple for the next almost forty years.

The anonymous photographer has vanished now, and in my mind I see Charlie carefully lay down the bicycle in the ditch beside the lane, then spread out a coarse wool quilt made of scraps from men's suits. It is a multi-muted-color assemblage of squares stitched together and tacked with red wool yarn ties. Inda sits with dignity on the quilt which covers a four-foot square patch of the dry, dusty prairie grass, directly across from the ditch where the bicycle rests.

A pair of prairie dogs have popped up from a hole near by, sitting upright on their hind two feet, their forepaws pointed toward themselves as if to say, "Are you two looking for us?" But the young couple pay them no attention and they pop back into their subterranean houses.

A fat grasshopper plunks himself down beside Inda. "Hey you little varmint. This spot is for my wife," Charlie protests gallantly, saying aloud proudly the word "wife." He has waited a very long time to be able to say it. The grasshopper spits a stream of brown juice, the color of tobacco chaw, as he catapults off. He narrowly escapes the maw of a sharp-eyed crow.

The couple sits shoulder-to shoulder, rarely speaking as they pick their way through the remains of the picnic lunch they have brought. They eat unhurriedly. They enjoy each other, their land, the silence — broken only by an occasional meadowlark and the subtle undertheme of unidentified insects. The day is warm, but not the unbearable Dakota heat of mid or late-summer. Perhaps it is now they decide to name the property *Fairview Farms*, although it was always just "the Farm" to the girls and me.

Happily they survey the vastness, albeit barrenness, of their new domain. In my scenario, my mother is conceived that night under a cloudless sky littered with stars and a full moon. As the young couple lie in each other's arms, they drop to sleep hearing the plaintive sound of a lonesome coyote, one of those lonely singers of the night. He sings wistfully, but none of his relatives answer. The coyote is not threateningly close; they sleep immune from roaming critters, surrounded by the spicy fragrance of wild roses. They have found blissful fulfillment.

In reality, the photo was shot by Charlie himself. He was an avid amateur photographer, who knew all about time-release, so he could be in the picture too. He had one other trick to make sure he was present visibly whenever he acted as the photographer — which was most of the time — and that was to have an extremely large, framed photo of himself positioned prominently in the background, his head size in the photo equal to the size of the heads of those he was photographing!

The young couple in the picture was actually nowhere near their homestead. They were just outside Bismarck the summer before their marriage took place in November, 1902. Charlie had bicycled the sixty miles up from his parents' farm in Emmons County just for a short visit, over country dirt roads and sandy hills, which made the going hard. He did this frequently over the years of their long courtship, and spoke in later years of how tired his legs got. My own legs hurt when I even think about how many times he must have made that trip.

The society editor of *The Emmons County Republican* reported the Charlie Pearson nuptials the easy way: she quoted in its entirety the fulsome coverage (in the effusive style of the day) of *The Bismarck Tribune*.

Another wedding of two popular and well known young people was that which occurred at Bismarck Tuesday evening, and mentioned as follows by the Bismarck Tribune:

At the home of the bride's parents, 216 Fifth Street, Tuesday evening, November 11, 1902, was performed the mar-

*riage ceremony which united Inda, daughter of Mr. and Mrs.
Wm. Conner, to Mr. Chas H. Pearson. The ceremony was that of
the Episcopal service and was performed by the Rev. Joss of this
city.*

*Miss Laura, sister of the bride, acted as bridesmaid and
Master Edward, brother of the groom, acted as best man. Only
the near relatives witnessed this ceremony... Many valuable
presents were received and hearty good wishes were
extended...Charles Pearson is one of the best known young men
in Northern Emmons County, and is a prosperous young
rancher, of the habits and disposition that will make cheerful the
home that his bride has consented to share.*

*The bride was formerly a resident of Emmons County,
where she spent a few years of her earlier life, and where she
made the many friendships which followed her to Bismarck in
later years. She is a talented young lady and will add both grace
and beauty to her chosen home.*

*The happy couple have begun housekeeping on Mr.
Pearson's ranch at Tell. The Republican extends congratulations
together with the best wishes of their numerous friends.*

Although the newspaper cites Uncle Ed ("Master Edward")
as best man, the marriage certificate lists Charlie's sister
Carrie's husband, Walfred Hoover, in that role. As for other
disparities between reality and the newspaper report, how Inda
and Charlie must have laughed at the word "prosperous," and
the description of their new life on the ranch at Tell. They had,
to be sure, received a $10.00 bill from Charlie's folks as a wed-
ding present, a generous, if not princely sum, given the times
and the difficulty of getting cash money together. Charlie's
mother wrote in a feathery script an endearing note for the
occasion, innocent in its assumptions, and charming in its
formality:

> *Dear Son*
> *You and your dear Inda are now united for ever.*
> *May gods blessing*
> *be with you and your wife.*
> *Please find herewith $10.00*
> *as a present.*
> > *Very respectfully,*
> > *Mr. and Mrs. Olaf Pehrson*

As for their "housekeeping on the ranch at Tell," the young couple had indeed erected a sod house on Inda's portion of their homestead, because it was required that you have a house to live in on your property, according to the Homestead Act of 1862, but although sod was an efficient cold repellent, it lacked almost every other nicety, and the couple opted not spend their first wedded winter in it.

No, Charlie was not prosperous — yet, but things were moving along pretty rapidly. Looking just a little into their future, by 1905 they were able to build a small frame house on Inda's property where Elsie was born in 1907.

Inda's homestead claim "proved up" on July 16, 1907. President Teddy Roosevelt (or the Secretary of the General Land Office signed the official certificate for him. Both signatures looked curiously alike.) Inda nee Conner Pearson now owned free and clear her portion of Fairview Farms "to have and to hold with the appurtenances thereof."

Now they were free to sell the first house built on Inda's property, which they did, to a Walter White who moved it away, a fairly common practice in those days. This, of course was only after they had built another small house, this time on Charlie's side of the property, where Agnes and Flora were born. This second house was in turn sold to neighbor Levi Thompson (who also moved the purchase to his own property) in 1915 when the comfortable house I knew and loved was completed. It sat on the same little hillock on Inda's property as the first house. This third house was where Charline was born in 1917.

Back before the Pearsons were quite so prosperous, shortly after their move to the 1905 house, Charlie's youngest sister Annie came for a visit, a visit long enough to prompt her humorous comment, "Let's vary the menu tonight, folks. Instead of our usual potatoes, eggs, bread, butter and milk, let's have milk, bread and butter plus eggs and potatoes." The sumptuous farm eating that I remember so well and fondly came well after 1907.

In 1903, however, in all probability my mother turned into more than the proverbial gleam in Grandpa's eye on a cold February night atop a spartan bed in the architecturally plain frame house that belonged to Charlie's parents. The elder Pehrsons (not yet spelling their name Pearson) lived in a white

wood house on the homestead a mile or so from Inda and
Charlie's two homesteads, and the young couple lived with the
elder Pehrsons for a year or two.

My mother was born very properly exactly eleven months
after they married.

6

You must have been a beautiful baby,
'Cuz baby, look at you now...
Popular song of the twenties

For the young Charlie Pearsons, 1903 was an exceptionally good year. For one thing, Olaf relinquished the office of postmaster at Tell, and Charlie took over the position officially, thus receiving the accompanying salary, although he had been doing much of the work for several years. It was a post he enjoyed until 1908 when mail distribution was moved to Braddock for more centralized control of delivery and Tell no longer warranted a postmaster.

However, it was my mother's timely arrival on October 12, the date of his own birthday that was cause for Charlie's exuberance. *The Emmons County Republican* noted on October 15, 1903:

Postmaster Chas. Pearson, of Tell, was in Hazelton Tuesday with a smile and a box of cigars. Inquiry elicited the fact that there was a new schoolma'am at his house — a fine eight-pound baby girl — born Monday. Dr. Snyder reports all parties doing nicely.

As with the birth of all five girls, Lucille's delivery was at home. "Where else?" Flora remarked when I asked about it. There were, of course, no hospitals in the middle of the prairie, but there were doctors. One was always summoned in the nick of time, although with all the deliveries of calves, colts, lambs and piglets Charlie had mid-wifed, I believe he could have handled it himself. (Well, maybe not the first time.)

Laura Lucille was named for Inda's next oldest sister

Laura, but no one ever called her anything besides "'Cille," or
Lucille, or in later years, "Lu." That she was unusually bright
was early apparent, and schoolmarm Inda was quick to spot and
nurture it. She drew the alphabet letters and put them on
cardboard in Lucille's crib, and began to teach them to her so by
the time the new baby was one year old she knew the ABCs.

Agnes loved to tell the story Charlie once told her about
Inda's lost comb. It was tortoise shell, and very special to Inda,
though in those days, any comb was valuable. It had totally
disappeared when Lucille was about nine months old. Three
months passed before Inda remarked quizzically to Charlie, "I
wonder whatever could have happened to my comb?" One-year-
old (plus) Lucille piped up, "Do you mean the one I put in the
organ pedals?" Sure enough, when Charlie opened the section of
the organ where the pedals sat, there was the missing comb.

One story that the girls swear is not apocryphal seems
almost too amazing to be believed, but they heard it as youngsters from the neighbors as well as from Charlie and Inda so I
repeat it here.

It seems that Lucille could read before she really talked,
and by the time she was two, able to read aloud creditably from
the King James Bible. On Sunday afternoons after church,
neighbors from as far away as Braddock would arrive, uninvited, to pay a call. They had heard of this amazing baby, and
wanted to see for themselves if the gossip was true. To be sure
that her apparent facility with the Bible was not a sham, or that
little 'Cille, coached by prideful parents, had not memorized
specially chosen verses by rote, they brought their own Bibles
and would choose their own citations for her to read. She
happily obliged, leaving the neighbors shaking their heads and
clucking in amazement.

She also had what today is categorized as an "eidetic"
memory, a phrase entering the psychological lexicon in about
1923, but in 1903, was called "photographic." As they grew up,
her little sisters would give her something to read (a letter,
perhaps) and she would glance at it idly, then hand it back
immediately. Heatedly they would say, "Well, READ it, 'Cille."
But she *had* read it and could quote it to them verbatim.

She had another talent — not too socially acceptable,
however. She was able to sit on the opposite side of a desk from
a person looking at a printed page in front of him or her and

read it from her side — never betraying that fact, of course!

No other sister was trained to perform quite so early in life as Lucille. That early requirement of her may explain why in college she would bargain with her teachers: she would write TWO papers to everyone else's one, if the professors would not require her to read her papers aloud to the class.

With no evidence of jealousy, however, and with great earnestness, each of my aunts has assured me that my mother was the smartest of the five. I'm sure it was a disappointment to her that her own daughter didn't learn to read until she went to school!

The births of Elsie, (1907) Agnes (1909) and Flora (1912) were also medically uneventful, and happily welcomed, though it can hardly be assumed that Charlie wouldn't have been thrilled to see the arrival of a boy somewhere along the line. How could he know so early what good farm hands the girls would turn into?

By the time the three younger sisters arrived, the extraordinary intelligence of all their offspring was taken for granted by Charlie and Inda; sadly, the amount of time and attention given to Lucille's unusually early reading talents had now to be divided among the rest of the girls, the farm, and the livestock. Nevertheless, all learned to read well before they ever went to school, taught by Inda from the *Rose Primer*, a slim little green book with a large pink/red rose on the cover. Inda would sit in the kitchen of a winter day with the oven door open to keep warm, while the youngest girl would read aloud her most recently learned pages, thus preparing her to start school at the age of five, ready for the second grade.

Almost concurrently with Charline's birth in June of 1917, 41-year old Inda very nearly lost her life. The birth itself seemed to have gone as well as the earlier four, but very shortly afterwards she developed a raging fever that reached higher than 106 degrees, and she became delirious. Childbed fever (*puerperal sepsis*) was not uncommon in those days, but today Flora and her two daughters, Carla and Connie, (all three nurses) suspect the reason for Inda's terrible infection was caused by the attending doctor himself. With gentle understatement they suggest that "maybe the doctor just didn't wash his hands well enough."

He had just come from a home where they had scarlet

fever, and he had many more calls to make after delivering
Charline. In a hurry, and not wanting to wait for the placenta to
eject naturally, he impatiently reached up and pulled it out. It is
known today that both scarlet fever and *puerperal sepsis* are
caused by the streptococcus organism.

Charlie was frantic because every bed in the Bismarck
hospitals was full. A world-wide pandemic of influenza was
rampant and North Dakota had not been overlooked by this
virulent killer. Valley City couldn't take another patient, nor
could Fargo. Finally he was able to get Inda a bed in the hospital at Jamestown — a four hour drive away. It had one other
disadvantage: it was the State's mental institution, not a
regular medical hospital. Notwithstanding that serious drawback, the Jamestown Hospital saved Inda's life, though it took
several months.

The telephone wires were quickly humming as the news
got out. The emergency ring (6 shorts) on the party line caused
even those not given to "rubbering" (listening in on calls not
intended for you) to tune in to the Pearson's problem. Hearing
the bad news, many called in to offer help in tending the newborn. One neighbor, a motherly soul named Mrs. West, was
overheard crooning to the furiously wailing Charline as she
washed her in a large basin on the kitchen table, "Well, it were
too baddy she were *so* maddy."

It was to the Swiss family Grunefelder (pronounced
Greenfelder) that Charlie entrusted the new baby, no matter
that Anton and Theresa were "Different." How different was
"Different" was clear to every Swedish immigrant, who knew
only Lutheranism, the State religion in Sweden. When they
spoke of it, they — *whispered* the word, *Catholics.*

There was not any subject that Charlie and Anton
Grunefelder agreed on be it religion, politics, proper farm
methods or farm subsidies (Charlie was agin' the latter). One
was an IVA (member of the Independent Voters Association)
and the other a FUR (Farmers Union Republican). Nobody
remembers who was which. Nevertheless, they were the best of
friends.

Rejecting offers from his sister Lizzie to take the older
girls, Charlie assured Inda in an August 8, 1917 letter to her in
the Jamestown hospital that he would only "separate the children from me when I cannot talk anymore."

He placed not-quite-14-year-old Lucille in charge of
tending the house and commissioned the younger three to help
him with the livestock until...until...when? At that point, he
couldn't allow himself to think anything other than "until Inda
comes home." The community buzzed. They knew she might
never come home.

Inda's next oldest sister Laura, and Charlie's baby sister
Annie, both living in Bismarck at the time, offered to keep the
newborn, but only for a short time was Charline allowed to be
that far away from Charlie. Theresa Grunefelder didn't like
that thought, either. Like a brooding hen, she had tucked
Charline under her maternal wing and would not give her up.
"Theresa has a good heart," Charlie wrote Inda.

So it was Theresa who bundled Charline up in blankets,
re-wrapping her in newspapers to ward off the chill when she
and Charlie and the four older girls set out in Charlie's *New Era*
open touring car — not really the ideal vehicle to drive the five
daughters and Mrs. Grunefelder the 100 miles to Jamestown to
visit Inda. It was a long and chilly trip at best, traveling 25
miles an hour. Mrs. Grunefelder's newspapers were an inspired
protection for the baby.

Flora, who was only five, remembers how sharp the cold
could get in the early morning (four o'clock) even though it was
summer, and how nippy in the evenings as they returned on
these one-day junkets. They could never spend the night because they had to get back to milk the cows.

All the girls did their best to keep up their own spirits as
well as Inda's that long summer and early fall. It didn't help
their pain to have heartless classmates taunt them at recess
with cries of "Your mother's in the Crazy House, nyaah, nyaah,
nyaah."

Flora, who hadn't been to school yet, scratched out in
jagged printing a letter every week, that always said the same
thing:

*"DEAR MAMA. HOW ARE YOU? I AM FINE. LOVE,
FLORA."* One week she branched out: *"DEAR MAMA. HOW
ARE YOU? I AM FINE. WE HAVE A NEW CALF. LOVE,
FLORA."*

Dear Wife Inda, Charlie wrote on August 8, 1917, upset
at the news he'd received from her about impending (unspeci-
fied) surgery, *I just wish I could come and see you right away.*

He wanted so to be with her, and yet loathe to leave his responsibilities at the farm. At the beginning of the letter he offers to come to her side, but by the end of the letter has talked himself out of it, unless she wants him.

The girls help milk the cows, feed the pigs and chickens he reports; even little Flora does what she can — swat flies, wipe dishes and collect eggs from the chickenhouse.

Flora observed later in life...

Of course gathering eggs could get old fast, unless the gatherer succumbed to the challenge of a soft dirt floor, a slight depression in it, and a perfect stick lying nearby. A small pail full of eggs, when dumped into said depression and vigorously stirred with the stick make a novel and intriguing creation — bright gold and white against the black dirt. An artist experiences joy in creating an entirely new and original sight. On the way back to the house, the empty pail swings lightly from the hand.

Charlie was in the midst of something called "heading," with which Lucille, Elsie and Agnes were old enough to help, but which they couldn't handle alone.

Wheat was a major source of income for the Pearson farm. But if the crop grew short, if it had been a dry season, for instance, it couldn't be harvested the standard way, using a binder, but had to be gathered with a cumbersome machine called a header, and this had been one of those ultra-dry years. You could accurately describe a header as a Rube Goldberg contraption.

A clumsy, heavy piece of machinery, Charlie had to drive the six horses pushing it, as he straddled the steering bar — which was nothing more than a wide board — simultaneously keeping an eye on the looming elevator attached to the machine, which delivers straw to the receiving wagon driven by one of the girls. The wagon driver endeavors to keep alongside steadily and not let the grain go strewn back onto the field, but it's a tough job, especially with flying ants aiming at exposed necks and scratchy grain beards working their way up inside the clothes to legs and arms. The other girls try, with pitch forks, to keep the load distributed across the wagon box and shout encouragement to the wagon driver, who is terrified at coming to the end of the field where she must make a turn — a major maneuver requiring a steady hand and a responsive pair of horses. How could Charlie leave the girls alone to handle this major job by themselves?

And best he not let Inda know just how much the girls *did* do to help him, for this was the one area on which they had major disagreements. She was greatly opposed to their daughters doing heavy farm work, especially lifting. The grain bundles spewed out by the reaper/binder at harvest time had to be lifted, carried and stacked *just so* into a rain repellent shock. It resembled a kind of cone.

It was Inda's belief that such lifting would disarrange a girl's internal reproductive organs. She urged — in vain — the hiring of a man to do this work.

So strongly she felt about this that once on a clear, full-moon-lit night she waited until Charlie was asleep, then silently left the house and walked down to the newly cut, but still not shocked, grainfield. All alone, she advanced on those rows of bundles lying flat on the stubble. Bent over, grasping two, she thrust them into a slanted vertical cone and then built around that core a compact grouping of the near-by bundles — that's how she did it. Then on to the next area she went and repeated the procedure over and over. A few hours later, the task was completed and her daughters rescued, at least that one time.

Charlie might have wanted to believe that trolls were capable of such altruism, but Inda had made her point. Not that she won the issue for long, however!

"*Do not worry about anything, Inda,*" Charlie continued in his anguished letter. "*I just made a deal with Mrs. Sparks to come over and help and show Lucille how to fry down a mutton that I will kill next week. We have not killed any yet. I told Lucille to save the chickens until you come home so you can get a taste at them. We are getting along real well when we consider conditions. Of course you know this is my busy time, but if we can lay low a little, I will soon finish some of this up. Now Inda, just rest easy do not worry about anything. Worry is the worst thing that you can do, so don't do it...the children are real good, they take care of themselves real well, and all of them are well, and have been since you left, you can trust me. When I go to town or any place I take them along, so they fare well and feel well. What we are waiting for is for you to get strong so that you can come home. I hope you can soon, from your chas.*"

Inda did come home that fall, not quite as good as new
— but nearly.

Charlie had one other major worry that summer — the
deadly Spanish influenza. Many of their neighbors were terribly
ill; a few died. But Charlie, who had strong opinions about
almost everything, gave his sure-fire medical advice on flu
prevention to the girls: "1) Never lie down on the ground where
you can get chilled and 2) gargle with salt water every day."
Well, it worked, that summer at least. No one in his family fell
sick with flu during the epidemic.

Nevertheless Flora, with her proclivity for scientific
experiments, decided to find out for herself if he was right. She
carefully conducted her test lying flat out on the ground behind
the lilac bush in the grove of trees beside the front drive for a
half hour one day. But there were no dramatic flu-like symp-
toms forthcoming so she disappointedly returned to the house,
wisely refraining from announcing her test results.

Insulated as they were, their mother's illness affected
the girls far more than the early part of World War I. But they
were intensely aware of what was going on, and would hear
Charlie discuss current events with various neighbors. The
girls overheard tales of the possibility of the enemy using poison
gas and that it would settle in the low places; safety lay in
getting above it. The younger girls reasoned that if they
climbed the windmill and stayed up there in the high pure air
they would be safe. Flora was sick with anxiety, not being
aware of the distances between the farm and the enemy, she
had pictures of herself forever living up there on the windmill.

Charlie was too old to be drafted, but busy as he was in
1917 and 1918 — he was school treasurer and township supervi-
sor — he found time to sell Liberty Bonds. No neighbor was
allowed to get out of buying at least one bond while he was in
charge of the community's goal.

A neighboring thorn in Charlie's flesh was his biggest
sales challenge. This was the farmer whose property abutted
Fairview Farms, and who *insisted* the earth was flat — which
drove Charlie right up the wall. This was also the same neighbor who deliberately planted his wheat right up to the very edge
of the Pearson cow pasture. His billowing grainfield of course
tempted Charlie's cows to break in and feast. Not good for the

cows, which bloated them and of course not good for the neighbor's harvest. Confrontation!

Charlie (with slight irony): "Friend, why did you plant your wheat RIGHT UP to my fence??"

Thorny neighbor: "The devil told me to."

He was a nay-sayer, noted for pooh-poohing every community project Charlie and Inda proposed, and he flatly refused to make the requested bond purchase. Charlie looked him in the eye and threatened, "If you don't buy at least one bond, I'm hauling one of your cows to town. I'll sell it and buy the bond *for* you. You know I'll do it too." The recalcitrant one bought.

Ironically, it was only two months before the end of the war, when the pain of an immediate family member being killed in action in France brought personal grief to the Pearsons. Inda's next to youngest brother, Lieutenant Arthur Conner, was reported killed in the town of Sechault, France. He was thirty-three years old.

Very little was known of how he met his death until Inda's baby sister, Faye, managed to track down his commander, a Captain William F. McCann. Her letter pleading for information about her brother's death finally reached him at his home in Framingham, Massachusetts, and on May 7, 1919 he responded at length.

Grandma (Lottie) Conner had been 43 years old when her youngest daughter Faye was born, and Faye never really knew her mother, nor indeed had she ever had a real home. Lottie was ill for most of the time after Faye's birth until she died at the age of 56, and Grandpa Conner had his hands full, caring for her while keeping his small hack business going.

There was no one to look after Faye except her 10-year old brother, Marshall, an unlikely candidate for surrogate parent. All the other siblings were grown and had families of their own, except for Arthur. Faye had no one in the family to cherish her except her adored bachelor brother Arthur, who returned the affection, though Arthur had enlisted in the army right after high school and was very far away — a career soldier stationed in Hawaii before the Great War began.

"You'll come to Hawaii and live with me, little sister, when you are just a few years older," he'd written to her from Honolulu. Shunted from place to place, including for a time, a Catholic convent, little Faye's sole hope for a happy future was

wrapped in her dreams of living in Hawaii with Arthur. The
war of course, had delayed the fulfillment of her dreams.

She was nineteen when she read the details of his death
from Capt. McCann:

*At the time of Lieut. Conner's death I was the Battalion
Adjutant of the 1st Batallion, 372nd Infantry, US, with the
French Army and in the Champagne Offensive.*

*Lieut. Conner with several other Officers, then just
commissioned from the Army Candidate School in France,
reported for duty with our Battalion as we were going into the
drive of Sept. 26th 1918, in the Champagne front. It was at the
town of Hans, France that they reported for duty. This town is
situated not far from the town of Ripent, then the German
Headquarters, or near to the Headquarters of their army, at
least. I tell you all this in order that you may become more
familiar with the last few days of your brother's life.*

*Miss Conner, you may well be proud of such a brother, a
gentleman, and a wonderful soldier, one whom I would liked to
have known better, brave and fearless, yet cool, always exercising
the best of judgement.*

*Unfortunately he met his death during the attack on the
town of Sechault, France on Sept. 30th 1918. Lieutenant Conner
met his death by Machine Guns while in the act of encouraging
his men after hard and fierce fighting across the flats in front of
Sechault, just as the Battalion was ready to rush the town. This
town was loaded with Machine Guns. Under terrific Machine
Gun fire, he held his men and talked to them in a way that made
us proud of him. I personally recommended him for the American D.S.C.*

*During this attack our casualties were very heavy, many
of the Officers having obeyed the Command of the Supreme
Commander of all men and soldiers; it seems a great pity after
having passed all the trials and tests of a soldier, starting from
the bottom, receiving as a final reward, his Commission, (an
ideal soldier) his ambition attained, happy and light hearted,
ordered to immediate action in the line during a great Offensive,
to meet his Glorious Death, in his maiden drive as an Officer.*

*After the town of Sechault was captured, I then being in
Command ordered a Lieutenant John A. Sullivan, the only
Officer left with me after the fight, to bury the dead.*

Lieutenant Sullivan reported to me later that all of our dead were buried, most of them having been buried by the French with whom our Regiment formed the famous French 157th Red Hand Division.

Faye and Inda grieved for Arthur; the older Pearson girls grieved more for their Aunt Faye, so close to their own age she could have been their sister.

7

When lilacs last in the door yard bloom'd
and the great star droop'd in the western sky...
Walt Whitman

From the very beginning the sturdy, brown eggshell with white trim house that Charlie and Inda built in 1915 was the talk of the neighborhood. Not huge by today's standards, it had a second story, and was rumored to have indoor plumbing with hot and cold running water. It did.

It also had a telephone. Our "ring" on the community line was one long and a short. A ring was produced by twirling the gadget that looked like a pencil sharpener on the right side of the phone, alternating the length of each twirl. Six shorts was the signal for everyone in the neighborhood to listen in for what might be important news or an emergency. One neighbor sometimes rang six shorts just because he wanted an audience while he sang into the mouthpiece. That forgivable fraudulence might actually have been appreciated by some, because nobody in the area had radios — though Charlie did own a crystal set with headphones. The drawback to this particular neighbor's six rings was that sometimes he just wanted to announce in basso profundo the very imminent *End of the World*. Nobody believed him, of course, and they wearied of the calls. Because of him, as in the story of the boy who cried "Wolf, wolf" too often, the six rings began to have less urgency.

The new Pearson house stood on a gentle rise of land facing west toward the sloping mound across the road. I always called that mound "Indian Hill," for as you got closer to it, and perhaps began to climb it, you were soon huffing and puffing. It was really pretty steep, though North Dakota's claims to anything approaching a mountain (i.e. White Butte, Black Butte and the Turtle Mountains) are not in Emmons County.

I suppose I thought it was Indian connected because
Charlie had a box of Indian arrowheads he'd collected over the
years and I imagined, rightly or wrongly, that they came mostly
from that hill. My imagination was buttressed by the presence
of a ring of stones near the peak of the hill that surely must
have served as the hearth of some long-ago tepee. The top of the
hill was high enough to serve as a brave's perfect look-out for
game — deer, antelope, and rabbits were plentiful. He might
also have been watching for signs of coyotes or wolves, also
plentiful.

As you climbed the hill, the aura of times gone by
washing over you on a clear blue Dakota day, you might even
have imagined yourself a young brave needing to catch one of
the wild eagles dipping and soaring overhead. You must have
eagle feathers, of course, for your ceremonial headdress. You
have no gun, naturally, so after you reach the top of the hill, you
cleverly scoop out a shallow trench, just deep enough to hold
your recumbent body. For concealment, you have brought leafy
branches from undergrowth near the Missouri River bottom,
and now you pull them loosely across yourself. On top of the
branches you securely tie a live rabbit. Then you lie quietly and
wait. A keen-eyed soaring eagle will note the twisting, strug-
gling rabbit, swoop down to grasp the poor creature in its sharp,
clutching talons. At that precise moment vigilant you thrust
your hands up through the branches and seize both legs of the
eagle, and as he flaps helplessly, you pluck the needed feathers,
then release the angry King of Air Currents. Fortunately, you
are wearing heavy leather buckskin and heavy mitts an adoring
maiden (Red Wing, perhaps?) has fashioned for you. But how,
you may ask your imaginative self quizzically, wending your
way back down the hill, did you catch that hapless rabbit in the
first place? A problem to be solved some other summer day.

Slightly north of the house was a front entrance road,
wide enough for a hayrack to straddle. It bent around a copse of
trees that Charlie had forethoughtedly planted thirteen years
earlier, and led from a county road to our verandaed front
entrance. Those trees emerged mirage-like in the middle of
untold miles of flat prairie land. The dense little woods was
made up of box elders of the North American maple genus,
poplars, and willows. It also hosted wild plum trees, wild cherry
trees, a few black currant bushes, a stand of rhubarb (rhubarb

pie being a family favorite) and wild prairie roses.

They called that tree area "the Grove." One winter the snow drifts were so high the girls cut through the woods and walked over the tops of the trees on their way to school. In the summer the Grove sheltered Ladies Aid picnics, occasional worship services and Farmers' Union picnics. Sometimes a make-shift platform was placed in the meeting area, and at one assemblage (the reason for the occasion no longer remembered by anyone) Charlie felt inspired to recite one of his favorite John Greenleaf Whittier poems:

> *Blessings on thee little man*
> *Barefoot boy with cheek of tan*
> *With thy turned up pantaloons*
> *And thy merry whistled tunes —*
> *With thy red lips, redder still*
> *Kissed by strawberries on the hill;*
> *With the sunshine on thy face*
> *Through thy torn brim's jaunty grace*
> *From my heart I give thee joy —*
> *I was once a barefoot boy!*

Whittier rambles on for another 92 lines, and Flora once opined that both Whittier and Charlie should have quit while they still had an audience.

Our front stoop was guarded by what grew to be a wonderfully lush lilac bush at the south side of the short sprint of steps leading to an elegantly carved oak door. That lilac bush was my special friend, and we sat together many a night and watched the sun dip down behind Indian Hill, before Grandma hoo-hooed, "Bedtime, Kay."

I am not the only one for whom that bush had special meaning. Homesick Charline wrote to Charlie a few years after her 1941 marriage and permanent migration to California, "Smell our lilacs for me, Papa." It was then a few years after Inda had died, and Charlie was living with Flora and Jake in Bismarck. He responded that he would indeed go home to the farm to smell them for her. Any excuse to go back to Emmons County suited him to a T.

On the left side of the stoop as you faced the house was a small rock garden, Flora's special project. After she graduated from nursing school in 1932 and began taking short trips around the Dakotas, the rock garden expanded every time she came back to the farm for a visit. Latter-day Pearson girls like me and assorted visiting cousins were fascinated by her gatherings from the Badlands, the Black Hills, and Lake Sakajawea: marine fossils from the lake, rose quartz, shale, agates, and one cone-like sandstone formation about two feet high. Uncle Ed contributed some fairy-tears — a local name for small oblong sandstone concretions which had their beginnings around some nucleus — plus other geological oddities accumulated from his travels about North Dakota. Not included in this collection were any huge two-foot round "cannon balls" to be found along and in the Cannon Ball River about 50 miles south of Mandan. These sandstone monsters were avidly collected and used as yard decoration by many North Dakotans, but we were not among them.

Long before my time there had been a large flower garden sloping down southwest of the house. It was memorable for a stand of cosmos, a mix of cerise, yellow, and pink. Cosmos grows tall and small girls could almost be covered by it, so playing hide-and-seek of a late summer evening in the flower garden was almost as popular a playground as the cornfield.

As you stepped up onto the veranda, a large oval pane of glass in the center of the front door allowed a visitor to peer into the homey living room. The inquisitive one could see an upright piano standing along the north wall, and in the southeast corner of the same room, a floor model wind-up Edison — the Victrola predecessor. A small cot was visible, as were two rockers and a large oak reading table almost library size, strewn with a mass of periodicals which included *The Dakota Farmer, Successful Farming, The Pathfinder, The Home Friend, Literary Digest, Review of Reviews* and *The Scientific American.*

I have a hard time imagining who on the premises had time to read any or all of these magazines but the girls remember particularly an ongoing column in *The Home Friend* about a domineering husband named Warren and his too self-effacing wife Helen. Inda would be furious at Helen on a weekly basis for putting up with such a boorish man, but each week waited eagerly for a new incident to be riled over.

If the visitor pressed his nose up close to the oval glass window, he might see beyond the living room into the sunny dining room, separated from the front room only by a pair of highly polished Corinthian style wood colonnades. In between the piano in the living room and the north colonnade was a minuscule space where small girls could curl themselves into invisibility — a place to pout, nurse wounded feelings, hide from chores, or enjoy a rare moment of sister-free privacy.

The colonnades framed a room that held a large round oak table, expandable to the point of accommodating everyone Inda invited home for dinner on Sundays after church to a full threshing crew. Sunday dinner usually included a table's worth of the congregation and the pastor, who immediately after being fed dashed off to his second service in Temvik 20 plus miles away. An array of unmatched chairs, mostly ladder-back, surrounded the table.

On the north wall of the dining room was a built-in cupboard/sideboard with paned glass doors. Behind the glass doors sat the Good Dishes — a full set of Chinese blue Willowware, the arrival of which, via Sears Roebuck of course, is memorialized with triple exclamation points in Charline's written memories.

Below the sideboard were three built-in drawers, connected on either side to a small vertical cabinet. The top tier of drawers was too shallow to hold more than the jumble of a farm family's predictable collection of clutter — rubber bands, string, stray Mason jar lids, nipples for catsup bottles to feed orphan lambs, pliers, scissors, spools of black and white thread, and assorted safety pins. In my day there might also have been white paper paste, but when the girls were growing up, paste was made with a glutinous mess of flour and water.

The middle drawer, being quite a lot deeper, held the Good Linen. Deepest of all was the bottom drawer, Off Limits to the girls, for it held Charlie's School Treasurer papers and Other Important Stuff.

The two vertical cabinets on either side of the drawers were Off Limits to all but Flora (the right side) and Agnes (the left side) where they secreted private treasures. Flora once became heir to an empty red talcum powder can made of tin. Besides its sprinkle top it had a lid which, with difficulty, could be pried off. Into this unique bank Flora stored her *money* — any small coins she could acquire, some of which she may have acquired the same way I did.

Charlie liked to play a game with me, and I'm sure it started earlier with his daughters, wherein he would open his three-compartmented long, leather purse, carefully extract two coins, extend his palm and offer a choice of nickel or a dime. If you chose the nickel, thinking because it was larger it would buy more, he would cackle happily; it really tickled him. He pulled this ploy often enough so that I caught on, but I also learned that if I amused him by choosing the nickel, I usually got the dime, too. I let him laugh at me, greedily accepted both the nickel and the dime and ran for my small red purse with its fake gold chain. Unlike Flora, I didn't use banks, although Elsie's favorite gifts to me were always some form of bank, including one that looked like a miniature cash register. It stood idle and lonely most of the time.

I suspect that Charlie's game might have been the way that Flora got her money, too, though in earlier, less prosperous years it was probably not a game he played too often. She also earned 25¢ a day for what she calls her "desultory" sheep herding, not her favorite chore.

In any event, one day Flora couldn't find her talcum can. She went about the house wailing and moaning over her loss. Inda would patiently query, "Well, Flora, where do you *keep* your money?" and Flora weepingly replied, "In the can." After several such dialogues, exasperated Inda expostulated: "Well, *Jiminy whiz, kid*, where do you keep the *can*???"

This exchange so amused observant Agnes, an able and talented mimic, that she went about the house doing perfect imitations of Inda's Jiminy whiz kid outburst, which of course only increased Flora's agitation.

Agnes the sociable, Agnes the talented cook, Agnes the always prepared, had other uses for her private cabinet. It was where she stored her luscious white Lady Baltimore cakes with brown sugar frosting, baked not for the tastebuds of her salivating sisters, mind you, but for any potential company who might happen to drop by. Unfortunately, drop-bys in the middle of the prairie were not all that frequent, so often her cake dried out before it could be eaten — except for peeling off the brown sugar frosting and eating it like penuche fudge. (Plain penuche fudge, a heavenly concoction of brown sugar, cream, butter and nuts, was Charline's specialty, and I was usually her biggest customer on the rare days she and I shared alone on the farm. Her

penuche making was usually followed by a marathon of maga-
zine reading in companionable silence.)

A long, horizontal waist-high mirror was housed behind
the sideboard's serving ledge, visually doubling the size of Inda's
sun-drenched indoor greenery located on the opposite side of the
room on a long oak bench beside the large bay window facing the
south quarter of the farm. That bench had been hand-made by
Olaf as mealtime seating for his seven offspring, in later years
passed along to Inda and Charlie.

There were other plants, but I remember particularly
several giant rubber plants (very ugly) and two or three large
flowing ferns (very beautiful). The other girls remember most
especially an array of brilliant red geraniums, a few pink and
white as well, all sitting in old tin tomato cans of assorted sizes.
The outrageous vigor of these rambunctious plants was attributed by Inda to the nail she placed in each tin can, giving a
healthy shot of iron thereby; who knows what nutrients the tin
cans might have contributed. More iron, most likely.

Beneath both the larger window in the living room, and
on the east wall of the dining room sat an ugly but comforting
little hot water radiator (heated by the basement furnace) which
alternately clanked, burbled, hissed, and burped. It required a
small key with scallops around its edges to help it noisily and
unashamedly release its excess air.

At the east end of the flower bench was a small, solid
oak table — wash-stand type — holding Charlie's Oliver typewriter, which he plied with two forefingers at a clattering speed.
The table had come from the Campbell sheep ranch west of
Kintyre where Charlie worked as herder and shearer when a
very young man. Kintyre, another name of Scottish origin, was
originally named Campbell for the most important rancher in
the area, a practice of nomenclature quite common around the
state.

On the east wall sat Inda's rarely idle treadle sewing
machine; in a small corner on the southwest wall next to the
greenery bench was what Charlie called his "secretary." It was a
tiny but functional drop-leaf desk, full of pigeonholes and secret
places to store important documents. Its lower shelf held
Charlie's well-worn complete set of *Ridpath's History of the
World*.

Above the secretary a motto painted in dark green

cursive lettering on a small sheet of tin hung on a nail. Some
seed company had sent it to him as a gift early on in his farming
career, when it became apparent that Charlie would be a customer worth cultivating. It read: *Plan Your Work, Then
Hustle.*

Charlie lived by that motto, and presumed that because
of his example the girls would all go and do likewise. Fatherly
lectures at the supper table gave further impetus to their
collective lifelong tendency to make to-do lists, followed by
hustle, whizz and dash. His *Save Your Money and Never Never
Touch the Principal* lecture, however, was the most frequent,
and no doubt led to Flora's tenacious protection of her talcum
can.

Stepping from the dining room you would find yourself
in Inda's domain, a large, airy kitchen dominated by an enormous black coal range on the west wall. You could almost never
be too young for the chore of shoveling out its perpetual accumu-
lation of ashes. This grandiose stove had a built-in heating
device which supplied hot water for the upright hot water tank
directly behind it. On the south side of the stove in its fire box
was a series of hollow projections through which the cold water
would enter, circulate and then flow into the tank. On broiling
summer days when heating up the stove was unthinkable, the
family had to be content to bathe in luke-to-tepid water.

A modern white porcelain sink replete with a wide dish
draining area and two long spindly front legs, remarkable only
for its size in comparison with today's space-saving models,
stood against the west wall next to the range. Next to the sink
between two windows on the north wall was the milk separator,
the source of never ending chores for the girls. Hanging on a
wall on the northeast corner of the kitchen was the wooden
telephone, an apparatus a foot-and-a-half tall, and about ten
inches wide. A sturdy invention, that one.

Extending not quite to the center of the room stood a
husky square table covered with practical but unprepossessing
yellow-flowered white oilcloth. Pushed back against the north
wall unless all four sides were needed to seat the diners, the
table was surrounded by chairs of many lineages and heights,
plus a backless high stool or two. These metal stools were a
hardy breed — one of them lives in Flora's kitchen today.

Just off the kitchen to the east was the walk-in pantry

whose handsomely carpentered shelves held edible treasures. All of Inda's summer canning — corn, tomatoes, string beans and peas plus prize-worthy (though never entered in a fair) canned beef and mutton. The meat, its juices, and some water had been put into pint jars, placed in a boiler and boiled in water for four hours, then sealed up. Months later, one could open the jar and find what had been fluid now to be a shimmering dark gelatin, with juicy, tender meat buried in it.

Also standing at attention on the shelves was an army of glass Mason jars full of grape and bullberry jelly. Both wild grapes and bullberries (too tart to eat but great for jelly) were gathered on the annual Pearson trek to the Missouri River bottoms every autumn. With seven eager pickers, the family returned home with baskets, tubs and boxes flowing over with purple-black grapes and orange-red bullberries that would be trounced into jelly the next day by Inda and her merry elves. Native Indians in days gone by once pounded bullberries into venison suet as part of a preserving process, but jelly was all Inda used them for. A light, orangey red, the tangy bullberry jelly was spread generously in sandwiches, a staple for school lunch pails.

Grapes for eating (juicy purple Concord grapes) were bought at Falgatter's General Store in handled baskets — the latter adapted later into cradles for dolls and kittens — and were a special treat, pure eating pleasure. The technique was to pop one into the mouth, squeeze out the cohesive center containing the seeds and swallow that ball whole. Then suck out the sweet juice remaining in the vacated skin and discard the too-tart purple left-over.

High on a top shelf was Inda's medical book with marvelously graphic anatomical pictures, thought to be safely out of the reach and eyes of the young and curious — not altogether a safe assumption. "The vivid *Doctor Book* was furtively perused only when Mama was safely out of the house," according to Flora.

Staples from Falgatter's store in Kintyre such as salt, oatmeal and coffee beans were also visible on the open shelves of the one-windowed pantry. One-hundred pound sacks of sugar and flour — sacks that were ultimately bleached and made into dishtowels — sat side by side on the floor, along with a wooden crate of dried fruit — apricots, prunes, figs or apples. The

Watkins man's visits were visible, too, with large bottles of pure vanilla and lemon extract in plain view.

A special air-tight crock was visited frequently by one and all, for it held the brown sugar. One day when Inda and Charlie were going to Kintyre they were mightily surprised when Agnes and Flora declined to go along. (Not go to Kintyre? Were they sick?) The conspiring two waited only until the Model T Ford rounded the bend by the Grove; then as wickedly planned, they raced to the brown sugar supply, dipped up a goodly amount into large porridge bowls, added a small amount of water, stirred it all together into a nasty brown paste, and with no oatmeal to mitigate the sweetness, began to stuff their small selves. The joy was short lived. Quickly sated with the sickly sweet stuff, the small culprits wanted no second helpings. Heartsick, they grieved and regretted. For this short-lived, dubious pleasure they had sacrificed a trip to Kintyre!

The bulging pantry gave ample testimony that the *Emmons County Republican* had been prophetic back in 1902 when they called Charlie a "prosperous" rancher. The comment was just thirteen years early.

A large, windowed back porch-room just off the kitchen, parallel to the pantry, functioned as an unheated catch-all, which every farm house needs. It housed another modern gem: a motorized Maytag washing machine, galvanized into action by a gas motor and sporting a rugged wringer through which the sodden but clean clothes were hand fed. Small girls were charged with retrieving the clothes as they wormed and squished through to the opposite side into the tub of rinse water, then wrung again into the basket, making sure they layered neatly into the waiting clothes basket. Later the wash would be hung out to dry by the older girls, tall enough to reach the clothesline. The weekly laundry was usually too much for the clotheslines, and so the girls made use of the sheep fence where they draped the heavy work clothes and bibbed overalls. Tedding, or spreading out to dry, wasn't just for newly cut hay.

A noisy appliance, that Maytag. No one was ever in doubt about when it was washday, and if you happened to be on the outside of the house when it was time to disgorge its bellyfull of lye-soapy, hot water, you'd best not be close to the back stoop, where its long black hose hung obscenely from a hole in the porch and spewed dirty water like Mt. Vesuvius lava into the backyard.

Clean, empty cream cans waiting to be filled with sour cream and hauled to Kintyre to sell, lined one wall of the back porch along with another choremaker, the butter churn, though the latter lived sometimes in the pantry.

Walking west from the kitchen down the windowless hallway you came first to the sole bathroom in the house, whose only claim to fame was that it existed at all. A marvel of the neighborhood in 1915, it was complete with flushing toilet, hot and cold running water in the footed bathtub, and an immense washbasin where one could take sponge baths with water heated atop the range in a big copper tea kettle if the hot water tank had not been heated up.

The reason the Pearsons could have indoor plumbing was that Charlie had dug a series of trenches reaching from the house southwest down the hill away from the house. First was the septic tank, then the trench which somehow (underground) received the effluent and disposed, disbursed or decimated it all in a manner incomprehensible to me.

Before those trenches were built and the septic tank carried the whole load by itself, there would sometimes be a slow response to the indoor plumbing. Then Charlie would have to bring a portable hand-operated pump (big and effective) to pump out the contents to run down the hill. The girls would pray for no south wind that day. Nevertheless, even with an unwelcome wind, it was better than the aroma of the "Littlehouse," the family nomenclature for a diminutive two-hole retreat out on the far side of the chicken coop. There, with the door left open, one could sit in privacy with the Sears Roebuck catalogue, or gaze in dreamy solitude into the sheep pasture, and on beyond to the rippling fields of grain.

A large single-paned bathroom window looking out on the north side of the property gave a full view of the big, red barn to any enthroned sitter on the "thunder-mug." Several hundred feet farther and to the left you could also see Charlie's "shop," about the size of a single-car garage, where he plied his smithy talents, repaired broken machinery, sharpened plow blades, mower sickles and hoes, and replaced horse's shoes. Once in the early thirties he even repaired what was probably a broken motor for a barnstorming pilot who had been forced to land unceremoniously in one of our fields. Though Charlie had repaired many an ailing auto (neighbors' as well as ours) he

certainly had never repaired an airplane, but he didn't let that
daunt him. Flora amplifies:

> *I vividly remember the day we heard an airplane over-
> head, sputtering and then descending into the pasture just north
> east of the barn. An airplane! A most rare sight, and then to
> think of it landing in OUR backyard! Several neighbors as well
> as Papa came running up to it, but we kids were forbidden to go
> close. Soon we saw Papa and the pilot come hiking over to our
> blacksmith shop, and after some time, go hiking back to the
> downed plane. I think I was too young to understand what it
> was that had broken, but I well remember seeing the repaired
> plane finally get airborne.*

A large set of bellows was mounted on the ceiling of the
shop with a rope pull hanging down. When the forge was
glowing with red embers a pull on the rope sent a blast of air
into them, increasing their output of heat onto/into the object
being prepared to be re-shaped or re-sharpened on the anvil
under Charlie's heavy sledge hammer. Watching this operation
was a source of never-ending fascination for all of us.

Returning to our house tour, the next door down the
hallway from the kitchen led to the basement, that wonderfully
horrible, tantalizing, black, scary realm of The Pump, without
which the house would have no electricity. Actually, there was
no electricity when the house was first built, but it was wired
with great expectations for some undesignated time in the
future, but privately known that it would be when Charlie had
the cash to do it, for it was against Charlie's Monetary Creed to
buy anything on credit. For at least two years after the
Pearsons moved into the new house, switchboxes stood naked
and open.

"Can you remember getting electricity on your farm?"
my cousins Carla and Connie queried of their mother Flora in a
now family-famous taped oral history garnered during a
breadmaking session in her kitchen.

> *Very well. At first I really hadn't wanted electricity. I had
> always enjoyed the evening hour when the kerosene lamps were
> turned on. I liked to watch the flickering light reflected off the
> glass chimneys of the lamps and lanterns, which I had some-*

times helped to polish. The lanterns, of course, were usable for outdoor chores. Exposed to the wind, the globe had to be set into a metal frame which had a carrying handle; the globe's open top was protected from the wind by a metal shield.

But on the evening of the day when those lamps became obsolete in our home, I was about five. To my great pleasure, I had been invited to go with Papa in the pick-up truck to the home of Mr. Kelsch in Napoleon. Mr. Kelsch, you see, had battery cells for sale, because the Rural High Line had recently brought electricity to the town of Napoleon.

We went inside and Mrs. Kelsch served us wienerwurst, mashed potatoes and sauerkraut. The bargaining between the men in the next room wafted to my ears as Mrs. Kelsch entertained me in the kitchen.

Evidently Mr. Kelsch's price was too high, because finally my dad said, "Come on, Flora, we are going home."

I was terribly disappointed. I remember how sad I felt at the failure of our mission. I had so looked forward to telling my sisters that we were finally going to get our electricity. The house had been wired for electric current when it was built in 1915, but for a long time the exposed wires simply protruded from the wall and from the ceiling. Now Papa and I had gone on this important errand, and we were leaving empty handed. But as we drove out of the yard, I turned around for one last look and saw Mr. Kelsch.

"Papa!" I cried, "He's waving at us to come back! Maybe he wants to give you your price!"

And when we returned to our farm I did get to tell my sisters that now we would have electric light. What we had brought home with us were large battery cells that we stored in the basement. After the bare light bulbs had been installed at the end of a drop cord hanging from the ceiling, Papa would go down in the basement, start a little gas-driven two-cylinder engine that would re-charge those 14-inch rectangular battery cells. Then for several days we would have a faint little light at night that came from the dreary low-watt bulb hanging so forlornly from the single drop cords — one in each room — a far cry from the cheery illumination of the old kerosene lamps.

Gradually, as the charge wore down, the light would get dimmer and dimmer. Then we girls would be admonished, "WHO has been using too much electricity?" Well, it wasn't on

*any electric appliances in those days, believe me! It was all on
those little electric light bulbs.*

*Papa would then have to go down into the basement and
start up the motor. Some of the smoke from the motor was
filtered off through an exhaust pipe that went out the north wall,
but not all. We loved to go down into the basement after Papa
had been charging the battery cells because then the cellar was
filled with thick blue smoke whose aroma was intoxicating.*

*When we were outside and the motor was running, we
could hear its baritone voice:*

*"Surrey-LUNG-lung-lung, surrey-LUNG-lung-lung,
surrey-LUNG-lung-lung" it sang to us through the heavy, wide-
diameter exhaust pipe that extruded from the side wall of the
house.*

Quite apart from the magical pump that made wonderful
smells and sang "surrey-LUNG-lung-lung" to you, there were
spooky Things in the basement that anyone under the age of ten
knew very well lived directly behind the open-riser stairs
leading down to the coal bin.

What those Things looked like, or where they came from
was never known, but it WAS known that an unwary child, sent
downstairs to fetch a scuttle of coal, or enough potatoes for
supper, or perhaps to turn the eggs in the incubator, could be
snatched by the ankles, dragged through the open-backed risers
and carted off to the black environs of the Things who would
probably eat you immediately.

There was a way out, however. The more savvy child
knew that They could not grab you from any higher up than the
fourth step. Therefore, if you *jumped* from the fourth step over
the last three stairs, the Things were stymied and had to scurry
back to the coal bin, or wherever it was They slept. One other
way to keep Them at bay was to persuade Inda to stand at the
top of the stairs until you finished your appointed errand, for it
was known They were deathly afraid of Inda, a veritable
ghostbuster if there ever was one.

Beyond the cellar door entrance, parallel to the living
room, was Inda and Charlie's small bedroom, which contained
very little: their iron painted-white fourposter with its four
brass knobs, a medium-to-small wardrobe, a dresser with deep
drawers and a mirror and a tiny night stand. On the latter stood

a huge Big Ben alarm clock that ticked so loudly you could hear it from outside the room. It also held the barrel-shaped tumbler with water where Charlie put his false teeth at night or whenever they became too painful to wear. The shape of the tumbler and the water magnified those "choppers" as he called them, turning them into objects of horrid fascination to me. I would stare at them as though those bright pink and ivory plates were some alien species in an aquarium.

Just outside their bedroom door was the stairwell leading to the upstairs and the east and west bedrooms. The landing was spacious, its two windows facing out toward the barn, the shop and the trees. It served youthful imaginations as a playground of many purposes. Sometimes it was a cruise ship, sometimes a doll-house, sometimes a huge game-board where dominoes and checkers could be spread out, as the players lay stomach-down facing each other. But always it was an aerie safe from adult eyes.

My cousin Gregory — Agnes's son — and I once used it as a crow's nest from which we could watch all the adults outside the Norwegian Lutheran church, attending a funeral from which we had been excluded. We didn't care. Much.

At the top of the stairs, if you turned right you were in the west room, which for a while was Lucille and Elsie's room, but then abdicated by them for Grandpa Conner. In my day it was the hired girl's room. It, too, was sparsely furnished, though it had a walk-in closet at least half as big as the room itself.

The hallway between the rooms held floor-to-ceiling built-in drawers (what else, with carpentry the family talent?) and a sizeable linen closet.

The east room, which during the Grandpa Conner sojourn held all five girls, was furnished with two white painted wrought iron four poster beds, and a small dresser. Period. But it, too, had a very large walk-in closet, AND, happy shudder, two unfinished side closets on either side of the room, hunkered down beneath the slanted eaves. These closets, like the cellar, were also suspected of harboring Unnamed Beasties. However, they held heavenly treasures; for instance, ancient magazines, years of *National Geographic* with pictures of chocolate-colored bare-breasted women living on exotic islands, untold boxes of books, and most enticing to me, boxes of ladies' shoes, party dresses and hats packed in trunks by the long-gone girls, just waiting to be used for playing dress-up on rainy days.

These attractions warranted persuading Inda to disperse the Beasties prior to the entrance of a youngster by whom they were presumably not intimidated.

Finally, but hardly least, was the large veranda off the east bedroom which covered the unheated porch below, and from which one could survey all of the Pearson farm and on into forever, across the unending plains beyond our property. The veranda had been made safe for the girls by the erection of a three-and-a-half foot railing, but it was possible to climb over the south side, which had a wider ledge, with room to sit or stand outside the rail's protection.

Neither Agnes nor Flora would ever admit to observing the act personally, but they were, nonetheless, challenged by tales of young boys who wrote their names in the snow when peeing behind the school-house. So the two girls made up their own version of the game: unable to write their names as the boys did, they climbed out to the edge of the veranda, faced the empty air in front of them, squatted into position and vied to see who could pee the farthest away from the house. They watched with fascination the sparkling arcs they created. Their efforts spurted far out, never striking the side of the house, which might have imperiled their clandestine contest. Agnes, being three years older and that much longer of torso, usually won.

Oh, it was a wonderful house to grow up in, all right.

8

Vengeance is Mine,
Saith the Lord.
Romans 12.19

There are some Pearson girl stories I know so well,
surely I must have been there when they happened. How could
I not have been, when right this minute, I can tell you the other
Pee Story to its tiniest detail: the room, their beds, their night-
gowns, even what they are saying, because I hear them. I see
them. I can smell the pink calomine lotion they all daubed on,
therapy against the mosquito bites accumulated through the
day.

It is 1921. Lucille, at eighteen, is home for the summer
from her second year at Ellendale Normal School.

It is only dusk, the sun has not yet set, though they can't
see it drop like a mammoth penny on fire behind Indian Hill, for
they are in the east bedroom, looking out from the foot of their
beds at the first faint Evening Star. All five have said their
ritual "Star light, star bright, wish I may, wish I might..."
standing just outside their bedroom on the back veranda over-
looking the backyard, the chicken coop and the Littlehouse.
Some nights the girls drag their comforters out onto the railed
porch, and lie out there communing with the star-sprinkled
black sky, wondering if they have soul-sisters somewhere on
another planet. Sometimes they count shooting stars and
speculate on the composition of those myriads of stars and on
whether they really are just openings in the sky to let them see
the shining lights of heaven coming through. Sometimes they
fall asleep and get rained on; then they have to sleepily drag the
bedclothes back into the house.

When the stars are dimmed by the light of a bright
moon, Lucille frequently keeps her little sisters in cowed awe by

telling them that the occasional dark shape flitting across the
face of the moon is in truth a *SEMI-LUNAR* who will come down
and snatch her away from them and take her up to the moon
unless they keep their proper place in her retinue. And THEN
who would they have to tell them wonderful stories at bedtime?

The flashing antics of some little night-flying creature
are often accompanied by the hollow hooting of a great owl.
Those eerie night sounds, plus the sudden screams of a prairie
burrowing owl give them all the incentive they need to obey her.
It is a wonder they ever fall asleep.

On this particular night there are too many mosquitoes
for either their own or 'Cille's outdoor fantasies. All five are
already in bed; they try to keep their voices low so Mama won't
call up to scold from the foot of the stairs.

Oh, oh, too late.

"Girls, settle down. Papa has to be up before four
o'clock; he needs his sleep. Don't be selfish."

They fall silent.

They can hear Grandpa Conner across the hall in the
west bedroom, snoring his whistle-like snort. It sounds like a
sick tea kettle. If it weren't for him coming to live with them,
mean old coot, Lucille and Elsie would still have a room to
themselves.

They are all five crowded into the little east bedroom.
Lucille and Elsie whisper and giggle in the white-painted iron-
frame double bed on the south wall; Flora, Agnes and Charline
are cramped into the other double bed with the harder mattress.
Agnes has to sleep in the middle tonight; it's her turn to be the
"butterball."

There are sounds of stifled laughter. Flora, squeezed
against the wall sits up, wide awake.

"What's funny, 'Cille?" she asks finally.

"Nothing. Go to sleep, honey."

"Something's funny. You and Elsie are laughing and I
want to know too."

Agnes is sitting up now, all ears. She props a pillow
behind her head — a pillow whose blue-stripe ticking is beginning to let the feathers pop out. She settles in for an evening of
fun.

Lucille has a dilemma. She has hatched a scheme to get
even with Grandpa Conner for keeping *both* the new Monkey

(Montgomery) Wards and Sears-Roebuck catalogues to himself this entire week. She is dying to share the plan with her sisters, but Charline, at age four, has a tendency to blab. Not that she means to. It just rolls out of her mouth under the most superficial interrogation.

With her resourceful imagination always in high gear, Lucille says, "Charline, I have to pee. I am so tired tonight. Would you go downstairs and do it for me? You may wear my gold locket to Sunday School this week if you will do that for me."

Charline is delighted. She has to pee herself anyway, and to wear 'Cille's locket would please her mightily. She slips into the too-large blue felt slippers that both Agnes and Flora have outgrown, and scampers downstairs.

Lucille whispers hastily. "Since Grandpa Conner loves to get packages in the mail, I say we should make him happy. Let's send him a package he won't ever, ever forget." She is so amused at her own idea she can't stop giggling, or get the words out fast enough to unveil the plan to her admiring audience.

Charline has been too quick; she is already flying up from the landing. They know where she is because she has hit the third from top stair, the one that squeaks and should be stepped over if you don't want to be heard coming.

"Ssssh. Here she comes. I'll tell you in the morning."

But Elsie is too curious to wait.

"Oh, Charline. I too, have to pee, but I cut my big toe this afternoon. Would you, just as a big favor, go down again and pee for me? I will help you clear the table after breakfast tomorrow, if you will."

"Okay." Charline is cheerful. She especially loves Elsie and would go just to oblige her, but the added promise of help to take the breakfast dishes off the table in the morning (her main chore, with more to come as she grows older) is irresistible.

Once more she heads downstairs.

"What will be in the package, 'Cille?" They know it will be something wonderfully terrible. Flora shivers with anticipation. This could be better than 'Cille's ghost stories.

"It's going to be an enormous package. We'll gather up everything we can find out in the back yard — chicken feathers and old bones and dead mice, and cow patties and turkey turds and ...."

But Charline is back. Agnes is ready for her.

"Ooooh, Charline. I wish I'd thought to ask you to pee for me, too. Would it be too much to ask...?"

Charline gives her a baleful look but trudges back down the stairs.

By this time the girls are all so convulsed with Lucille's plan and how they have hoodwinked poor little Charline they must sssh themselves severely to be quiet again.

Charline is back, her bounce almost gone; she starts to pile onto the hard bed with a self-righteous sigh.

But Flora doesn't want to be left out of this great game.

"Charline," she begins, "would you....?"

A lower lip begins to tremble. Charline bursts into tears; between sobs she says sorrowfully "Flor, I sorry — I just don't have ANY PEE LEFT."

Inda looms in the doorway.

"What's going on in here? Why is Charline crying?"

A guilty silence falls on the little dormitory. Finally, with cool head, Lucille responds.

"She may have been having a nightmare, Mama. She'll be all right."

Inda looks skeptical, but Charline is weeping silently now, her tears hidden by the dark. Something's going on that she doesn't understand, but whatever it is she's not going to spill any beans or be called a crybaby or worst of all, a tattle tale.

The two older girls pull up their covers as though to sleep; Mama withdraws; the three little ones turn over on their sides all in the same direction, like three demitasse spoons. Tomorrow is going to be a big day. They have Grandpa Connor's surprise package to prepare.

The next day is bright and cloudless, a normal hot June Dakota day. Grandpa Conner sits on the top step of the back stoop, as is his daily wont, whittling on a small piece of wood, whistling tunelessly, his game leg held out straight in front of him. A long time ago he broke it, and it was never properly set, causing him chronic pain and aggravation.

Elsie is strewing grain nonchalantly for the ever-greedy mob of chickens clustered around her feet. Agnes and Flora are hidden beneath the stoop in their favorite eavesdropping position.

Lucille sails into sight like a heavily laden prairie schooner, cutting across from the big front drive, as though having just collected the day's mail from the mailbox a quarter-mile away.

She is all innocence. "A package has come for you, Grandpa Conner. Here it is," she says sweetly. All but smirking, she hands him a heavy parcel, neatly wrapped in brown paper, tied carefully with heavy twine, and knotted at the crosspoints.

Grandpa Conner looks up at her cautiously with his one good eye, the other long gone from a wood chip hitting it while chopping wood many years before. His long, slender face, at first disbelieving, breaks into a barely discernible smile. He carefully lays down his whittling on the back stoop, hefts the package in his two hands. Lucille and Elsie wait expectantly, politely, to watch him open the package.

But Grandpa Conner will not give them that satisfaction. Why should they be allowed the pleasure of watching him open this wonderful package? After all, was it not just yesterday that the girls locked him in the the grey-weathered two-holer Littlehouse *again* — locked for hours (seemingly) with the wooden bar from the outside, in his only refuge from these youthful tormentors? Exactly which imps were responsible he is not exactly sure, but he suspects these two as the most likely candidates.

"Hey little gals, lemme out, lemme out!" he'd yelled hoarsely, his plaint falling on no one's ears but the callously indifferent barnyard fowls. Nary a girl around to save him.

And wasn't it only last week that at least one of the littler scalawags had poked his angular, unpadded rump with a sharp stick through the spaces between the slats of the wooden steps? He well knows that three of them hide there daily just to annoy him as he sits on the stoop with his ever present whittling. Where else was an old man to go besides the outhouse and the back stoop?

But now his attention returns to the package.

What could it be? He scratches his head, trying to remember what he might have ordered from Sears or Monkey Wards catalogue, which he studies so carefully day after day. But it's for him all righty, addressed in big, bold print: Mr. W.H. Conner, c/o C.H. Pearson, Fairview Farms, Emmons

County, North Dakota.

His weathered face is slightly flushed, he finger-brushes his long, droopy black mustache absent-mindedly, then with great dignity picks up his whittling and with his package, retreats into the house.

Agnes and Flora emerge from their hiding place to cavort on the dry grass in uncontained hilarity. Elsie and Lucille sit on the stoop, their own shoulders heaving, as they laugh silently, hands cupped over their lips.

"'Cille, this is the best you've ever thought of," Agnes crows, as she and Flora fly up the steps, two at a time, to join the other two on the top step. Lucille tries not to look smug, but fails. Only Charline is not present to share their short-lived glee.

In a moment the east bedroom door is flung open and with a comanche yell, Grandpa Conner gallops thunderously out of the bedroom to the veranda just over them, leans over the rail and pours five pounds of barnyard detritus, the entire contents of the surprise package, on their unwary but deserving heads.

Lucille thinks with sudden insight of the citation in the book of Romans. *Vengeance is MINE, saith the Lord.* Actually, she reflects with a wry smile; it was Grandpa Conner who struck the retaliatory blow. God had nothing to do with it.

Poor Grandpa Conner. The girls as adults viewed their bedevilment of their mother's father with regret in rueful hindsight.

He had come to their home for a refuge, probably as reluctant to be there as they were to have him. His resourceful wife, Lottie, had died in 1913. He had nursed her through a long and painful illness; his children were grown and gone, none zealous to have him as a perpetual houseguest. He had led a life of vocational frustration, and now he was the unhappy recipient of the charity of his oldest daughter and her energetic, successful, no-nonsense husband, taunted by their five boisterous daughters. It was no wonder that not too many months later he packed up his bag and headed just across the border to Montana, where he lived out his days with his bachelor rancher son, Uncle Charley. He might have had to help with the cooking there in Wibaux, but there were no vexing little girls there.

He had one last small triumph. That same summer

before he left, he led little four-year old Charline, his one friend and ally, gently by the hand to Charlie's blacksmith shop. There he took a deck of cards out of his hip pocket, placed the cards in a vise, and filed off the edges of one side, all except for a small portion about a quarter-inch long while she watched with awe. He then instructed her in the art of locating any card selected by an audience. You put the card in the deck the opposite way so the high edge can be felt by a finger. You shuffle the deck a lot, but take care not to switch ends.

Charline says, "I surely enjoyed the bafflement on the faces of my sisters that afternoon and he did too, for it was quite a while before they found the clue to my bewildering facility."

Grandpa Conner died in 1932 when he was 82 at Uncle Charley's ranch. Death was caused by "the infirmities of old age," according to the omniscient *Bismarck Tribune*.

9

There was a little girl who had a little curl
Right in the middle of her forehead
And when she was good, she was very very good
And when she was bad, she was horrid.
Children's Nursery Rhyme

Agnes, where do you suppose Charline is?
I don't know Mama.
Elsie, have you seen Charline?
No, Mama.
Lucille, do you know where Charline is?
Haven't seen her lately Mama.
Will someone please try to find her? The company will be
here any minute and she needs to get cleaned up. Will someone
please look in the laundry pile?

The family is a-twitter. The visitors from Bismarck are
due any minute. The blue Willowware has already been set on
the table for company dinner. The house sparkles and everyone
is dressed but Charlie, who is shaving, with half a shaving
cream-covered face to go. But where can Charline be? She
hadn't buried herself in the laundry pile behind Inda's wardrobe, the girls' favorite hiding place; she's not down at the barn,
she isn't in the tiny corner beside the piano, she isn't in either of
the east room closets. They have hoo-hooed all over the yard
until their throats are hoarse. Where could she possibly be?

I found her, Mama.
Where, Flora?
(Sing-songy) *I think you'd better come see!*

A large lump inside Inda and Charlie's bed moves ever

Charlie Pearson and Inda Conner, summer of
1902, outside Bismarck.

Charlie's motto, sent to him by one of his seed suppliers. It always hung over his little "secretary" in the dining room.

Air view of Fairview Farms—probably shot about 1948, after the sale to the Stroms. Note the Norwegian Lutheran Church visible in the background, later razed. A small graveyard is still maintained there.

The Fairview Farm buildings: The barn faced
south, towards the east side of the house.

Note the chicken coop in the forground. The door is open. Inda used this visual aid to signify to Charlie out in the field that the time was 11:30 a.m. and he should come in soon for "dinner." (He had no watch.)

Front view of the house, which faced west towards "Indian Hill." These shots were taken shortly after 1915.

Stairsteps, l. to r., Lucille, Elsie, Agnes; Flora in front with doll. Photo shot in front of Charlie and Inda Pearson's second house, about 1914.

Agnes, Lucille, Elsie, Flora in lap, all in Sunday white. About 1913. Photo was made into postcards.

"Nooning" at the hayslough, about 1919. Uncle Ed, Inda, Charlie, Flora, Agnes, unidentified horse.

Picknicking with the Grunefelders down by the Missouri River, 1915. Pearsons in the autocar. Emma Grunefelder is with them in the Pearson car.

Charlie feeding the sheep,
mid-thirties.

Grunefelders in their Buick. Elsie's notes say
that Elsie, Agnes and Lucille are in rear seat of
the Buick.

harlie has just caught a fish at Seeman Park in Linton on a "Play Day."
da will pan fry it immediately over an open fire. Note how dressed up
harlie was! (He had no play clothes!) About 1923, the summer Charles
onner spent with the Pearsons, with Flora playing baby sitter.

Charlie and Flora (in head scarf) on a
berry-picking day at the Missouri
River, west of Hazelton.

Elsie, Flora and Agnes in Charlie's invention, the hollow "Horror."
December, 1919, outside School #3.

Flora, Agnes, Elsie, winter 1919. Playing in front
of house. Note The Grove visible in the background, filled to the top with snow. Charlie was
the photographer.

Entitled "Lunch Bucket" by one of the girls. L. to R., Agnes, Elsie
and Chubby, the Indian pony. Summer of 1920. Elsie in 7th grade,
to start 8th in the fall. Notes on the back of the photo in Elsie's
handwriting:
*We went to Tell School (Amy Engsell, teacher) after our (regular)
school was out "to make up for the day we lost because of bad
weather," per Mama. A couple of summers we went to Goose Lake
School—same reason. Here, we had just come home from school
and were putting Chubby on a picket chain to get his supper.*

Agnes, Elsie and Flora, about 1924. Knit caps of Agnes and Elsie were brand new. Lucille's friend Julia Brandt had taught them how to make them. Flora wore her "plain old hat," probably a hand-me-down.

A windy Sunday summer gathering, about 1923. L. to R., Cousin Joanne Hughes, (Aunt Laura's daughter); Cousin Charlotte Kent, (Aunt Faye's daughter) Charline, Flora, Otto Bauer, unidentified swain, Elsie.

Another Sumday gathering of the girls' friends, to play on the swing, about 1921: L. to R. Cora Kuntson, Elsie, Carrie Knutson (Cora's sister), Louise Grunefelder, little Charline amused and mystified by unidentified giggler (possibly Agnes?) in front. This group of young people had come to visit and swing on our tall telephone pole swing.

The girls in their "frocks" about 1928: Lucille.

Elsie and Lucille.

Assorted swains—Flora's. Probably 1928. Left to right: Edward Horton, Lester Daniels (bent over), Sievert Moe, George Hogen Collings. In front, right, bent over, Otto Klaudt.

Agnes, Charline, Elsie, about 1926.

Ellendale: One of the main classroom buildings.

so slightly, as Inda follows Flora's voice to the master bedroom. Flora is peeking under the covers; Inda follows suit, and drags one chagrined four-year-old out from beneath the sheets.

Inda pales.

Charline! What have you done to yourself??

Charline manages a crooked smile, trying to charm her way out of this confrontation, then breaks into tears.

I cut my hair Mama. Are you going to spank me?

She has by now worked herself into anguished sobs and gasping intakes of breath. Inda gazes in controlled exasperation mixed with amusement at her baby daughter. What was once Charline's just-below-ear-length Buster-Brown bob is now half a Buster-Brown bob, one side of her head shorn as short as any boy's, but jaggedly. Inda pulls the bed covers back and stares at a pair of kitchen shears and short brown hairs scattered indiscriminately across the entire bed; she has a sudden preview into discomfort and pain not unlike saints of the hair-shirt persuasion. Well, she would have to deal with those sheets later.

Her face becomes more grim, and she answers in a dangerously calm voice.

No, Charline, I am not going to spank you.. Your punishment is .....that you will wear your hair exactly as it is until it grows out.

The genius of that inspired punishment did not sink in until Charline saw herself in the mirror and had to endure for weeks the cat-calls and jibes of her heartless siblings. Nevertheless, Charline seemed perennially disposed to giving haircuts to various of her favorite dolls and animals. The above event did not prevent a good clipping for her teddy bear shortly thereafter. She writes...

The area which comprised the top of his head, around his ears, and in fact all of which would be the natural hair area on a person was cut as short as scissors could do on the already short hair he bore. It didn't seem to bother him much.

Charline's naughtinesses were never really bad. None of the girls was more than occasionally out of line, though to hear them tell it they were the champion scalawags of the neighbor-

hood.   The fact is that it took only a severe look from either
Charlie or Inda for them to be devastated for a week, or that
most dire warning of all from Inda, "You just wait until your
father comes home." Somehow that paper tiger threat never
failed to throw them into terror, though the razor strap in the
bathroom was used strictly for Charlie to sharpen his razor; no
one ever got spanked, not even an occasional back-handed swat.
Scolded, perhaps; punished, or given a ferocious parental
glower. But *spanked*? A Pearson girl? Never!

The sisters remembered their occasional misdeeds into
adulthood with the sharpness of regret felt those many years
ago, especially Charline — specifically the Gum Incident.

*It was a cold day, no snow, but rainy looking, some old
snow on the ground. Papa came from town and handed me a
package of gum (five sticks) and said to keep four for the other
girls when they got home from school. Gum was a great treat as
not always did Papa bring something home from Kintyre in the
nature of "wasteful" things. Usually he would bring bananas or
something more wholesome to his way of thinking.*

*I chewed my stick for awhile, playing in Mama and
Papa's bedroom with my rag doll, Sally Anne. After awhile the
gum lost its nice flavor and I wondered how TWO sticks of gum
would be in my mouth. It smelled so good! The second stick
quickly joined the first and I chewed them both together quite
awhile. The flavor evaporated and those others smelled so
enticing. It was not long until the third stick joined the others in
my mouth, then the fourth....and then the fifth! By this time my
mouth had quite a time to encompass all that gum and not
drizzle.*

*When I heard the girls getting home from school I quickly
opened the window and the storm window and hastily dropped
the big mess onto the dark, dirty snow. Then the girls came in
eagerly anticipating their treat Papa told them was waiting for
them...what sorrow ensued when they discovered that I had
selfishly chewed ALL five pieces of gum. My guilt endures to this
day.*

One of Charline's peccadillos resulted in quick retribution. The proud possessor of a beautiful new set of crayons, she
allowed her curiosity as to how such colorful things would taste

overwhelm her caution. Surely it wouldn't hurt if she just
nibbled off the top of each crayon, to find out if taste changed
with each color. After her experiment, the results of which were
disappointing to say the least, the possibility of parental disap-
proval washed over her. She darted to the bathroom to flush
away the tell-tale bottoms of the crayon remnants, but Inda
caught her in the act.

How many had she eaten? Inda bore down. Charline
didn't remember and the evidence was swirling away into the
great beyond.

*I heard them call Dr. Simon and I heard the words
"castor oil" and I went and hid. Flora either came with me or
had to find me, I'm not sure which. Of course THE hiding place
when it was dark — and it was dark by the time Dr. Simon came
— was behind the wardrobe in the bedroom, under all the clothes
— piles to be mended, piles to be ironed, piles to be washed. I
scrounged down beneath ALL of them. They looked there at least
twice before they found me. Papa had to hold me between his
knees (me standing) and Dr. Simon (when I refused to open my
mouth) just held my nose until I had to open my mouth to
breathe and in the horrid stuff went! TWICE!*

Cats were generally not allowed inside the Pearson
house — at least until the advent of an elegant white angora
named "Pancho" somewhere in the early thirties. Pancho was
the daughter of a beautiful black/gray/orange calico angora
named Oscar, belonging to Uncle Marshall and Aunt Esther. (It
has been only recently that I have become curious as to why
these two fertile females both received masculine names, and
now of course it is much too late to find out.)

Pancho was all soft fluffy white except for a dark grey
patch at the very top of her queenly head. She was the Jackie
Onassis of all the cats, much too hoity toity to associate with the
barn cats, except for an occasional romp in the hay with a tom-
cat version of Lady Chatterly's lover, resulting in a frequent
pregnancy which produced at least two all-white short-hair
kittens with a single grey patch on top of their heads. Something about Pancho's regal bearing made Inda break her own
rules, and Pancho became an aberration otherwise unheard of
on our farm: she was a House Cat.

Prior to Pancho, spiriting a cat into the house was a stealthy affair and once resulted in mortification to the conspirators, but since sufficient evidence was lacking, there was no punishment, however merited. There were a few days, of course, when Inda was feeling mellow — or perhaps just worn down by the pleas of the girls when Charlie was safely out in the fields, not to return until mealtime, that two or three kittens were allowed in just for an hour or so. The girls sometimes amused themselves by dressing the kittens in doll clothes, then letting them run on the dining-room sideboard to watch the startled felines see themselves reflected in the sideboard mirror.

One year when their little cousin Charles from Bismarck spent the whole summer with them, Charles and Charline conspired to get two kittens upstairs for a more leisurely stay. They rigged a lidded grape basket with a rope from the upstairs veranda off the east bedroom. Charles would lower the basket to the back porch below, where Charline loaded it with kittens, scooped from their barnyard frolicking. The cats and whatever they were playing with were promptly whisked to the veranda upstairs on the improvised elevator. Voila! Kittens in the house without ever entering a door.

On one of these surreptitious occasions, a sudden shower drove the two cousins off the unsheltered veranda into the east bedroom, along with their forbidden visitors and their basket of barnyard toys. Play was resumed; later the showers dissipated, and the kittens were once more lowered to the yard before Inda was due to come out and stand on the back porch, ringing the big old cow bell to summon Charlie to come home for supper.

In the fall of that year Inda did an all-points search for a foul smell that emanated from somewhere in the vicinity of the east bedroom. After turning the room and closets of that bedroom inside out, she made the linen closet her next target of investigation. Shake shake — towels. Shake shake — sheets. Shake shake — pillowcases. And what should roll out of one pillowcase? The head of a very dead gopher, much atrophied and excruciating to smell. Inda was appalled and at a loss to explain to herself how that desiccated head could possibly have gotten into her *linen closet*!!! Charline had a very good idea but wisely kept her own counsel; Charles was safely back in Bismarck and she did not care to be a solo culprit. Confession is not *always* good for the soul.

The barn cats, while not at all pampered, didn't lead too rugged a life. After all, there were field mice for the taking, and free milk every night. After the milking was done (they got a squirt or two in advance from Charlie down at the barn) and the kitchen separator completed its divisive work, aside from the blue skim milk and the cream-colored cream, there was a third product: a two or three-inch froth of foam on top of the pails containing the skim milk.

The girls skimmed off the foam, deemed detrimental to the calves, bawling for their supper at the barn, and offered it to the cats waiting at the back porch, where it was lapped up eagerly. Then, feeling very full indeed, with bulging bellies from all that ingested air they waddled away for a big bath and a long sleep somewhere in the hayloft. Who wanted to be a House Cat, anyway?

They were all nameless, these barnies, except for Old Silver, whose devotion to Inda was remarkable. Silver would come daily from the fields carrying a limp field mouse in her mouth, never relinquishing the almost-comatose animal until she could find the girls' mother. Then she laid her offering at Inda's feet and waited for a petting and praise, (always given), after which she picked up the day's catch and headed for the haymow and her current batch of kittens.

10

Flies in the buttermilk, shoo shoo shoo
Skip to m'Lou, my darlin'
Song for country dance

It is no wonder the world equates food with love. Anyone who has experienced it can tell you that there is no sense of security equal to the well-being that engulfs your soul as when the yeasty fragrance of bread rising in a country kitchen wafts your way. Pure joy pervades as you bite into a slice of new bread with thick cream spread on it, the cream so thick that it will not penetrate the bread.

Food has never tasted so good to me again as it did on the farm in the '30's. This is not just the gilding of memory. What I am remembering is pre-cholesterol cookery, pre-Weight-Watchers, pre-Dr. Pritikin, and pre-nouvelle cuisine. The chief secret to Inda's success as a cook was her lavish hand with double thick fresh cream and home-churned butter slathered on whatever came to hand, plus a wanton attitude toward eggs.

Day-old brown-shell eggs (scrambled or fried in hot butter — I doubt that any of our Pearsons had ever heard of omelets before 1940) accompanied by bacon and cinnamon rolls was a favorite breakfast for special occasions, but standard fare was oatmeal. Not just ordinary oatmeal — oatmeal swimming in cream that today would be sold as whipping cream; it was laced with dark, lumpy brown sugar. If there were oatmeal left over from the day before, Inda shaped it into patties, fried them in butter and served them with brown sugar syrup.

Who would not feel loved after one of Inda's breakfasts?

If you were still quite small, you might be rewarded for your diligence in hand-grinding the coffee beans that morning in the dark wooden grinder with the little drawer at the bottom. You would squirm happily as an eighth of a cup of the thick black coffee that bubbled so tantalizingly in the huge enamel pot was poured just for you — in my case into my blue glass Shirley Temple mug. Of course seven-eighths of the mug was filled with Guernsey whole milk.

Just before Inda poured the boiling coffee into the waiting thick white mugs everyone else drank from, she broke an egg into it. I've never been sure why — perhaps to settle the grounds, for this was not percolated brew — it was boiled vigorously within an inch of those coffee beans' lives. If coffee could have grown hair on the girls' chests, Inda's certainly would have.

Her most memorable specialties included homemade doughnuts. I think Inda's culinary secret here was extra nutmeg in the dough, which she deep-fat fried in a big, round three-legged black kettle that I always supposed was a twin to the pot of gold at the end of the rainbow. The fire in the big range had to be burning at just the right amount of heat, because the black kettle would be lowered down close to the burning coal to rest in the circular hole left by the removal of one of the stove lids. Setting the pot just an inch or two above the coals was necessary, because its legs made too much distance between it and the hot oil and the range surface.

The process of readying pot, oil, stove, and fire was not a job allowed small girls, but they watched the process with utter absorption. Inda making doughnuts was like a major stage production, and the girls had front row seats.

One of the jobs for small girls was to cut the doughnuts with the doughnut cutter, and push out the little inner circles that would be fried later and turn into round, bite-size morsels called doughnut holes. Small girls could also roll the doughnuts in sugar mixed with cinnamon after they cooled down a bit, and bargain their help into a doughnut hole or two before supper.

Inda cooked corn on the cob picked and husked by one of the girls not more than twenty minutes before dinner, and she added a sprinkling of sugar and a cup or two of fresh milk to the boiling water. Corn-husking was a little scary in those pre-chemical treatment days, because one never knew when a furry little corn-borer would have taken up residence. He of course would have to meet his maker in short order, and the end of the ear to which he had helped himself had to be amputated. Even more startling was to meet an ugly case of "smut," a grayish blob of blight which also had to be dealt with summarily. Nevertheless, the end result of the remaining ear was better than anything available today.

Baby peas, which small girls picked and then shelled, sitting on the back stoop, were cooked the same way as corn — sugar and milk added to enhance their already perfect flavor; string beans picked and stringed by small girls, were set a-wallowing in butter and flavored with a hunk of home-cured bacon, salted and smoked in our own smoke-house.

The tasteless, juiceless, cardboard produce hawked in today's markets as tomatoes are horrifyingly bad imitations of what grew in Inda's vegetable garden. But then, most farmers today don't have thick, black North Dakota soil to provide the plants their proper flavor-giving properties; nor can most people walk into their side-yard, to pick their tomatoes on the very day of perfect ripeness. Inda served them in slices in the summertime with no added embellishments. What the family couldn't eat she canned, and in the winter served cooked up with hunks of home-made bread and thick cream. Inda called the dish just "stewed tomatoes," but totally unlike any stewed tomatoes I've ever met since.

We all had a sweet tooth, and Inda catered to us shamelessly. Charlie's favorite flavor was always lemon for desserts — lemon cookies and lemon sponge cake being tops with him. The girls all inherited Inda's "Cup-of-Everything" cake recipe whose key secret ingredient is molasses, but the all-time family favorite was the "Lady Baltimore" cake, which Agnes excelled in making. It was a light, white cake with brown sugar frosting.

Charlie allowed himself few indulgences, but one of those few was a frequent purchase at Falgatter's of a short, squat wooden tub full of salt herring in brine. That and summer sausage (a variety of salami) for which we all had a taste, were treats from the trips to town. None of us cared for lutefisk, the traditional Scandinavian treat that was trundled out by other families at neighborhood and community gatherings.

When they became young matrons with homes of their own, each of the girls went way beyond "good cook" status in the eyes of their offspring, though I must in candor note, that while Lucille (the class valedictorian) took a "with honors" degree in home economics, her heart was never in the kitchen.

Notwithstanding latter-day culinary prowess, in their early years on the farm there were a few kitchen disasters along the way for these future stellar cooks. One of them took place when for some reason Inda went to Bismarck for a few days leaving small Flora in charge of the kitchen.

Knowing that Charlie loved boiled potatoes and salt herring, Flora, the tyro cook, served them for supper every night Inda was gone. Charlie never complained, and may even have been secretly delighted. After the success of her first dinner of potatoes and herring, she decided to be a little more adventurous for the first solo breakfast meal. Inda had left the recipe for pancakes: so much buttermilk, so many eggs, so much baking powder, and some sugar. Flora tells the story herself:

So I said, "Are you ready, Papa?" Yes, he was ready. I took my frying pan over to the stove, heated it properly hot — testing it with a drop of water to see if it popped as I had seen Mama do it — took my mixture, ladled some into the pan and it BLEW UP ALL OVER, clear to the ceiling. My dad calmly asked, "Well, how much flour did you put in?
"FLOUR?? She never said anything about FLOUR!!!"

(Inda had evidently mistakenly assumed that the key ingredient of flour could be omitted from her instructions — didn't *everyone* know you put flour in pancakes??)

Buttermilk is an acquired taste nowadays, but it was the Pearson drink of choice. One day a burly young woman who lived several miles from the Pearsons, stopped by our house on her way to Kintyre, for the day was hot, and her horses tired. Hospitable Inda asked her to sit down, and thoughtfully brought their guest a large tumbler of cool, fresh buttermilk. The young guest raised it eagerly to her face, drank it all down without a pause. When the glass was brought down to the table, her upper lip was coated with white almost to her nostrils. The girls were too polite or too shy or too amused to suggest she wipe her mouth, so the young woman headed to Kintyre still wearing her new white mustache.

Having a cold could be a rather marvelous thing, especially in winter. Not only did you not have to go to school, but Inda pampered you with tea kettle tea, perhaps more commonly

known as Cambric tea, which is nothing more than hot water
mixed with milk or cream and plenty of sugar. If your throat
were too sore for real food you were given a dose of milk'n'bread,
in my case with plenty of sugar, also good for just-before-bed
snacks even if you weren't sick.

Flora, as a 5-year-old, once announced her idea of perfect
meals for herself when grown and free to choose what she ate,
would be milk'n'bread (no sugar) for breakfast, milk'n'bread for
dinner and milk'n'bread and butter for supper.

I was almost an adult before I learned that most of what
America calls "lunch" was what we called "dinner." What we
called "supper" the rest of the world calls "dinner." Suppers, in
the more urban areas, I knew because of Grandma's ladies'
magazines, were late evening functions like grand fund-raising
events or other galas of some sort. Maybe even a small tryst à
deux. Whatever that was.

The Pearson kitchen was the hub of most of the indoor
activity, and of course no one wanted to be totally out of the
action, even if sick. An ailing girl could place the small living
room rocker in front of the cooking range, open the oven door,
prop her feet up on it, and bask in the heat, alternately dozing
or rocking. She would be swathed in Charlie's batten flannel
bathrobe and shod in his sheepskin slippers, wrapped in what
can best be described as a "Depression" quilt — the kind put
together with scraps with no attempt at artistry, but a wonderful relic to be wrapped in. You might say, a hole-y comforter.

If the ailing one were not too ailing, she could entertain
herself during the day by "rubbering" (listening in on the party
line) to see if anything interesting was going on in the neighborhood. The telephone on the north wall next to the square
kitchen table was hung so high that anyone under four feet tall
was compelled to stand on a chair to reach it. Unhappily for the
would-be eavesdropper, there was rarely anything really worth
listening to, but it alleviated the loneliness and boredom just to
hear other voices. If it was *too* boring, like the daily calls between the two neighboring sisters (one had married and moved
to the next farm) the rubberer would quickly hang up.

Well, so....How goes it?
Oh, yah, well, all right. So....how goes it with you?

That was hang-up time at the Pearson end. Even more frustrating was when the neighbors chattered in Finnish or Norwegian or Swedish. Swedish was never allowed to be spoken in their home, for fear the girls would have an accent and say things like "yello" for Jello and "Root" for Ruth. Charlie Pearson was determined that his daughters would speak accent-free English.

But oh joy of joys! Once in a great while the phone ring was a long and a short — someone was calling US! The ailing girl would have a miraculous recovery:

I'LL GET IT, MAMA!

11

Just a song at twilight, when the lights are low
And the flick'ring shadows softly come and go...
G. Clifton Bingham, J.L. Malloy

Always there was music in the Pearson household. In the
early years there was only Inda singing as she peeled the
ubiquitous potatoes, or whistling as she fed (or beheaded)
chickens or diapered a daughter. She could draw her lips
together, barely separated into a tight-lipped almost-smile, curl
her tongue and produce an incredibly beautiful musical sound, a
talent no one in the family could ever emulate.

As the daughters came along, and a modest improvement
in finances, so came the musical instruments: a small pump
organ, a violin Charlie taught himself to play — though there is
no record of his achieving memorable music, two of the earliest
Edison phonograph players (in sequence, not at once) and most
important to the prairie family, a Kimball piano. These all
arrived, not necessarily in the above order, during the girls'
growing-up years.

The earliest instrument in the house was a large ma-
hogany table model music box which played very large metal
discs, perforated and pointed to strike the metallic keys below.
When it was replaced by the floor model Edison, the music box
was sent to Inda's younger brother Tom Conner in Wibaux,
Montana, which the Pearson girls' younger cousins promptly
loaded onto a little coaster wagon, entered in the town parade
and became stars of the event.

The Pearson piano made its appearance while Grandpa
Conner was still living with them. Charlie had ordered it from a
catalogue (Sears, undoubtedly) and it was shipped in a handsome wooden crate. Grandpa Conner was not terribly interested
in the piano — he had his eye on that crate; he confiscated it

quickly and converted it into a small smokehouse.

One would think that it would have burnt up, but he kept the fire low; it never even got charred. It was a solidly built box, open on one side so that he could insert the smoking frames. Where it slanted down to accommodate the keyboard, there was an opening from which he could somehow hang meat from the ceiling of the box, ready to be smoked, and then later be able to reach in to retrieve it after being sufficiently "done." As a rule, hickory wood is used to do the smoking; Grandpa Conner used corncobs. Unhappily, his well-intentioned frugality was none too successful, for no one will admit to eating anything he smoked in the piano box.

One of Inda's ploys to keep her youngsters distracted until supper time when Charlie would finally come in just as it was beginning to grow dark, was to sit down at the big new Kimball and start them all singing. The girls made up their own words for an old schottische tune called *Autumn Leaf* and sang lustily to ward off their hunger pangs:

> *Clifford, don't you eat yet*
> *Clifford, don't you eat yet*
> *Supper'll soon be ready*
> *Supper'll soon be ready......*

How they came up with the name Clifford, since there were no boys in the family, nor did they know anyone named Clifford, can only be left to speculation. Perhaps the beat of the rhythm coincided with the beat of CLIFF'-ord. The schottische is a dance not unlike a polka but slower, with gliding and hopping steps, perfect for energetic, hungry little girls. The original tune and words were written by one D.W. Crist and "Respectfully dedicated to Miss Anna C. Bates, New Franklin, Ohio."

I don't know how early Inda started to teach Lucille to play the piano, but when she had taken her as far musically as she could herself, once a week she hitched up Fleet or Dolly or Chubby to their one-seated buggy; mother, daughter (tightly squeezed together) and pony trotted off for further lessons for my mother from Mrs. Anna Peterson, who lived seven or eight miles west of our farm.

Lucille proved to be more than an apt pupil. She was truly talented. The rest of the girls say they "took" but the lessons didn't "take." At least, they did not have the enthusiasm that Lucille displayed. In this area, too, I must have been a disappointment to my mother. She squeezed out money from her tiny budget in the thirties for piano lessons for me, but my exasperated teacher finally told her to "save your money and give her acting lessons." The teacher was actually quite right, for my later interests and career for a long time lay in that area.

The younger Pearson girls were delighted to be relieved from such dreary chores as scales and etudes. In the early evenings after supper they coaxed Lucille to play for them; they would be glad to do her share of the dishes, they offered, if only she would entertain them with her sprightly repertory, an exchange of duties she accepted with alacrity. Although steadfastly denying vocal talent, she also sang when requested. Inda always asked for one particular hymn: *It is well, it is well with my soul*.

All of us girls wax nostalgic, for of course by now I have proclaimed myself to be a Pearson girl, but our hearts kindle to different songs. Flora mentions *Somewhere a Voice Is Calling*. My own favorites were *Nola* and *Kitten on the Keys*. Charline remembers one memorable night three or four years after the end of World War I when their neighbors the McAllisters came for a visit from two farms away. Charlie and William McAllister had worked shoulder to shoulder as young boys on the Dugald Campbell sheep ranch, and their friendship continued throughout their lives. Charlie and Bill McAllister's daughter Katie played their fiddles while Lucille held forth on the Kimball. The rest of the group sang along lustily to the tunes of current favorites:

> *K-k-k-Katie, Beautiful Katie,*
> *You're the only g-g-g-g-girl that I adore—*
> *When the m-m-m-moon shines over the cow shed*
> *I'll be waiting at the k-k-k-kitchen door.*

and
> *Good-bye Ma, good-bye Pa*
> *Good-bye mule with the old heehaw.*
> *I don't know what this war's about,*
> *But you bet by gosh I'll soon find out.*

and

Keep the home fires burning
While your hearts are yearning
Though your lads are far away
They dream of home —
There's a silver lining
Through the dark cloud shining,
Turn the dark cloud inside out
Till the boys come home.

The Pearson parlor was always a gathering place for some kind of musical session, but choir practice for the members of the little Norwegian Lutheran Church just a quarter mile away, was the most frequent.   Lucille, protesting she couldn't sing, though Flora says she had a lovely soprano voice, played the piano while Charlie stood close by holding a kerosene lamp so she could read the music. Another lamp stood atop the Kimball, which was all the light the choir had, but it was enough.

Charlie always requested his favorite hymn, not without reason. It was written by a pioneer Swedish preacher's daughter, who must have known first-hand about the terrible, predictable Dakota droughts. Summer after summer Charlie would look out over his parched crops, shake his head sadly and murmur, "It can't rain. It just can't do it. It just can't rain." Then he would get the choir to sing, *There Shall be Showers of Blessing* and he would have hope again:

There shall be showers of blessing—precious reviving again;
Over the hills and the valleys, sound of abundance of rain
Showers of blessing, showers of blessing we need:
Mercy drops round us are falling, but for the showers we plead.

Sometimes in mid week Agnes would trudge the quarter-mile from the Pearson house up the dusty road in the burning mid-summer heat to the little Norwegian church. As she was waiting for the mail delivery (the Pearson post-box was directly across the road from the church) she would slip in the front door, which was never locked, and both play the tiny pump organ and sing the *Showers of Blessings* hymn all by herself. In later years she told her son — my cousin Gregory Meyer — that in those rain-parched days in the thirties at Sunday service, after the last hymn had been sung, some desperate farmer in the congregation would trumpet loudly a variation on the theme of, "How about some *real* rain, Lord, a real gullywasher?"

Once in a great while it would rain hard, though more often than not, Charlie and the other farmers had to conclude that the Lord, for reasons known only to Himself, said no.

Long after my mother had died, Flora wrote me what she termed a "visualization" of one of Lucille's youthful days of performance.

I want you to look into my mind and see the picture that flashes there so frequently.

I am a lowly high school student in Ellendale, attending the Academy, an adjunct to the State College there. Twice each week the total enrollment of College and Academy, plus the entire faculty, file into the stately chapel at 11:00 a.m. for wholesome edification. This morning I am tensely expectant for I know what will soon be filling that huge room — the magic of Franz Liszt.

From behind the curtain at one end of the long stage I see my sister Lucille quietly come toward the center. She wears a demure pink dress all spangled with tiny green leaves. The hemline is low, but not really a line at all — rather a series of points and angles.

She walks to the big grand piano, takes the seat, is silently still for a long moment looking down. I hold my breath. She lifts her beautiful hands (I am still not breathing). When she at last lets them fall crashing to the keyboard, the drama begins. Out pour the long anticipated contrasts in the "Hungarian Rhapsody;" the gentle promises, the racing, chasing melodies and the thundering booms.

I know it all so well, but I shiver with each change of mood. Her hands fly. Her silent energy is transformed by the piano into a flood of overwhelming sound and enduring memories. That sound now, so many years later, often comes back to me, and brings with it the vision which I wish I could adequately express to you.

You must look into my mind, for there it remains fresh and wondrous and true.

This is Lucille.

My mother told me herself of the days when she and my father played together in concerts and at dances all over our part of North Dakota. My parents were already married, working on their college degrees at Ellendale State Normal School where they had met. After graduation they took teaching positions in Braddock (about 12 miles northwest of our farm). To augment their modest teachers' salaries, they put together a tiny orchestra and thus enabled all the local youth (largely Swedes, Norwegians, Finns but with a healthy mix of Swiss, Germans and Russians) to dance away the twenties.

Lucille played the piano and sang, while Otto played several other instruments including the sax, and sang in a full, rich baritone. He achieved some degree of fame, singing on the Bismarck radio station KFYR. My mother always spoke matter-of-factly about those days, glossing over as much as possible whatever part Otto Bauer played in her life. I once bemoaned the fact that not only could I not play the piano, but I couldn't even carry a tune, much less sing well — so unfair, since my father (whom I never heard sing) reputedly sang so magnificently.

"Well," she said scathingly, "would you want to be a baritone?"

Lucille's disdain for my father went so far as to cause her to clip Otto's face from her photo album so the book I have today, filled with her college and family photos, shows one male individual always beheaded by a pair of manicure scissors. I do have pictures of my father, though, thanks to my less scissors-oriented aunts.

Flora, probably in deference to the memory of my mother and Lucille's deliberate avoidance of any recognition of the existence of Otto Bauer, omits in her Franz Liszt memory of my mother, that it was a two-piano concert and Otto also performed that day. Lucille played primo and Otto secundo. Perhaps Otto's secundo status was what eventually brought about the divorce. Who could live up to Lucille?

Otto and Lucille were not the only musicians in southwest North Dakota. An ambitious young man named Lawrence Welk was causing quite a stir among the locals with his dance band, playing primarily around a town named Strasburg. Long after Otto and Lucille had disbanded their small group, Lawrence Welk was still holding forth to the admiration of an ever-growing fan club, including the Pearson girls, who danced to his polkas, schottisches, waltzes and foxtrots in their salad days.

Many, many years later when Lawrence Welk and his Champagne Music were a big draw nationally, he and his group paid a visit to Roanoke, Virginia to perform in the newly-built municipal center in nearby Salem — crowd capacity of 10,000. It proved to be a sellout house.

At the time, I was hosting a TV interview/talk show on the local CBS affiliate station in Roanoke. The station manager instructed me to cancel any other interviews for the day: Lawrence Welk et al would be my guests. Groans came from all my crew, with the loudest from me. Who would want to interview such a cornball? we queried each other from our musically highbrow perches.

As it turned out, Lawrence Welk could have given professional lessons at any charm school, any public relations school, and/or used-car dealership. He had the entire station staff eating out of his hand before he had even reached the studio doors. I groveled mentally for having been so snippy about him beforehand.

To get the conversation going (he arrived 5 minutes before air time and there was no opportunity for pre-show chit-chat) I whispered to him just before the stage manager gave us the last minute "in 5-4-3-2-1" countdown, that my mother and her sisters had danced to his music in North Dakota back in the twenties. His beam broadened. The interview went well.

Afterwards, John Harkrader, the station manager called me into his office to chat with him and Lawrence Welk, to discuss my command-performance invitation to sit with Welk on the platform as his special guest at his group's performance that night. (What would a non-musical person add to his show? queried I of myself. But I did as bid.)

I was introduced by the King of Champagne Music to an ebullient crowd as "the daughter of a girl I used to date," at which point he hugged me and then deftly led me into a spirited polka, with the crowd by this time in near hysteria. One of Roanoke's own dancing with Lawrence Welk! (Then did I mentally thank my Uncle Leo, Elsie's husband, for including polkas in his dance lessons he had given me so many years ago. Polka-ing, like riding a bicycle, is a skill that never leaves you, I have decided.)

How Lucille had advanced from having danced to his music to being one of Lawrence Welk's girlfriends so instantaneously, I will never know. Chalk it up to canny showmanship, for the crowd loved it, and so did I. For weeks afterwards, I was stopped in the streets of Roanoke.

"What does it feel like to dance with Lawrence Welk?" strangers would ask. "Very nice," I would respond smugly. After all, it was a Pearson Girl tradition, dancing with Lawrence Welk.

Flora's instrument of choice (not counting her wonderfully smooth, sweet alto voice) was a Spanish guitar. How she had *yearned* to own one. For months she pored over the Sears catalogue, and finally earned enough money to buy it by husking corn. Charlie paid her 25 cents a bushel, as corn husking didn't count as normal (unpaid) chores. But at 25 cents a bushel, it was taking a long time to accumulate the exorbitant $14.95 required.

I asked Flora more than once, "What was Inda really like?" Although I spent my earliest years in Inda's care, my memory of Inda has never been so sharp as that of Charlie, who lived twenty years longer than she, and whose voice I can pull into my mind in an instant. With Inda, it is much harder. Flora's answer, in part, was a story about money for the guitar.

There I would be after supper in the early evening just before the sun set, bone-tired after all the regular chores were done, sitting on top of a high stack of corn bundles, wearily husking just a few more ears to try to earn that guitar. Many was the night that Mama would come out of the kitchen — more tired even than I was. She'd climb up on the corn stack with me, and we would husk together silently until it was too dark to see any more. It wasn't much longer before I had my guitar. That's what Inda was like.

A Finnish neighbor family named Jutila (whose mother was the local mid-wife) played a significant role in the Pearson family life, not only because their son Eino, (pronounced Ay´-know You´-till-a), a big, beautiful blond young man who owned the community threshing machine and brought it to the Pearson farm every threshing season. Much more important as far as

the girls were concerned, he built a radio, and kept it in the
Jutila attic, where Flora and Lucille were occasionally invited to
come and listen to music. It was Eino's sister Helen who frequently coached Flora and gave her help in fingering and
strumming during Flora's lonely struggles to learn to play her
new guitar all by herself.

With their ears inclined to hear and make merry with
anything musical, the sisters loved to sing-song the Jutila name.
When Eino's sister, Celia Jutila, got married, the girls made a
chant of her names on their way to school. Merrily they trilled
"Celia Jutila married Jack Allila (pronounced Al-lee-la)—

Cee-lee-ya-you-till-la married Jack Al-lee-la

That was almost as much fun as quickly counting from one
to ten in Finnish, an equally chantable liturgy that made the
long walk to school pass more agreeably:

Ixxi	*(icksy)*
Cocksi	*(coxy)*
Columnen	*(cole-yume-nen)*
Nelli	*(nelly)*
Viese	*(vee-see)*
Gose	*(go-see)*
Satsamen	*(sat-sa-men)*
Yestickson	*(yes-tick-son)*
Oodeck-san	*(oo-deck-san)*
Kuminin	*(ku-men-nen)*

Flora quickly built up a repertory of three songs on her
new guitar. To her great delight, Lucille, "the real musician" by
then teaching English in the Braddock High School 12 miles
away, invited Flora and her friend Ruth Fuller to put on a little
show for her class. The two friends strummed away and sang
Fandango, Aloha Oe and a third number, now buried in the
bottom of memory's stubborn warehouse. Flora described
herself at Lucille's Ellendale piano performances as "beaming
and very, very proud." In turn, Lucille, being something of a
sober-sides might not have openly beamed, but she was, nonetheless, very, very proud of her little sister's demonstrated
talent with her brand new Spanish guitar.

The first phonograph in the Pearson house was a cylinder Edison, table model. A handsome floor model eventually replacing it, was Charlie's pride and joy. Playing a song or two before bedtime was his night-cap before collapsing in fatigue onto the wrought-iron four-poster with a bright brass knob on each post — a bed that he and Inda shared for almost 40 years.

The round playing head was fitted with a diamond needle which never needed to be changed, as did the Victrolas'. The girls were sternly cautioned to never, NEVER touch that diamond point, never to touch the playing arm and to always use the operating device in the front right corner. The records, as opposed to those for the Victrolas, were heavy and very thick, almost half an inch. They were stored in the lower section of the cabinet, always on edge, in separate compartments. The girls were never to touch the grooved playing surfaces, only the very edge of the record.

Duly briefed on the care and handling of the records, little Flora was finally allowed to play the Edison all by herself. It is a wonder that her favorite, Handel's *Messiah*, didn't wear out, she played it so often. The family marveled at her early taste for that classic; she loved especially the *Hallelujah Chorus*. It was revealed finally that it was because of its familiarity that she was drawn to it. Hadn't she been hearing Grandpa Conner yell "Hi-yah-YAH, hi-yah-YAH" to the horses for most of her young life? She was almost an adult before she realized that Hi-yah-YAH and Halleluljah are not quite the same thing.

My favorite was a record by a Scot named Harry Lauder who twanged out something in a high-pitched voice that sounded to my ear like "just a weak dock and dorra" but was in fact some kind of a drinking song and the real words were "Just a wee doch and dorris." Why Charlie had it in his collection is open to question because although the family were not teetotalers, exactly, they just didn't drink. A drinking song in the Pearson house? Amazing.

Inda was proud of her hardwood floors in the parlor and dining room, and frequently would roll up the green paisley carpet in the living room, and lather both floors with paste wax. An equally hard chore was the polishing that came next (even though there was electricity in the house, no one had ever heard of floor polishers in those days). She would put a double pair of Charlie's worn-out woolen sox on me, wind-up the phonograph player and set me skate-sliding over the waxed floor around and around the rooms to the accompaniment of Harry Lauder and his drinking song, thus keeping me entertained and her floors receiving at least a modicum of polishing. This was not a paid chore — it was too much fun!

12

Dashing through the snow
In a one-horse open sleigh
O'er the fields we go
Laughing all the way...
     J. S. Pierpont (1857)

Say what you will about North Dakota winters, and no one will deny that they are c-o-l-d, at least there is never any danger of Christmas being anything but white. If it doesn't actually snow on Christmas day itself, there is always plenty left over from the week before.

I remember a particular Christmas at the farm, probably one of the last times the family drove the five or six miles to Maria Lutheran for Christmas services in a horse-drawn sleigh, because after 1935 tires, as well as roads, were less iffy and Charlie could both safely and proudly drive his latest automobile instead.

My most specific memory about that special ride is of freshly hotted bricks which Inda retrieved from the bowels of the big, black range and then wrapped in old towels to be placed as foot-rests in the sleigh so our feet would be warm at least as long as the trip going to church. Presumably our elevated spirits from the church service would keep us warm coming home.

Recalled with equal nostalgia is the tinkle-jangle, tinkle-jangle of real jingle bells on the sleigh as Jane (or was it Maude?) tossed her head, whinnied and nickered through steamy nostrils, and pranced as briskly out of the driveway as a plowhorse could prance in new fallen snow.

Charline captures Christmas at the farm through childhood's eyes in a letter she wrote in 1963 to my cousin Connie, Flora's younger daughter.

When your mother and I were little, Christmas was always an EVENT because it meant that the big girls were coming home. There was the big bustle of trying to time the house cleaning as late as possible so it would last, but as early as needed to get everything done — the kitchen floor got dirty so fast, 24 hours would have it right back where it started.

The popcorn had to be popped on top of the range in the heavy cast-iron pan Mama used for frying chickens. You shook the pan constantly, so that no stray "old widow" would burn on the bottom, one hand covered with a thick potholder and a firm grasp on the lid with the other equally protected hand.

The product of these labors was to go with the store-bought'n cranberries to be strung alternately (two cranberries to four popcorns) on thick black thread, making long swags of holiday color to serve as tree decorations — a culinary treat tossed out for the birds once Christmas was over. The needles to string with were never sharp enough and I could never find a thimble, so my fingers began to look like pin cushions.

Mama would be baking things, and outside there was such a cold, cold wind, and the snow blowing. Sometimes Papa had to take the older girls to Kintyre in the sled on secret errands. Mama would have had a hot rock in the oven all the night before so they shouldn't freeze their feet.

The tree was carefully chosen by Charlie and perhaps a daughter or two, on a special trip to Falgatter's General Store in Kintyre. Our property boasted not even one lonesome pine, and if it had, would never have been chopped down. The tree was NEVER put up until the 24th. Then the candles had to be placed just so. The placing of the candles was a strategic ritual you weren't allowed to perform until you were quite old — ten at least. A candle had to be more than eight inches away from the branch above it, or fffffttttt! Up in flames everything would go, so we were warned. It never happened at our house, but we knew of places where it had.

The actual lighting of the Christmas tree was so much more eventful than today's mere flick of a switch. We all stood at attention, really in awe at the spectacle of lit candles in our own home! Papa was always standing at the ready with his bucket of water lest even one ambitious spark leap beyond the taper and its holder-clamp. The lighted candles were a twenty-minute, once-a-year ceremony, over all too soon, but no one wanted a disaster at Christmas tide.

One year when Elsie was first teaching at a near-by one-room country school, Papa was Santa for her school children and he wore — instead of the traditional red suit — our old, old ratty muskrat coat that everyone in the family wore at one time or another, and a red mask and red cap (all one piece). One of the little boys said after he left, "It was too the real Santa, I saw his sleigh and reindeer go over the hill." I suppose in the late afternoon shadows, with a lively imagination, you could think that Jack's long mule ears looked like antlers.

Some years we had to learn "pieces" (little Christmas poems) for the church Christmas party. I was too shy, so one of the other little girls (Helen Hanson was her name) and I went up in front together, holding hands. We took turns speaking, clinging to each other for support to face what seemed to us a vast audience — there were maybe 20 families at most.

Before the girls got old enough to have jobs and had money to bring home toys at Christmas, our presents usually consisted of the tree, the candles, and the individual bags of candy and nuts that Papa provided. These he thought were sufficient. Papa sent away to Sears for our candy.

Flora remembers a year when Agnes got a black and red fire engine with four high-stepping horses attached. That was the same year she herself received a two-wheeled yellow metal cart with a donkey attached. Very small. But she, like Charline, recalls the Christmas candy most vividly:

When the bounty came from his order from the catalogue, he would stash it high on top of the wardrobe in his and Inda's bedroom, saving it for Christmas. But I saw where he had hidden it. So when it came time to go to school each morning, I would stand on a stool, reach up high, and get a little of the candy to take to my classmates for lunch. Gradually the supply dwindled and when Christmas came, I remember hearing Papa shouting, "Inda! Come here! We've got a mouse!" I couldn't imagine that I could have taken so much it would be noticed — after all, I only took such a little each time. I never confessed, though.

Charline's letter also includes a story about the annual candy:

One year the candy came in little tin boxes about twice the size of the kitchen match boxes and they were stuffed full of ribbon candy. The outside of my box was painted red and on it were stencils of nursery rhymes. I LOVED that box. Flora's was blue, I think. That must have been about 1920.

A postmortem to the tin box story is the following: Sometime after that particular Christmas, on a "let's pretend" day, Charline and Flora played "Funeral." They buried two small china dolls who had long blonde hair, blue eyes and painted shoes and socks. They used Charline's beloved red tin candy box as the casket. Charline reports that it was "a *lovely* funeral."

They intended to exhume their toys the next day but something intervened and they didn't do it. When they got around to recovering the dolls, they searched in vain for the burial plot. They KNEW they were buried north of the house near the cellar door, but WHERE? The dolls and Charline's tin box remain today somewhere on the farm in Emmons County, still waiting for a resurrection seventy years after the fact.

Charline's letter continues:

Santa always came while the folks were out milking on Christmas Eve. The big doors were shut to the living and dining room, and if anyone peeked, Santa wouldn't come. That was an awfully long hour.

The worst Christmas was the year Flora informed me there wasn't any Santa Claus (she said she never ever believed in St. Nick in the first place, and that none of the other girls did either). I was getting used to having the girls tell me terrible stories that weren't true, like the time they told me I didn't belong to the family but the gypsies had left me and the folks took me in so I wouldn't starve to death. With skepticism born of experience, I demanded that Flora PROVE there wasn't a Santa, so she took me to the cellar and showed me the little door on the bottom of the chimney where the ashes come out....obviously this was the only outlet of our chimney, and obviously no Santa could come out of a door one foot wide and 15 inches tall. There was nothing I could do but believe her.

As the years advanced and everyone got older, the Christmas reunions got better and better. At least in loot. Agnes and

Elsie bought me a teddy bear one year — maybe it was the same year Flora got her Minerva doll, but the following year — my Mama doll! That year I have no recollection of any other present anyone else got — just my doll from Elsie! She was almost as large as a real baby, but fatter. Her eyes opened and shut and she said "Mama" when tipped first back and then forward. She had seams across the bottom of her body where the legs began, so by holding her beneath her arms I could make her walk — sort of. Her face, arms and legs from knees to feet were all an imitation china (probably plaster of paris). Her two teeth fell out early on, but her red tongue stayed in place, and I didn't mind about her teeth. I loved her anyway.

She wore a yellow dress with white trim on the hemline and edging the neckline. On the white part little blue ducks sailed along in single lines. Her yellow bonnet had a white back to it. Her hair was black and "real." Several years later Flora cut her bedraggles so she looked neater, but that hair never did respond to well to combing and brushing. I don't know why, but she was unnamed all her lifetime. She spent her last years in Flora's basement in Bismarck.

Flora remembers her Minerva doll almost as well as Charline remembers her mama doll. Minerva had a bisque head and a beautiful painted face with a tiny perfect mouth, a hint of two teeth and a tip of red tongue showing, painted eye-lashes, delicate china hands, dark brown *real* hair, eyes that opened and closed, and a jointed kid-leather body.

Charline's new teddy bear took a back seat any time she got to hold Minerva. She was required to sit primly, with older sisters carefully supervising how she handled her and severely limiting her minutes of holding. Minerva was removed from Charline's grasp before she got out of her chair, to avert any unfortunate accident imperiling that delicate china head.

Flora also remembers an earlier doll that Elsie made for Charline in the days when none of them had cash to buy gifts. Elsie drew an outline of what was soon to be "Sally Anne" on white cloth, probably a bleached bag that sugar came in which they usually used for dishtowels. She stitched the outlined body, trimmed the edges, stuffed it with cotton batting and painted her face and hair with watercolors from school. Poor Sally Anne was relegated to the bottom of the toy drawer after Charline got her mama doll.

I still have my checker set Agnes got me the year Mama taught me to play checkers on an up-ended orange crate with the squares crayola-ed in. We used buttons for checkers, a rare commodity in our house. Finding enough buttons to play the game was always a time-consuming preliminary. The set from Agnes folded in the middle and latched with the checkers nestled inside.

One memorable year Flora made me doll house furniture out of match boxes. The boxes were the kind that held matches that were little two-inch wooden sticks with ignitable ends, which you scratched along a sandpapery strip on the outside of the box to get them to light. The boxes were about four inches long, two and a half inches wide and two inches deep. By cutting some ends and refolding and glueing, Flora was able to make chairs, tables, and beds.

Of course there was the year that the girls all brought home candy and I ate so much I was too sick to get out of bed Christmas Day! I never lived that one down.

Oh, the Christmas smells — the cooking — fresh bread and cinnamon rolls stuffed with brown sugar, ginger cookies and fudge; pine syrup dripping from the tree which traditionally stood in the dining room until New Year's Day, the girls' perfume ("Evening in Paris" that came in a beautiful dark blue bottle with a long tassle hanging from its side); Christmas sounds — the girls' party dresses swishing, and their feet running up and down the bare stairs, their voices all raised in competition to be heard first and above the other one — all too difficult for me to keep up with — the conversations upstairs and down. Sometimes I did it by hanging in the landing where I could keep tabs on both, but usually I vacillated between the ones up and the ones downstairs — always pushed a little by the ones who were trying to get rid of me. I can't imagine why.

Oh, Charline — how much alike we were — little you pining to be in on the excitement of whatever the Big Girls were up to! But you were blessed. You were already growing into the real thing, a Pearson Girl, those many Christmases ago.

13

The friendly cow all red and white
I love with all my heart;
She gives me cream with all her might,
To eat with apple tart.
            Robert Louis Stevenson

Whenever tempted to think I am brutally busy, assaulted by more duties than one person can reasonably be
expected to address in one day, or feeling stressed out by sub-
way trauma, and begin to whimper that week-ends ought to be
three days and not two, I reflect on the 52-weeks-a-year routine
of Inda, Charlie and the girls. For them, there was no such
thing as a week-end off.

"Vacations?" they might query incredulously, "What are
they?"

The Pearson family observed four holidays a year:
Christmas, Thanksgiving, the Fourth of July, and the annual
all-day "Play Day" outing held for all the schools at Seemans
Park in Linton, the county seat. Sundays were special, of
course, but not actually holidays. On Sundays no one was
allowed to do what qualified as "work." Unless you counted
"chores."

Chores, the girls explained to me, were daily obligations,
no matter the holiday, no matter the Sabbath, no matter WHAT.
Chores included making beds, cooking meals, setting the table,
doing dishes, separating the milk and cleaning the separator
afterwards.

Even on Sundays after milking was finished, the cream
had to be separated from the milk, a fairly arduous and boring
task. The twist of a little screw caused the stream of cream to be
thinner or thicker as it poured out its separate spout. On the
other side would flow the fresh, faintly blue, skim milk.   Flora
describes how the machine worked:

A series of cone-shaped disks fit onto a spindle with a covering on it. The large vat on top of the machine contained the spindle, and the disks were whirled at a very fast speed and the milk would go through there as it whirled — a sort of centrifugal action. The cream would rise to the top and come through a small hole and then down the spout into a waiting receptacle. It took a while to get the machine started. You pushed and pushed and pushed to get it to turn even the first cycle. It would start out with a very low groan. As you increased the speed, you could hear it reach the proper pitch, then you knew it was time to turn the spout and let the milk and cream start pouring through their respective spouts. This huge machine had to be taken apart, its pieces washed and put back together again every time you used it. That wasn't work. That was a chore, endless it seemed.

Charlie's prime concern was for the feeding and watering of the livestock, especially in winter. And the milking. Whenever they went to an event — like the Fourth of July celebration at Linton, 20 miles away, the girls would always complain because long before anyone else left, long before the games and festivities were over, Charlie would announce, "Time to go now, girls." And they would always protest, "Oh, we can't go NOW, papa, it's so early." His scornful retort was, "Well, do you want to stay 'til the last dog is hung?" His theory was: get there first before anybody else, and leave first. A dozen or more cows were anxiously awaiting their return. The most onerous chore, and the most inescapable, was milking the cows daily at both dawn and dusk. If you were late, a herd of Guernseys, Herefords and Jerseys (or intermarriages thereof) with swollen, heavy udders would bawl and bellow with outrage. Not even Charlie could make you feel as guilty as they could.

If you think that milking cows is easy, let me enlighten you. It isn't. There were many small triumphs in my childhood that I enjoy even now in retrospect — the thrill of first being able to skip; the joy of balancing on a bicycle without an uncle holding onto the carrying rack; the success of making it to the top of the climbing rope in gym class, the victory of the first face-size balloon of bubble gum, the ecstasy of a real whistle coming from my pursed lips. These cherished achievements all pale when I remember my elation the first time a small stream of rich white milk tinkled into the bottom of the big tin pail pressed precariously between my knobby little knees. Charlie's final girl-child student had almost gotten the hang of it.

There are several things to learn before you actually put hands to teats. Getting "Bossy" into her stall and safely closed into her stanchion comes first. Don't even think about putting her in any stall but her own, because if you do, not only will she refuse to enter it, but the entire herd will become distraught. Cows do not like change, especially at milking time. (People too — have you ever noticed the glare you elicit when having innocently sat in a church pew someone else sits in regularly?)

You must approach your client always from the right side, not the left, as when mounting a horse. "So, Boss," you say and try not to sound tentative. (Why are all cows, even ones who have personal names, usually addressed as "Bossy"? One of our family wordsmiths has theorized that it is because cows belong to the genus bos, family bovidae.) "So, Boss. Easy girl," you croon.

There are a few anxious moments at the outset while Bossy turns baleful brown eyes in your direction, as though to say accusatively, "Who are you, insignificant intruder, and *where's Charlie?*" Mournfully she soon turns back to chewing her cud, with a flick of her tail that says, "Well, if it has to be you, pray get on with it."

You then hunker down onto the little 3-legged stool that stands just inches from the floor, tilt forward on two of the legs, lay your head against the hollow of her upper thigh and flank, and firmly grasp a teat in each hand. Gently/strongly you begin to massage/pull the milk down from the top of the teat, (close to her bulging udder) and point the ensuing thin stream you have successfully suctioned out, downward to the side of the pail nestled between your knees.

Above all, you must do this with rhythmic quickness and authority. Rapidly massage/press with the left hand downward, one, two, three; then with the right hand, one two, three, alternating so quickly it almost seems simultaneous.

Never mind Bossy's brillo-like tail swiping your face now and again — it's nothing personal, she's just whisking the bothersome flies away. Nor should you be startled on the not infrequent occasions when she raises that same tail high and lets go with a loud pee or cow-patty that lands in the barn-length pee-trough behind her. She's not bashful. But the milker must react instantly if this happens, quickly standing up, holding the milk pail safely away from the area of "fall-out."

What is really most disheartening, even to a veteran milker, is to be almost done with one cow and just before the last stripping is to have her abruptly thrust her right rear leg forward, knock the pail out from between your knees, with the foamy milk flowing over the floor and you.

I don't remember how long it took me to get even a half pail of milk but I do remember that Grandpa would have had all the rest of the herd milked before I finished my half pail, and then he would polish off my unfinished assignment. I never got really good at this chore, and certainly never good enough to aim a stream to the mouth of a waiting barn cat sitting expectantly across from the pee-trough. He and the girls could, though, without missing a stroke.

Flora, primarily because of her skill as a milkmaid, was the only one of the five girls not sent away from home for her first year of high school. Lucille went to Ellendale, the State Normal School, which had a high school connected with it. Elsie and Agnes went to live with their Aunt Laura (one of Inda's younger sisters) to attend Bismarck High School. These were places large enough to attract teachers Inda and Charlie thought worthy of their precocious offspring.

In Flora's case, she and a neighbor named Carl Pearson (no relation) were privately tutored for 9th grade at the local Tell School by a lady named Julia Holihan, noteworthy for her black, black hair and Irish blue eyes. "She really knew her stuff," according to Flora. "Stuff" was Ancient History, General Science, English and Algebra.

The reason for this change in educational pattern was that Charlie out of necessity, had conscripted Flora as his sole milking partner and fill-in field hand for her first year of high school, a recognition of her milking prowess, but more importantly, his need to down-load some of the responsibility for the work that provided the family income. Who else was left? The big girls were gone, Charline was too little; Inda had the house and the chickens and the turkeys to handle, though she pitched in frequently anyway, especially for the evening milking.

One can feel Flora's anguish in the cold, dark Dakota winter mornings before she prepared to trundle off to school, there to tilt with Carl, her learning partner, with whom she was

engaged in a spirited academic competition. Which was worse?
To face the cold and the milking chore, or school with the now
suspect Carl, who had been reported to Flora by tattle tales in
the lower classes that Carl was heard to say, "I wish Miss
Holihan would get sick and have to go home and then they
would appoint me teacher. And the first thing I would do is
send that Flora Pearson *home!*" That (unverified) report deep-
ened the ongoing rivalry and Flora wouldn't have minded at all
being the teacher in charge who could then turn the tables and
send Carl home. Miss Holihan, being a hardy sort, was never
absent, however, and the dueling academics plowed on under
Miss Holihan's aegis.

They made it up later, though. Seventy years later.
Flora returned to Emmons County for a family reunion in 1996.
While attending the tiny Lutheran church in Kintyre, she was
stopped at the rear of the sanctuary by a dapper, slender,
silver-haired gentleman who bent down from his over six-feet
and said softly to her, almost shyly, "Are you *Flora?*" Instantly,
the ancient feud was over. Someone snapped a photo of them,
the first photo of the members of that unique 9th grade class of
two.

Time dropped away, and Flora's memory returned her to
those cold winter mornings before school.

*If you want to know what pure torture is, hear your name
called at 4 a.m. every black winter morning; try to force yourself
from a deep sleep under cozy covers, to respond to Papa's ONE
TIME ONLY wake-up call. The agony and great disgrace if
derelict in duty hung like a threatening cloud in my mind, so
shaking off the desire to sleep was counter-balanced by known
duty, but it was not pleasant. The shadows cast from the lantern
Papa carried on his way to the barn flickered against the railings
on the porch outside my bedroom window, an eerie reminder that
I, too must brave the cold and the dark.*

*When I finally staggered down the stairs and out into the
frosty dawn, I hastened over the snowy frozen path to the barn,
slid back one of the heavy doors and entered with relief into the
welcome animal-warmed air. Relief quickly changed to chagrin
as I saw that Papa had already milked at least three cows before
my arrival.*

Sitting close to a placid cow, my head leaning comfortably against her broad side, assuaged my guilt. I'm sure I dozed off more than a few times, relaxed by her warmth, my hands in third gear — automatic. All was silence except for the sound of milk rhythmically hitting two tin pails, an occasional soft moo, and the rustle upstairs in the haymow of a host of resident barn mice. Faintly, across the barnyard we might hear the rooster announce triumphantly that he had seen to it that another day had begun.

14

Baa, baa black sheep, have you any wool?
Yes sir, yes sir, three bags full!
Traditional nursery rhyme, origin unknown

The principle of diversified farming is quite simple to a
farm girl. If you've ever been responsible for collecting the day's
eggs from the chicken coop and had the misfortune to stumble
and fall, you know how fervently you wished all the eggs had not
been in one basket.

Charlie ardently believed in spreading risk. If one year
were bad for hogs, it might not be so bad for wheat. If it were
bad for wheat, at least he could count on the sheep. For his
black-faced, droopy-eared, fleecy white Shropshires' pleasure
and sustenance (150 of them) he reserved 80 acres of pasture —
almost a sixth of the entire farm. The sheep, like the hay
meadow, were reliable, and supplied three crops for selling:
lambs, fleece and manure, "the best fertilizer there is," according to Charlie, plus furnishing mutton and tallow for the household.

The Pearson sisters flowed seamlessly back and forth
between their roles as resident milkmaids and shepherdesses,
sometimes all in one day. Sheep must be moved from pasture to
pasture about every three weeks because they have the bad
habit of eating the grass right down to the roots, which is why
cattlemen traditionally feud with sheep farmers; the woolly
beasts can and do utterly destroy a range for any other animal.

The girls were responsible for herding them, helped by
the ever-enthusiastic sheep dog, Pendro, albeit (even in their
best of all possible worlds) with occasional sibling grumpiness
about whose turn it was to move the notorious pasture ruiners
after they had done their sheeply mischief.

In March sometime, the baby lambs made their appearance, and that was always cause for rejoicing, but preceded by a

great deal of vigilance on the part of everyone in the household. If a ewe produced more than one lamb at a birthing, very often this mother sheep did not have enough milk for both. One of the twins would be raised on a bottle because the stronger of the two would butt the weaker out of the way of the mother's udder.

To save this lamb it was necessary to bring it into the kitchen where Inda would lay the little animal on a pile of old blankets or shirts in a box near the stove. Sometimes there would be two or three at a time in the kitchen, but they didn't need to stay long — only until they were dry from the birthing. After that they could go out to the sheep shed to be with their mother. Or if they were orphans, they had to live in the orphans' pen where the girls lavished special attention on them.

Though the lambs may have left the safety of the house and stove, the girls would still have to continue to feed them, using cow's milk in an old catsup bottle with a tough, black nipple on it. Once you start nursing a lamb you have to continue until they can eat other foods by themselves. Like human babies, little lambs love to suck, and suck *hard*. Sometimes they pulled the bottle's nipple right off, spilling the milk and causing the surrogate feeder to have to trudge back to the house for a refill.

If you went to the barn just for a sociable visit to your adoptee, no milk bottle in hand, the lamb would make-do by sucking one or two of your fingers. That gentle/hard, persistent tugging on my fingers was, I think, the clue I needed to understand how to milk a cow.

It was a problem of course, when the lambs became too attached to the girls, or when the girls became too attached to the lambs. Charline, who more than once had an orphan lamb, still recalls the pain of the inevitable parting. Being in an "Indian" frame of mind, she once named an orphan "Two Bars" because she had two white bars on one ear, and Charline loved her on sight. Then came the black day when Two Bars was sold.

The fact that the folks took the money and bought me a coat with a mouton collar was no balm at all — even though it was the only NEW coat I ever had until my last year of high school. I always thought of my lamb whenever I wore that coat, and to this day I distinctly dislike mouton fur.

I too, once adopted an orphan, and in the short time she was mine, changed her name daily, with the result that today I can't remember what I finally chose. At any rate, my lamb was not a strong baby and she died within a week. That experience was painful enough for me to have written a "personal experience" poem requisite for some grade school publication a few years later. Two lines and the pain remain with me still:

And like the broken-hearted child I was, I cried
Because my black-nosed orphan lamb had died.

Agnes's adoptee was immediately named Billy the Ram, who became the farm character. Unfortunately, his name eventually had to be abbreviated to just plain Billy, for Charlie not only chopped off his tail (as he did all the lambs, to keep them cleaner), but he also "wethered" (castrated) him. A "wether" could look forward only to becoming lamb chops. Only a few rams were kept for breeding; indeed, foreign talent was frequently imported to prevent inbreeding. The interloper, old "Love 'Em and Leave 'Em's" happy annual tour of duty l'amour with any one flock was not lengthy.

Agnes managed to save Billy from lamb-chopdom, and made him feel so special, he thought he was a member of the family. When newly born he was unusually small and weak, and thus spent the first few weeks of his life nursed tenderly in the farmhouse, longer than most others. When it came time for him to join the flock down at the barn, he went reluctantly, but soon found ways to escape from any enclosure. Eschewing the icy cold water tank in the barn, he would make his way to the back porch of the house every morning, and stamp on the wooden porch outside the kitchen door until some tender-hearted member of the family would come out to bring him his accustomed warm water in an aluminum saucepan.

Agnes and Billy could most assuredly have been the inspiration for "Mary had a little lamb...."

"What makes the lamb love Mary so?"
The children all did cry
"Why Mary loves the lamb, you know"
The teacher did reply.

About a month or more before shearing, usually June when it was warm enough for the sheep to go bare-naked, they became so laden with their heavy coats that if for any reason they fell down, lay down or got themselves prone somehow, they could not get back up by themselves. If not found within a very few hours, they would of course die. And so it was that the girls were assigned an additional task. For this one they were to earn a stipend.

Twice a day they were to circulate the edge of the pastures — they called it "riding the fence" — to make sure that no sheep had suffered this misfortune. The amount earned varied with how prosperous Charlie was feeling. By the time it was eleven-year-old Charline's turn at this chore in 1928, he was paying 25¢ a day. That year not one sheep toppled over, but he had to pay anyhow. The next year he made a new deal: 5¢ a day, plus another nickel for each sheep that had to be hauled to her feet. Again, no sheep had tumbled, and this time Charlie had only the modest nickel a day to pay. (The girls were never the hard bargainers that Charlie was!)

Although Charlie handled the shearing himself, the older girls did help. By the end of the First World War, he had electric shears, and with his old prize-winning speed from boyhood, he would reach down, grab the hind leg of a member of the flock, set it on its rear end, and begin to shear. In a trice, the sitting wool-bearer, legs floundering helplessly, would have been relieved of its precious coat, the fleece removed all in one piece. The poor shorn thing would struggle up and away, bleating miserably, sporting a few small bloody nicks where Charlie's shears had come too close.

Not too long ago I heard a South Dakota (townie) minister preach on the joys of getting rid of unnecessary baggage. He used the analogy of how happy sheep are after they have been sheared. All of us in the Pearson pew thought quietly he would have done well to leave that particular illustration alone, as our memories went back to the first few unhappy, shivering days of newly shorn sheep.

Charlie always started shearing at the top of the sheep's head, working downward in a consistent, circular direction so that the fleece fell away downward, with as little coming apart as possible. When the fleece was all off, Charlie gathered it up and took it to the nearby tying table where Elsie and Agnes rolled and compressed it into a bundle, tied it with twine, then packed it into a huge burlap bag.

This open bag (replaced by another each time it became full) hung from a scaffold about seven feet tall, into which each bundle was tossed by the girls. Because the wool was so fluffy, Charlie climbed into the sack when it was partially full and tromped *hard* to compress those bundles, thus putting as many bundles as possible into the huge sack. When the sack could hold no more, he sat atop the wooden frame of the scaffold and with a huge needle and twine, sewed the top of the bag shut, making a fist-size ear at each end of it for grasping and loading onto the truck.

Charlie hauled the fleece up to Bismarck for sale to his favorite client, one Sid Sloven, who in turn would sell it to the woolen mills back east. A visit to Sid, who was Jewish — no one ever knew for sure how he came to settle in primarily Christian-oriented North Dakota — would provide Charlie with yet another opportunity to cajole him to reveal the secret Charlie was *absolutely convinced* that Sid knew: the location of the Ark of the Covenant. No matter how firmly Sid protested that of course he didn't know where it was, he was never able to convince my grandfather. "I know you know, Sid" he would insist. And Sid would shake his head and laugh.

Both were hard bargainers; we never knew who got the better of the other (or fleeced!) on a deal with the fleece. Once Sid bought a lamb from Charlie, and our family, well-steeped in Old Testament lore and full of the Abraham/Isaac story, was convinced that Sid had wanted it for a religious sacrifice. My Jewish husband finds this story particularly funny, and my cousin Connie, a Bible scholar, notes that there was no more sacrificing of animals after the destruction of the Temple in Jerusalem, about 70 A.D.

As for the how of Sid Sloven's arrival in Dakota, my Uncle Jake (Flora's husband) once related that in his younger years in the early 1900's, a large group of Jews came from New York to settle near his home in the Wilton area (mid-Dakota) with the intention of becoming farmers. Sid's family could have been one of that group. Eventually most of them gave it up as a bad idea and went back east, though they stayed long enough for some of their group to have died. The Jewish cemetery is still there near Wilton.

When the Dakota summer set in, so did pesky ticks and other flying insects. This triggered the next ovine event: the annual sheep dip, an occasion no one enjoyed. Here again, Charlie bore most of the burden of actually dousing the poor beasts, but the girls helped herd them into the pen outside the trough. The trough was a partially submerged long, narrow tank with about 12 to 14 inches showing above the surface of the ground, which Charlie had filled with either an evil-smelling dark brown creosote dip, or an even more repulsive poisonous yellow concoction.

Charlie, by the way, used sheep dip as one of his famous remedies for anything that needed disinfecting, be it beast or human. The sisters were convinced that his theory was that if the treatment stung or hurt or smelled horrible it would therefore be enormously effective. Turpentine on an open cut was therefore *THE THING* to apply. Inda's treatments via the Watkins man were a drop gentler — carbolic salve that lived in a red and golden striped can in the medicine cabinet.

One of the side-benefits for Charlie during shearing season was the healing of his poor scraped, snagged, thistled, bruised and blistered farm-working hands. The days he spent handling the wool, holding down the reluctant sheep with his bare hands, resulted in his damaged hands being renewed to amazing perfection. They came out soft, unblemished and completely healed. After all the shearing and wool packing were completed, he would hold them out to the girls for their admiration; everyone was suitably awed by the miraculous change, thanks to the soothing Oil of Sheep.

At sheep-dipping time, the girls would herd them into the pen just outside the gate that led to the trough situated a few hundred feet from the barn. Then Charlie, in a crouched position, would grasp one sheep at a time as it skidded down the chute, clamp his hand across its nose and mouth so that none of the poison liquid would be ingested, and guide/pull the animal through the trough to the opposite end, where the trough had a sloped incline with cleats on it. The minute he brought them up and took his hand off their mouths they scrambled up the cleated board, bleating furiously. With a mighty shake of the body which sent flying a shower of bright yellow droplets, they tried to re-establish a modicum of sheep dignity. Whether the sheep were grateful or not, the pests would leave them alone for the rest of the summer.

In one other area besides shearing, Charlie humanely spared the sisters from participating: the slaughter of any of the animals raised on our farm — not counting the chickens, of course. But it was Inda who made certain the girls stayed in the house when the long tails of the lambs were amputated (leaving only a short stub) and saw to it that those pathetic remnants were buried at once.

The same evening as Charlie butchered a sheep — usually a yearling — because there was no refrigerator, he would lay all the cuts out on a big platter, take them upstairs and outside to put them on the second-floor veranda on the east side of the house so that they would chill over night. In the morning, lamb chops for breakfast!

Later Inda preserved the remainder of the lamb. Some she cut into pieces and cooked on the range, put it in stone crocks and covered with hot melted tallow, which cooled, congealed and sealed the meat off from air and contamination.

The sides of the sheep, comparable to a pig's bacon area, would be rolled up, tied with strings in rolls about 14 inches long, and boiled. These rolls would later be sliced and used in sandwiches for lunch in the hayfield. This portion of the meat had alternating streaks of lean, layers of fat, layers of lean, layers of fat, just like bacon. The girls *always* removed the fat before they ate it, but Charlie didn't, thinking logically that tallow on the outside of your hands was very beneficial so..... (who knew anything about cholesterol in those days?) At any rate, he never seemed to suffer any ill effects, nor did he ever gain an extra pound.

15

Train up a child in the way he should go
And when he is old, he will not depart from it.
Proverbs 22.6

Although Charlie and Inda were married by an Episcopalian minister, the church they belonged to all their 38 married years together was Maria Lutheran, organized by a group of Swedish settlers on May 8, 1890 under the Constitution of the Augustana Synod. Olaf and Karna Pehrson were among the 23 original members, and Olaf served on the committee which spearheaded the building of the original church edifice in 1900. Any child born of at least one Lutheran parent was automatically Lutheran according to the way it had been in Sweden (and continued until 1995), so all the young Pehrsons were considered to be included in the membership.

On June 10 of 1900 the little group had even more cause for celebration: they had called a permanent pastor, and he had accepted. It was an enthusiastic, if small, congregation that met every week on the windswept plains some five miles northwest across a prairie trail from the Pearson home. In 1948 the group disbanded, and the edifice was moved to Kintyre, leaving behind only a plaque with the names of the original members, and a small graveyard.

Prior to the erection of the church of Maria Swedish Lutheran, services were held in their own homes, with Olaf delivering the sermons. His father Olaf's predilection for preaching may explain in part Charlie's frequent sermonettes to the sisters, and occasional letters of fatherly admonitions, such as the one he wrote to my mother when she was nine years old:

Dear Daughter:-
Today I am alive and well, but we do not know how long we will remain so... . I want to tell you a few things that I wish

that you would remember all thru your life. I think that today,
as the saying is, if you hear the LORD'S voice calling to you
COME, do not stay away.

My wish is that you grow up and be a good woman,
always do what is right to every one, right will win even tho it
may not seem so at the time, but time will show that it will. If I
should die before your Mama does I wish that you would help
her all that you can, and if you can do any good to your sisters,
you should do so, since you are the oldest in our family, you will
naturely (sic) *be looked upon to that.*

Notwithstanding the fact that the family membership
was at Maria Swedish Lutheran, the girls grew up attending the
Tell Evangelical Norwegian Lutheran church only a quarter of a
mile up the road from their home. This might have been remarkable, given the feeling of competition and scant respect for
each other among the Finns, the Norwegians and the Swedes,
stemming from the same feelings held in their native lands, but
the Norwegian Lutheran church had a major attraction besides
proximity as far as Charlie was concerned: English was spoken
at the service. Since Inda neither spoke nor understood Swedish, and since Charlie wanted his daughters to speak nothing
but English, the choice was not too surprising.

Charlie built the fire in the Tell church furnace every
cold Sunday morning, and it was Charlie who saved it from
perishing by fire when lightning hit the belfry one summer day;
the girls attended Sunday School there, all went to the main
service every Sunday morning, and the choir rehearsed in the
Pearson parlor every week. The only thing they didn't do was
have family burials there. But join it? Never!

"Why not?" my cousins and I queried curiously at a
recent family reunion.

"Why," said Flora as though it were self-evident, "because it was *Norwegian!*" We all had another laugh when my
cousin Carla's Montana husband Ted (who is himself a minister)
then told of the day he brought Flora's daughter Carla (nee
Johnson) home to meet his grandmother, who was militantly
Norwegian.

"So, Carla," she began gently enough, "what kind of
nationality are you?" Carla adroitly answered, "Oh, Scandinavian, Mrs. Arthun," hoping that would end the interrogation.

The grandmother persisted, "Vell, I know THAT because your name is Johnson. Are you Norwegian?" (and she lowered her voice) "or the *other* kind?"

Carla passed muster anyway. And Ted was fine with our family too — after all, there was precedent: Elsie had married that Norwegian, Leo Burnstad and it turned out pretty well — they were married 58 years before Elsie died in 1991.

Tell Norwegian Lutheran was a friendly church and most every Sunday one of the women would invite the whole congregation home to Sunday dinner afterwards. Naturally she had prepared extensively ahead of time, but would extend her invitation in a manner indicating that she had *just* thought of it. Inda frequently did this too; furthermore, the Pearson home (and dinner table) was always open to stray preachers.

Pastor Vang (pronounced "Wong") of the Tell Church, whose appetite can most politely be described as hearty, was the most frequent guest of all. His portly frame was very... substantial. He always wore a black suit with a long, long coat, the swallow tail of which had to be flipped out carefully before lowering his reverend amplitude into the fragile ladderback chair and diving into a meal. How could Inda not invite him every Sunday, since following the services at Tell Norwegian, he served the Temvik congregation at an afternoon service, southwest of the Pearson farm about 20 miles. Our farm was the only home directly on his way. Consider the annoyance of the little girls who were instructed, when sweets were in short supply, to be sure to take only one of the bread spreads. Consider the temptation to mimic the good Pastor after he had left for his next assignment.

"Oh yessssss— I like yelly," (*take, take, double helping*) "and I like honey too!" (*take, take, triple helping*).

The sisters did not go so far as one shocked little boy of Inda's childhood acquaintance in Indiana, who loudly announced in the presence of the guest, "MA! He sopped his bread on BOTH sides and didn't let it drip!" (The dish of bacon fat was for all to use sparingly.)

When Lucille was a confirmation student, the class often met in the Pearson living room. One day while class was going on, unexpected visitors arrived at the front door. Not to worry, said Pastor Vang heartily, "Never mind us — we'll yust take our class upstairs to Lucille's room."

Horrified Lucille grabbed Betsy Sjerslee's hand and they galloped up the stairway. Her bed stood considerably higher after being stuffed, kicked and stowed under. Fortunately Pastor Vang moved ponderously and the stairs were steep, so he was forever oblivious to the unreadiness of a teen-age girls' private quarters for an unexpected confirmation class reception.

Pastor Vang exuded authority from his pulpit, and was known to be a bit imperious with his parishioners. But he was a pussycat in comparison with his dour successor, whose name has not been resuscitated for our annals. One Gus Swanson, whose long white goatee trembled when he was excited, during one of the successor's all-too-lengthy sermons, heard a sound outside the window next to his pew and feared that his horse (with buggy) had become untied from the fence where he had left them. Goatee a-quiver he stood up abruptly and ran to the window, just as the minister was reaching full crescendo and the crux of his sermon.

"Sit down, Swanson!" thundered the pastor, annoyed at being upstaged.

Abashed and cowed, Swanson sat. But all that anybody remembers of the sermon that day was that the preacher *yelled* at old Mr. Swanson.

The girls took turns at saying grace at every meal ("First you give thanks" was the by-word for everything, but most especially meals). Elsie's prayer never varied, and with her tendency to sing-song, caused Lucille to naughtily, with eyes open and a fore-finger at the ready in order to conduct — as if leading an orchestra — while Elsie rattled through with heavily marked cadences,

Dear Heavenly Father up above
We thank Thee for Thy care and love
Bless this food before us spread
And feed our souls with heavenly bread.

This of course convulsed the other girls, whose eyes were also open, and the meal would begin, if not so full of gratitude as Inda would have liked, certainly in high good humor. After all, "a merry heart maketh a cheerful countenance," and the girls certainly qualified on that score.

Elsie did her own share of mimicking, and frequently

entertained her little sisters on the way to school with her
version of the latest visiting evangelist's performance. One
winter two young women came to the nearby Lutheran church
to conduct a series of meetings with zeal, enthusiasm and
awesome oratory to promote their cause. Flora writes...

*I am now not sure what their inspiration was, but it may
have been a stand against the use of alcohol, for soon after their
campaign, the Women's Christian Temperance Union (W.C.T.U.)
was established in our community. Blonde, plump Miss Holland
and tall, black-haired Miss Meekle held forth for several days,
mightily impressing us children, though not necessarily with the
message. It was their bodily vigor, passionate vehemence and
vocal virtuosity, the likes of which we had never heard before.*

*For days following their departure, our daily walks
across the prairie to Country School #3 were enlivened by Elsie's
memorable histrionics. Whenever we approached a high rock or
hummock, she would run ahead, mount the make-do podium and
begin a loud gibbering declamation in the manner of the recent
crusaders. Her act was short, but a remarkably realistic replica
of the recent meetings, for she built up to a pulpit-pounding
finale.*

*Her final pronouncement was accompanied by a slowly
rising right arm with clenched fist, and delivered in a loud,
rising crescendo of "Hobbelty, Hobbelty, Hobbelty, E-E-E-E-E—
EEE POOM!!" as the right fist came crushing down into her left
palm. There was no mistaking that Elsie had given less than
full attention to the message of the evangelists, but she certainly
had absorbed their hypnotic, evangelical delivery.*

Charlie was certainly a good example of everything he
believed in, but he always gave full vent to well-placed lecturing
as well. Inda, on the other hand, was more of the "by their
works shall ye know them" school of spiritual teaching, and I
believe it was from her quiet generosities that every one of the
five sisters grew up *truly believing* that it is more blessed to give
than receive, a belief they never relinquished.

While purchases made with proceeds from the farm
came about through the mutual decisions of Inda and Charlie, it
was Charlie who did the actual spending. But Inda's "turkey
money" was hers and hers alone to decide how it would be spent;

she also made the disbursement, with no say-so from Charlie. The turkeys were her private project, and they thrived under her husbandry.

In my book they were probably the least charming of any of the barnyard population. The gobbler strutted about arrogantly fanning his tail at the least provocation, and shook his wattles at me if I came too close. I also thought he and his harem were pretty dumb, literally not bright enough to come in out of the rain. They would raise their little bald heads to see what was happening, and the rain would pelt into their two nostrils, slide down into their lungs and drown them, causing Inda to always keep a fretful eye on the rainclouds if they were too far afield.

When her baby turkeys were too frail to withstand a cold rain or hail, she gathered them up and put them in a box in a warm oven, with the door open of course until they dried out and perked up. Charline says...

It was strange to see these little birds so limp and apparently dead, revive and start peeping. I also seem to recall Papa bringing some new born pigs in one night — their mother rolled over on them, but they recovered too. Heat (in moderation) is wonderful!

Dumb those turkeys might be, but profitable, and Inda gave them as much TLC as the lambs, or for that matter, anything alive that came into her range of concern.

No one remembers that Inda ever bought anything for herself from her turkey money, but they do remember examples of her largesse, and on one unforgettable occasion Charlie was the beneficiary. She sent away to Sears Roebuck and got him a magnificently elegant knee-length blue wool coat, the first time the sisters had ever seen him in anything other than a woolly sheepskin-lined leather jacket.

When Grandpa Conner died, he left an insurance policy of $600 to Inda. She promptly sent half to Uncle Charley because their father had been living with him in Montana from the time he left our farm. The other half went to Aunt Annie (Charlie's youngest sister) who always had a special place in her heart, starting from the days when she secretly toted Charlie's "love letters" in her school lunch pail to Inda, extending into later years when she became Charline's godmother. Aunt Annie married a farmer and moved with him to Alberta, Canada a few years later. The year of Inda's inheritance, the first planting of wheat of the young Canadians was frozen out, but Inda and her turkeys plus the rest of the inheritance saw to it that there was a second planting. And that took care of "Mama's Bank Account" for the year.

And why not? says Flora. "We had everything we needed. We were fortunate. We should share."

16

Rock of Ages, cleft for me —
Let me hide myself in thee...
Traditional hymn

There is a new wrinkle these days in the way curious children absorb what their parents and grandparents can tell them about their own youthful adventures, "when I was your age...." Because of the presence of a tape recorder our whole family is able to experience the same pleasure my cousins Carla and Connie did when they first elicited a series of historical anecdotes about "the girls" and "the farm" in a conversation with their mother Flora not too many years ago.

They were all in her kitchen one Saturday, and my cousins were asking her about "when she was a little girl," the same way she and her four sisters had frequently quizzed Inda and Charlie.

Up to her elbows in flour, kneading bread for her version of Inda's cinnamon rolls, Flora was telling them about the rocks at Fairview Farms.

The fields were filled with rocks, deposited, no doubt, by the ancient glaciers thousands of years ago. Once a year, before planting could begin, we would hitch the horses to the stone boat, a flat toboggan composed of several wide boards that curled up at the front.

The horses would drag this boat across the fields, stopping as we rolled up the heavy stones and rolled them on. Sometimes we had to use crow bars to loosen the bigger rocks, and occasionally we would even have to fasten a chain around a large boulder and have the horses pull it out. These stones were then piled up at various places in the field, eventually becoming monuments several feet high.

"Why did the stones keep coming up year after year?" asked Connie, the born interviewer, as she discreetly increased the volume on the tape recorder.

I suppose it had something to do with the freezing and contracting and melting and expanding of the earth. But whatever the reason, each year there were new stones to be removed. Besides the piles of rocks in the fields, we had also made a long wall of these stones that extended east between our house and the granary, where we made up games to play while we ran across their tops, a line which ran north and south.

It was that portion of the taped conversation that must have returned to Flora's mind after she had received a distressing phone call from Agnes in 1992.

"It is the custom in our family," Agnes announced that day in a firm voice, with her customary older-sister authority, "to die at 84." (Agnes was in her 83d year at the time.) The truth of what she said could not be too far gainsaid, for she listed at least four members of our family who had shuffled off this mortal coil at the age of 84, and had herself just been diagnosed with a painful (and terminal) illness called myleo dysplastic anemia.

Flora, with her medical background, knew that Agnes would be in pain in her final days. The years and miles and circumstances had kept the once-close sisters apart for a long time. What to do to make Agnes's last days easier? A favorite poem by Elizabeth Akers Allen flashed across her mind:

> *Backward, turn backward*
> *O time in your flight*
> *Make me a child again,*
> *Just for tonight.*

Perhaps the happy memories of their childhood together would help to distract. How else to share them across the miles but to write about them? Out came her trusty Smith Corona my Uncle Jake bought her in 1967. The memories flowed as Flora's fingers flew, writing to her sister....

Let's not go to school today, Agnes. Let's instead go down to the granary area where there stretches out a long line of rocks which have been hauled out of the fields. Big rocks, all sizes, all piled up three or four feet high, rumpled, uneven, jutting out and up. We climb up on one end, then see who can traverse that obstacle course to the far end, in a race.

But we may not leap from one rock to the next without calling out the name of a city or country for each step we take. Look at me, falling behind competent you. I am teetering on one foot, waving arms and the other foot in the air, trying to think of a name that will legitimize my next step. So quickly have I used up "London" and "France" and so tardily do any others come to me. "Braddock," I suddenly think of, and "Kintyre."

By that time you have nimbly skipped almost to the end, and the air above you sparkles with "Vienna, Moscow, Edinburgh, Africa, Berlin, San Francisco, Scotland, Wales, Timbuktu..." and here you come making the return traverse, and still emitting these strange sounding names of far away places.

"Let's go into the granary," I say in defeat, "and play in the oats bin. Maybe we can find the slabs of bacon stored there." (No competition in that, I think wisely.)

Smell those oats! So pungently identifiable — fresh and, well, OATY. Mixed in, of course is the slightly more pungent smell of the mice who have shared in our livestock's winter meals. Some might think it odd that these "timorous, cowerin' beasties" show no interest in Papa's bacon slabs which he has also housed in the granary. Perhaps, while they are opportunistic, they nevertheless have some built-in mouse-health radar that steers them away from salt-filled, cholesterol-filled, nitrate-filled, fat-filled bacon! Especially when they can dine on an ample supply of pure, healthful, unrefined unprocessed OATS!

Or no, better still, let's go back to the house, make bullberry jelly sandwiches, and head out east via the cow paths along the fence and go clear out to Bed Rock — that huge shattered boulder that you can crawl right up into its heart, lie back and watch the clouds make pictures while we savor and dawdle over our bullberry treat. How I would love to see it again — we never speculated on its origins as I do now. Did it come from outer space, the asteroid belt, and shatter on contact?

Remember the day Papa got his binoculars (only he

*called them "field glasses") and how he set them on a fence pole
one night and pointed them up at the stars so we could see for
ourselves the wonderful closeness of those far-away constella-
tions?*

    *Our fertile imaginations converted Bed Rock to our own
purposes these many years ago — to us it looked like a bed with a
headpiece and a footpiece, a shortened bed, perhaps. It had a
large crater around it, a depression —so maybe it was a meteor.
Isn't it great that time and space are erased by this wealth of
memories we have at our command?*

    The Bed Rock area was not always so serene a haven as
recalled for Agnes. The bouldered section of the farm stretched
all the way out to the cow pasture. One morning before school,
Charlie sent the two girls (Flora about 12, Charline about 7), out
to drive home a cow who had given birth out there. Although he
supplied the girls with a pitchfork, Inda was furious when she
heard where they had gone. She knew all too well which cow
they had been sent to retrieve.

    A mother animal with a new baby is always defensive,
and this particular cow, not noted for her gentle nature, was so
out of favor with the girls that she didn't even have a name —
no "Crocus" or "Lily" or "Molly," she. Inda's worries were
justified. The ornery, annoyed mother cow took one look at the
girls, and without a moment's hesitation butted Charline,
knocked her over and stepped on her forehead. Then she turned
on Flora and knocked her over, forcing the pitchfork to fly out of
her hand. The two frightened girls managed to scramble to
their feet and raced in terror for home, without the cow, without
the calf and without the pitchfork.

    That was one of the times that Charlie should have re-
sorted to his Swedish *"tust now, gamla,"* which the girls noticed
he always said when gentling Inda. But he didn't this time.
Assaulted by Inda's wrath and irritated Southern sensibilities
regarding proper work for girls, he retreated into silence.

    No chauvinist was Charlie Pearson. Girls were just as good
as boys, just as capable and he was only helping them prove it,
wasn't he? It was an ongoing dispute between these two strong-
willed individuals, and one of the few areas in which they were
in never-resolved disagreement.

    The taped kitchen interview came to an end when the

bread came out of the oven. Carla wrote:

> *Six golden loaves filled the whole house with the warm fragrance of muti-generational memories and urgent present anticipation. There was also a pan of steaming cinnamon rolls coated with caramel and a tub of butter nearby. Glasses of milk were poured and we began eating the rich rolls, still thinking about the wheat fields and hay meadows of Emmons County, North Dakota.*

17

Where 'tis smooth and where 'tis stony,
Trudge along, my little pony.....
Old German folk song

The Pearson girls had a habit of giving the name of a
beloved horse to another down the line, perhaps not immediately after the demise of the first, but not too long thereafter.
There were at least two Dollys: Dolly I was the horse Inda rode
in her school-teaching days; Dolly II was among those who
chauffeured the girls to Tell and Goose Lake schools, first as
students, later as school marms.

There were two or three Janes, Maudes, Ladies, Babes,
Toms and Bills. One of the Janes had hooves too small for her
feet, and the girls felt sorry for her — her feet seemed to hurt all
the time. The Daisy that I remember was a soft mottled grey
workhorse, gentle enough for me to ride bareback at age five.
The Daisy Charline remembers was an Appaloosa colored mare
given to jumping fences, much to Charlie's aggravation. Appaloosa, besides being the name of an Indian people of Washington
and Idaho, is also the name of a rugged saddle horse developed
in the west, having small dark spots or blotches on a white coat.
Charline writes....

*Papa cured our Daisy the Appaloosa of her jumping by
attaching a rope around her neck with a heavy lead drag attached to it the size of a sewer top, and she couldn't jump with
that load. After a period of this discipline, one day Charlie put
her in the pasture without the lead drag, and she didn't try to
jump the fence. She'd forgotten that she could! Never again did
she have to wear the weight.*

Then there was Chubby, a small brown pony, unremarkable for his looks, but in whose horseshoes no ordinary horse could follow. Like Billy the Ram, although technically belonging to the farm at large, everyone knew his heart belonged to Agnes.   Agnes and Charlie were the only two on the premises who could outflank and outfox the wily Chubby. When either of them rode him, or required him to do any of his workhorse chores, none of his pranks were in evidence. For them, he was the model of horsely decorum.

He was an Indian pony, by definition a small, hardy, vigorous and not especially graceful horse of Western-North American descent, bred from stock introduced by New World Spaniards and re-domesticated by the Northwestern Indians. These ponies were considered valuable as range horses and for cross breeding.

Chubby could perform any task the farm demanded. He was the riding pony, the buggy pony, and an excellent herdsman, not just an ordinary cow pony. The girls could signal him which cow they wanted singled out, and he did it all by himself. No need for them to ride him to get the desired results. If a cow jumped a fence, Chubby would be right on its tail, bringing the recalcitrant beast back home in short order. Chubby never suffered the Daisy treatment of being trained not to jump fences, since it was part of his job.

But ornery? Well I guess! And smart. Chubby had a mind of his own, and if he felt like being fed and no one was attending to his wants, he would extract himself from his stall and stroll to the oat box, located in the third step leading to the loft in the barn. With his teeth he pulled up the strap that held the lid closed and helped himself, eating as many oats as he pleased, which may account for his name.

Being a true free spirit Chubby didn't care to be picketed out in the yard. The girls would put a stake down into the ground about a foot deep. They would tie him there, fastened to the end of a long rope, thinking he would stay put, and graze the prairie grass circumference available around him, as any normal horse would. Not Chubby, who learned to pull the picket pin out of the ground with his teeth and betake himself to more succulent, if not greener, pastures of his own choosing.

Occasionally the girls would ride him bareback. For a

while he would gallop along gaily, even enthusiastically, then pull one of his favorite shenanigans. At full speed he stopped abruptly, lowered his head and the unwelcome passenger predictably sailed off into the air, landing on her aggrieved rump. Charline says, "The last time I rode him he did that to me. No more brown sugar lumps for him, let me tell you — at least from me!"

Agnes, born with a competitive spirit inherited from Charlie — who had been addicted to bicycle races in his youth and reportedly always won — would often inveigle little Flora into a horse race. Agnes of course rode Chubby; Flora got to ride Fleet, ("the relic assigned to me. She was quite a lot older than I was, quite old for a horse.") Fleet succeeded Dolly I as Inda's school-marm horse, a gentle sorrel who early in life may have been worthy of her name. By the time she was Flora's steed, however, her lack of fleetness guaranteed that Agnes and Chubby would win any riding competition.

The naughtiest thing Chubby ever did was *perhaps* unintentional. Elsie, Agnes and Flora were students, on their way to Tell School, with Chubby at the helm, Elsie driving, clipping along at a good speed, when they came to a hill with quite a steep slope. At the foot of the hill was a neighbor who had gone to his mailbox. As the buggy approached him, he gallantly doffed his hat to the young ladies. Chubby interpreted this as a threatening gesture, and tripled his speed, galloping hell-for-leather down the hill with the buggy swaying wildly back and forth until it finally completely toppled over.

Flora got badly banged by the buggy hood, which was folded down. When the buggy tipped over, the hood caught her under the chin and she was dragged along for several feet by her chin, but suffered no broken bones — only bruises and damaged dignity, also sustained by Agnes. Elsie, though, emerged with a badly broken collarbone. Chubby was in disgrace for some little time thereafter, though in the hindsight of passing years, the girls agree that just that once he *may* have been frightened, not (as suspected) pretending to be. Flora wrote of the incident in one of her "remember when" letters to Agnes:

Would it make you tired and cold if we were to bring back the scenes of an early evening in winter, darkness about to descend — supper not quite ready — and forward thinking

Agnes has put on her coat and gone down to the barn. She gathers up big armloads of hay, carries it out and "stuffs the buggy." She packs the small jutting-out box at the rear of the buggy for the horse's next day feed, while we are in school. Why, I wonder, is it always Agnes who gets this job? No other volunteers? One of those buggy rides leaps to mind: we turn west at the church, headed for Tell school. Who knows what goes on in the mind of a horse as he sees himself day after day put into confining harness and steered by a bunch of little snippets?

What was in his horsey thoughts as he came to the brow of the hill? Was Chubby really feeling threatened by our neighbor or had he just had enough of us for one day? Had he decided to brush away these young annoyances behind him? The best way to do it of course is bolt madly down that slope, twist, whirl and zig-zag until that load behind is disconnected and he can head out into the wild blue yonder, forever free. Did he gloat as he saw his load upended behind him, the snippets being dragged along on the ground? What dismay and disappointment did he feel when he discovered himself still snared by all that harness and trappings? Not free?? After all that effort??? Oh well, he can go home again, do cute and clever things the snippets will brag about. He will take an ear of corn in his mouth, maneuver it into a longitudinal position along his cheek interior and expertly chew off those kernels one row at a time, rotating the ear with tongue until all kernels are off, then eject the bare cob from his mouth and accept another, if offered.

I am seeing only darkly through the glass of memory into the balance of that scene. Does a white knight come galloping up to our rescue? Or is it whiskery neighbor Levi Thompson who sees our plight? How do we get home? How does the buggy get uprighted? Is the buggy still usable? Did we get taken to the doctor or did he come to us? Was that the end of our buggy-ing to school? I certainly remember a lot of walks from then on!

All of the Pearson horses were valued not only as workers, but family treasures. Charline recalls that she went to spend the night — her first night away from home — with the girls' cousin Mildred, close to her age and the only daughter of Uncle Ed (Charlie's carpenter-farmer brother) and Aunt Minnie, who lived on a neighboring farm about two miles away. Little Charline got homesick in the middle of the night and begged to be taken home.

Uncle Ed, bless his heart, got out of bed, dressed and walked me home. He wouldn't take a horse as he said his horses had to work the next day and needed their rest!

In another letter of memory to Agnes, Flora wrote...

In the winter dark, we go down to the barn, slide the heavy doors open, step inside, feel the warmth of the animals, smell their barny smell and hear the coaxing whicker of horses as they turn their heads in our direction as far as their roped halters will permit. We know what they want, even before they whinny and look pointedly at the third step in the stairway going up to the loft. It is a joy for us to be able to pour into their feed boxes their favorite sustenance, for we have grown up hearing Papa preach the virtues of oats for man and beast. They nuzzle our hands with their velvet noses, hoping perhaps for a rare treat of apple, or better still, a nugget of brown sugar we can be counted on to spirit to them from Inda's pantry.

18

Husha-bye, don't you cry
Cold is like a sorrow
Sing a song
T'won't be long
You'll be warm tomorrow.
The Ballad of Hazel Miner (Chuck Suchy)

As a rule, the girls tended all their lives to be like sundials, recording only sunny hours. Nevertheless, for all their golden memories — and memory does tend to cast a golden veil — they knew many deep fears shared by parents and offspring throughout homesteading communities in the north, not the least of which were the often unpredictable blizzards, the legendary accuracy of *The Farmer's Almanac* forecasts notwithstanding.

An experienced rancher like Charlie could stand out on his back stoop, put a finger to the wind, sniff the air, glance at the sky and announce with authority that it felt like snow to him. That was about as accurate as weather predictions were going to get in those days. How heavy the snowfall would be, not he nor anyone else had any way of knowing.

Winter storms caused hardships never to be forgotten, as Charlie could attest. He loved to tell the girls about one particular winter in the late 1880s when a storm drove snow in drifts so high he and his brothers couldn't get out of the doors of their house, so they took a portion of the roof off the storm shed attached to the house, and climbed out the top of the shed in order to get to the barn to feed their livestock.

The whole Pearson family was all too well aware of what could happen, and *did* happen much too frequently, should a normal snowfall turn into a furiously blinding blizzard, especially if the children were still at school. An incident in March of 1920 is harrowing for them to this day.

Hazel Miner, a not-quite-sixteen year old farmer's daughter from the town of Center in Oliver County (in the west central part of North Dakota) had gone one day to the area's one-room school as usual with her younger brother and sister. Late in the afternoon it began to snow at first softly, then heavily. Fearing a blizzard, the schoolmarm worriedly dismissed class, and everyone hustled to get home. Some kids' parents came for them; some lived close by and could walk home, gliding gleefully atop crusted snowdrifts, delighted to be let free from onerous classes for the day. Others, like Hazel Miner and her siblings, had come in a horse and sleigh. Hazel bundled up her little sister and brother, harnessed their pony, and the group of three headed for home at top speed.

The snow turned rapidly into a blinding blizzard with heavy winds. It grew steadily worse; dark came early and suddenly. Not surprisingly, Hazel lost her way. The little pony with his precious cargo plodded wearily on, all believing they were at least headed in the right direction. After several hours, Hazel realized with horror they were hopelessly lost; her little brother and sister were crying bitterly because they were so cold and so frightened.

Finally Hazel stopped the pony, and helped the children out of the sleigh. They burrowed a hole like rabbits in the snow under the sleigh, and Hazel told the children to lie down. Then she lay down over them, shielding them with her own body from the cold, like a mother hen. That whole night long she sang to them and told stories to keep them awake and moving, their blood circulating, so they wouldn't freeze to death. Everyone knew the one thing you must not do is fall asleep in the snow, or you would surely freeze.

At dawn, when a weary search party found them, the horse was still standing, his eyes and nose frozen shut. They lifted Hazel up, but only her hair was limp. The younger children were alive, but Hazel had died, frozen sometime in the early morning hours.

It seems strange that I can watch quite tearlessly the deaths of hundreds on television in wars all around the world, but am moved to sobs by this story of the brave Dakota girl who

The Ellendale years: Lucille and one of her very
best friends, Betsy Sjerslee—probably 1922 in
their dorm, Dacotah Hall.

Elsie and Agnes on the campus—Probably after 1924.

Flora studying in the dorm—1927 or 1928.

The Burnstad family, 1919. *Left to right:* Mother Victoria (née Day), pregnant with last baby Basil Burdette ("Bud"); Helen, Lorna, Leroy ("Pat"), Norman ("Mike"), Grace (died at 18 in 1925), Iva, Ted, Leo, Ralph, Harold, and father, Christian.

Lucille, at one of her early teaching assignments. She appears to be holding a puppet. (Lettering overhead says "Third Class Standard School.") About 1921.

Elsie's class at Gooselake School. Elsie's note says 1925 or 1926. *Left to right: First row:* Elmer Johnson, Clarence Magrum, Harold Kleppe, Martha Edholm, Ruth Edholm, Charline Pearson. *Second row:* John Magrum, Emery Edholm, Roy Broburgh, Josephine Magrum, Jenny Edholm, and Elsie Pearson.

1926. Agnes, Flora (in the red one of her three Ellendale dresses—the others were blue, and green), Elsie and Lucille.

Lucille, Elsie, Agnes, Flora, Charline—about 1936.

Charline, Flora, Agnes, Elsie, Lucille—about 1933.

Lucille, Elsie, Charline, Flora, Agnes (Kay in tree)—about 1935.
Taken in Napoleon.

Lucille, Elsie, Agnes, Flora, Charline (Kay in window). 1940. Taken in Wishek shortly after Inda died.

Kay and "Benny Blue," the baby skunk found by the CCC boys while planting our shelter belt. About 1935.

Lucille and Kay at Bismarck photographer's studio in a "ping pong"—about 1933.

The finalists (except for Harold Falconer, who came after Otto was gone.) Left to right, Oscar Meyer, Otto Bauer, Jake Johnson, Leo Burnstad. About 1933.

Sitting in grass: l to r., Joanne Hughes, Wallace Pearson, Charles Conner, Charotte Kent. *First row l. to r.:* Otto Bauer, Agnes Meyer, Aunt Esther Conner (Uncle Marshall hidden behind her), tall gentleman and his wife probably Oscar Meyer's parents, Elsie, Inda, Charlie. *Third row, l. to r.:* Two hidden, unidentified men, Aunt Mabel Pearson. Agnes and Oscar's wedding, July 3, 1932 at the farm.

The girls and their new husbands.
(Wedding dates noted):
Lucille and Otto Bauer—
April 24, 1924.

Elsie and Leo Burnstad—August 3, 1933.

Flora and Jake Johnson, September 12, 1940.

Charline and Harold Falconer, March 12, 1941.

Agnes and Oscar Meyer, July 3, 1932.

Charline is an aunt—
finally. 1931.

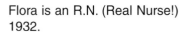

Flora is an R.N. (Real Nurse!)
1932.

The League of Republican Women of Washington, DC dinner at The Statler Hotel, February, 1948. Five seated at center table, left side, moving right: Congressman George H. Bender of Ohio, Lucille's boss, Kay, Lucille, Elsie, and Leo.

Kay (then Thornton) and Lawrence Welk, 1975.

Agnes hosted a family reunion at her home in Denver in 1944 where the last photo of all five sisters together was taken. *Left to right,* Charline, Flora, Agnes, Elsie and Lucille.

would, as the balladeer sang, *never see the young girl dreams her 16th year would bring.*

Charlie was moved, too, but not to tears. He was moved to build a special sled for his daughters, his own private invention, a thing of practicality if not beauty. Flora called it *The Hollow Horror.*

It was a hollow cube of windproof compra-board with a seat for three (if you were small), mounted on sled runners. It had a set of shafts attached off-center so that one horse pulling it could walk in the wheel-track instead of the center of the road, which would be filled with snow and where horses didn't like to step anyway. This way the horse and the sled runners both had tracks to move through instead of piled-up snow.

The Horror had one small plate glass window in front on the driver's side. Unfortunately it was only ten inches high and twelve inches wide, large enough for the driver to see where the horse was going (barely) but not for a passenger to see through as well. There was one sliding door for an exit, and a two-inch slot just wide enough for the reins to come through. While it offered protection from the cold, the Horror did not provide a cure from the resultant seasickness that the small passengers suffered as they rocked, bumped and churned their way to school through mounds of snow, bobbing up and down up and down up and down like surfers in an ocean. All the wretched passenger could do was peek out now and again and catch a glimpse of Dolly's rear end with her hooves kicking up snow, and hope not to throw up.

As the older sister, Agnes managed to pilot the little cube of transportation with professional aplomb, while Flora sat bleakly at her side praying for an end to the miserable rides to County School #3. A few years later, when Elsie was teaching at Goose Lake School five miles from their home, Charline was one of her fifth grade students. It was Charline's turn to be the unhappy passenger while Elsie played the masterful pilot to and fro, ten miles a day in all. On some evenings as they flew home over the drifts, the moon would already be up, and Charline, peeking out occasionally, would see clusters of rabbits sitting in large circles on the hillside, as though performing some winter lapinary Druidic rite.

Only Lucille managed to escape The Horror by having left home before Charlie invented it. Inda was sure the mon-

strosity would tip over and trap the girls inside someday, but
Charlie was sure it wouldn't. It turned out he was right — and
whatever else they felt, the girls were always warm enough,
completely sheltered from the rapier-like winds.

Besides its predilection for causing *mal de snow*, The
Horror was the target of derision and the other school kids'
tricks. Light in weight, it offered no resistance when some of
the bigger boys would seize the rear end and rock it (and passengers) up and down, back and forward, impeding the girls'
departure from the school-yard. The girls foiled their tormentors though; they jump-started the horse with a sudden jerk of
the reins, which left the boys sprawling, chagrined, and out-
smarted.

Flora-the-soft-hearted always felt sorry for the horses
that had to wait for the students all day in the cold, with no
water in a barn that no one ever thought to clean. They had to
stand patiently...

*on an ever steepening slope from rear to front. At that time
we knew nothing of the Augean stables housing three thousand
oxen which had not been cleaned for thirty years. No Hercules
ever came our way to rescue our school barn.*

One winter was so bad Charlie and Inda decided that Elsie
and Charline should live at the Goose Lake school, sometimes
for as long as a week at a time where Elsie taught and Charline
was a student. They kept warm by the school stove, a coal-
burning mini-monster enclosed in a wrap-around shield to
protect the smaller children from getting burned. Charlie set
them up with a small kerosene stove for their minimal cooking,
a folding bed and bedding, a small kerosene lamp to read by, a
milk can full of water and enough food to last them a few days.
Charline remembers they ate potatoes mostly. Charlie also left
Elsie with his favorite .22 rifle which she was afraid of in the
first place, and didn't know how to use in the second place, but
he insisted. He probably thought if she waved it about with a
wild look in her eye, that would scare away any would-be
prowler.

When she thought their food was running out, Inda
would walk up to the mailbox by the Norwegian Lutheran
Church and wait in the cold for the mailman to hand him a

packet of fresh pork or a loaf of bread and ask him to "stop by Goose Lake School and leave this with the girls." He did it, too.

The coldest week anyone remembers was the week in 1932 when Grandpa Conner died in Montana. His funeral was to take place in Bismarck so Elsie and Charline took the Soo train to Bismarck from Napoleon. I always supposed that the name of that local locomotive was a bastardization of the Indian name "Sioux," but the historical fact, I find, is that the full name was originally the "Minneapolis-St. Paul and Sault Sainte Marie Railway." "Saulte" being pronounced "Soo" the Dakota populace found the abbreviation more user friendly. At any rate, the Soo was the train the two girls rode from Napoleon, which was where Elsie was then teaching, and Charline was rooming with her while going to high school. The train was supposed to leave at 6 p.m., but didn't even arrive at the Napoleon station until 10 p.m. with the two young women refrigerating in the unheated depot the whole while. After finally boarding the train for the 80 mile ride, they shivered and shook through all the stops necessitated by snow drifts heaping up on the train tracks which had to be shoveled off before the iron horse could start up again.

They finally arrived in Bismarck about 4:00 a.m. exhausted and miserably cold. It was all they could talk about. Inda's younger brother, Uncle Tom Conner, a Montanan like Uncle Charley (with whom Grandpa Conner had been staying at the time of his death) put them to shame, though.

"Cold? You think this is cold? I'll tell you about cold. In Montana we sometimes have to prop open our cow's eyes with twigs to keep them from getting frozen shut."

Charline regaled her friends and classmates with this horror story of coldness as gospel for years until one day Inda overheard her tale and laughed until the tears came. "Oh that Tom," she said helplessly, when she could speak again. "That's a Tom story if ever there was one."

It was Uncle Tom, too, who was the source of the stories about Indiana Hoop snakes which we all believed and re-told until some of us were grandmothers. Even Inda had believed it. Hoop snakes, according to Tom, could put their tails in their mouths, propel themselves upwards and start rolling away from any potential danger. I suppose this story could compare to the "snark hunting" gotcha-myths of my own childhood. At any rate, the Hoop Snake fable is sufficiently alive as to be found in a good dictionary.

If the word "blizzard" could grip the Pearson hearts with fear, "prairie fire" could paralyze them. Charlie's early experience on his father's farm in 1887 taught him a lesson that caused him to be almost paranoid on the subject of fire. It was a lesson repeated to the girls so often they wearied of it; each retelling of this cautionary tale increased their own paranoia.

Charline reports...

Prairie fires were always in Papa's mind when it got dry. Sometimes we were alarmed by phone calls about one in the area, and then the folks would go out and plow a couple of furrows around the place and get out gunny sacks and barrels of water ready to go — but we never needed them. Someone always stopped the fire before it got to us, though once lightning struck the little Norwegian Lutheran church close by our house and caused a fire in the steeple. Papa put it out.

Flora adds...

What a fear of fire was instilled into us! What admonishment we received about being caught in a prairie fire. "Lie down in a roadside ditch," we were told, "until the fire passes over." I lived my life in fear. When I was told to herd the sheep in the harvested field east of the granary, I would hollow out a hideaway for myself in the strawstack where I could avoid looking out at the horizon where there could be a lurking prairie fire.

And when there really was a prairie fire, neighbors would come streaming out with wagons of barreled water, shovels, mops and blankets. Mama would open canned jars of tomatoes, set out dishes, and plates of bread and butter to be ready for exhausted fire fighters. Darkness would fall and then the lines of fire showed more plainly, greedily devouring the area's livelihood. In the morning, blackened pastures, charred fence posts and the smell of burned-over fields faced us.

Fire-prevention memories cling to me from about 1936 on — the extreme caution that Inda and Charlie took before leaving the premises. We would be ready to leave, all duded up for a trip to Kintyre or Linton (going, perhaps — oh rapture unconfined — to a MOVIE, for Charlie doted on Will Rogers and

I on Laurel and Hardy.)

Every object in the house that had had a fire connected with it from kerosene lamps to the big black coal range in the kitchen had to be double-checked. The final safeguard was to fill the tea kettle and pour water liberally all around the range, even though the ashes had been well damped down. One never knew when some errant ember might spring to life and begin a fire. The floor watering left the kitchen soggy, but we never came home to a disaster.

The source of Charlie's fears was his own experience in April of 1887 on his father Olaf's farm, described by his baby sister Annie in her later years, obviously wood-burned indelibly into her memory. It was a fire accidentally started by a neighbor who was burning straw stacks.

Dad (Olaf) and Charlie were working about the barn when I saw a fire creeping along the hills west of us. They did not think it very serious, but the wind increased in speed. Dad built a fire guard but the wind became stronger and the fire jumped the guard. Soon the barn, with cattle, horses and sheep enclosed, was threatened. The roof was covered with straw and the fire soon licked it up.

Charlie had intended to head out to help the fire fighters so he gave his mother his all-purpose jacknife to cut the tied animals loose so they could get out of the barn.

But Mother got rattled and disappeared with his knife, so he ran into the barn himself to free the stock tied to the mangers. Meanwhile some were trapped and died.

Charlie got most of them out, and managed to get out of the barn himself, just ahead of a cow that fell dead in the doorway behind him. Of this, Charlie writes himself...

I could hear my father calling me to come out. As I passed by a calf he raised up on his hind legs and got his front feet in my pocket. I got loose from the calf but by this time I had trouble getting out of the barn as a load of burning hay stood between me and the front of the door; my hair and eyebrows were singed but I got out. The barn burned and we lost some stock.

He doesn't mention his long, beautifully silky mustache, though it too suffered more than a little singeing. His hair, eyebrows and mustache eventually grew back.

Annie's story continues...

Someone gave me a lively young horse to hold out on the plowed ground beyond the house. Brother Oscar was some distance away trying to keep the frightened sheep from venturing into fiery areas. Charlie took our faithful and speedy horse "Tom" out to give young Oscar instructions on how to guide the flock. When Charlie and Tom got back to the house and barn, Tom's muscles were quivering from running so fast.

The fire had come near to the house. Our root cellar, which was against the north side of the house, was covered with a straw mixture, and had to be watched. The fire smouldered on and on and there was a steady watch all night.

At some point in that awful night Dad was so tired and discouraged he told Mother to go in the house and get his purse containing $5.00 and "just let it all go." But mother didn't give up. The next morning we saw our old well lying wide open; it had to be fenced off. (It had been walled with wooden boards and when they burned, the well lay exposed. Charlie had stayed up all night to keep the stock from falling into it.) A curbing was erected and a pulley, rope and buckets put into it so the watering needs could be met. It was a dismal sight and only a pioneer immigrant could muster the needed courage to start over again.

Courage they had, and helpful neighbors. Olaf's determination returned. He rebuilt — not one, but *two* new barns.

19

Waiting for the harvest, and the time of reaping,
We shall come rejoicing, bringing in the sheaves.
Knowles Shaw / George A. Minor

In the evenings in late summer after the milking was
done, the Pearsons frequently assembled on the back porch to
make ice cream. As they sat, taking turns cranking the old
wooden ice-cream freezer packed with ice and salt, they gazed
eastward over the ripening wheat fields. Slanted sunlight
descending at their backs highlighted the wheat against the
slowly darkening blue sky. A ceaseless wind caressed the
goldening whiskered grain, which ebbed and flowed in the
breeze like a silken, undulating prairie ocean.

Charlie had cut and hauled ice the previous winter from
the deep, wide creek which meandered through the haymeadow
until winter, then froze quite solid. Charlie would cut great
blocks from it in two-foot cubes. He would first chip into the ice
with a hatchet, then saw the blocks out with a great saw.
Finally, using a large grappling hook like a giant forceps, he
would extract the blocks of ice, push them up a ramp onto a sled
on runners. When the sled was full, the horses would bring
home the frozen load.

Amazingly, the ice stayed frozen solid through most of
the summer, thanks to the insulation of a straw-lined six-foot-
deep pit Charlie had dug for this purpose, and covered with a
small wooden A-line roof. That little wooden shed, just steps
away from the back porch, served as an outdoor refrigerator
where the Pearsons could put milk or food or whatever needed
to be cooled into a tin container (like an empty Karo sirup pail),
scoop away a little hole in the straw, which had been piled at
least a foot or two on top of the ice, seat the container, and let its

contents keep wonderfully cold.

A portion of this frigid treasure, sawed out, and pounded into manageable pebble-size lumps, was now freezing the vanilla, lemon or coffee flavored mixture (eggs, cream, and sugar) that Inda had prepared earlier in the day. If, by any happenstance there had been a hailstorm, the sisters ("opportunists that we were") would race out with all the pans in the house to gather the hard little pellets — sometimes as large as snowballs — and use the garnered hail to use in place of Charlie's ice-house ice to freeze their dessert.

As they looked out at the cattle in the corral and the promising wheat, Charlie would take the occasion to call the girls' attention to their most fortunate lives and remind them that they were living *the very best life:* good home, good crops and NO DEBTS. As they eagerly spooned the creamy treat into their waiting bowls, they could only agree. No one spoke aloud of wishing there was enough extra cash around to have store bought'n clothes instead of an older sister's hand-me-downs, already handed down at least once before. The cash was there all right, but safely locked up in the Holy of Holies — The Bank — where it was now officially *Principal*, never to be touched, but only revered as a Producer of Interest. Only interest could be spent without retributive disgrace.

The NO DEBTS part of his evening commentary evinced his very real gratitude — verbal gratitude being a way of life at the Pearsons. "First you give thanks," was Inda's admonition, then it was okay to ask for more. The verbal thanks from the senior Pearsons went more frequently to God than to the girls, who were taught early to "trust God and pick up the hoe," if they wanted to get ahead in life.

Charlie and Inda were never more grateful than during the worst of the Depression when farmers were lucky to get 25 cents a bushel for even the best of wheat — and theirs was the *best*, Charlie assured his small audience. They grew rye, barley, corn and oats for the livestock, but it was hard wheat, Markus wheat, that was their good cash crop. Incidentally, the girls could tell you that in the summer time before it was ripe you could go out into the field, break off a head, rub it in your hand to get the grains out, and then chew it into a wonderful gum.

Giving God plenty of credit, it was nonetheless thanks to Charlie's own dawn-to-dusk daily labor together with the dawn-to-past-dusk labor of indefatigable Inda and their beautiful, husky young daughters that they were solvent.

A story, probably apocryphal, is revived now and again about a pair of touring urbanites who once drove by one of the Pearson neighbors' billowing wheat fields, and gasped in awe.

"Isn't it wonderful what God has done in these magnificent fields?" cooed the lady in silk chiffon, having stepped daintily from her touring car to get a better view of the awesome scenery.

"Yup," agreed the farmer laconically, "but you should have seen it when God was doing the farming all by Himself."

Early in the fall the Pearsons would be heading into threshing week. This was the payoff week for half a year's endeavors in the fields. There would be more feverish work than ever, but it was an exciting time of year for them all; adrenalin was spritzing into the bloodstreams and dreams of a big harvest galvanized them further.

As soon as the wheat was deemed ripe, Charlie would go to the wheat fields with the binder, the machine which cuts the grain, ties it into bundles with twine and disperses the bundles at intervals a few feet apart. Then it was up to the daughters of the house to do their part, which was to gather the bundles two at a time, stack them together to build a teepee shaped cone so that if the rain fell on the bundles it would slide to the ground and not rot the grain. There the bundles would stay until the threshers came.

Threshing could take place any time after the wheat had been cut, until mid-winter, even after snowfall, but at the Pearson farm it was usually done by October.

For days beforehand, when the threshing was expected to take place, Inda and the girls would put any whirling dervish to shame as they spun about the kitchen creating cakes, pies, cookies, doughnuts and bread to feed the voracious visiting harvesters. There would have to be enough to feed the 12 to 15 extra hands (all neighbors pitching in to help, as they did each for the other, taking turns within the community) because it was expected that a *hearty* snack (we called it "lunch" — both morning and afternoon offerings) would be provided after two and a half hours of hard labor starting at 7:00 a.m., or after the dew had dried, whichever came first. Snacks ("lunch") consisting usually of doughnuts and heavily sugared and creamed coffee, came at 9:30 every morning, dinner at noon, snacks at 4:00 and supper after dark, usually as late as 7:30 or 8:00, for their day was sun to sun.

None of this cooking could be done too far ahead of course, for all the cookery would go stale if for any reason the "rig" of neighbor Eino Jutila (whose sister helped Flora with guitar-lessons) was delayed by a breakdown of the rig, or if one farmer's crop took longer than expected to be harvested, or if it rained hard. The latter was not too likely but still a consideration, for if a drenching rain wet the waiting bundles, threshing would have to be delayed a week or more until the grain was good and dry.

Eino's early threshing rig was powered by a steam engine. This required the constant attention of a "fireman" plus a large water wagon, which periodically had to be dragged down to a nearby creek where a new supply of water would be hand-pumped into its round belly. Eino would have to be on duty by 4:00 a.m. to "get the steam up" in sufficient force to activate the loud rumbling, grumbling, shaking separator. Any conversation in its vicinity had to be conducted in shouts.

The young ladies of the household not only had their own usual chores plus Charlie's during the week of threshing, but the extra cooking, extra table setting, extra dishes to wash and the lugging of the snacks to the fields. It is not too surprising that they were delighted to be drafted into helping with the threshing itself, for then they would be treated like one of the men, sitting at the table with them at dinner and supper, and *being waited on* by their sisters.

The threshing machine itself was a monstrous dinosaur-contraption that shook and rattled but did not roll except when moving to its next appointed farm. Making loud clattery noises while it worked, it stood in a pre-selected spot and waited for the visiting members of the threshing crew, who brought their own haywagons and their teams of horses and their pitchforks, to go and collect the shocks from the fields. They loaded them into their wagons and brought them to either side of the snarling, ravenous threshing machine, which first gobbled the bundles into its cutter in order to cut the twine that held them together. Those cutters were mean things, and in later years we all heard the horror story of when Flora's husband Jake — as a very young man and long before she met him — was out running a threshing machine and while adjusting something on the machine, lost his balance and fell into the cutter, thereby almost losing a leg.

After cutting the twine, the threshing machine somehow flips and flails the grain from the chaff, and the grain pours thunderously like water released from a dam into a long chute pointed into a waiting grain wagon box. It blows chaff and straw through a very long pipe, whereby it builds up a huge, shining pyramid of golden straw — some of which would be used the next winter as bedding for the milk cows.

Charline relates that when she was quite small — about eight years old — she and Flora teamed together in the wagon that received the newly naked kernels of wheat.

You had to disperse the wheat as it poured from the pipe from the rig — the chute had an elbow on it that would turn so you could have the wheat run out the elbow and thus fill one end of the wagon, then thrust the length of pipe as far as it could reach to fill the other end. If you did it right you weren't supposed to have to shovel much. However, you had a big shovel for that job, and unhappily I needed it all too frequently. A good yield made it hard to manage the pipe right, because the grains came flowing through fast and furiously, making glad the heart of the farmer, but often consternation in the heart of the little girl in the wagon box.

Centering the wagon for the grain to flow into was a precision task for Papa and sometimes the grain fell a few inches too far one way or another, so he would have to back and fill until he got it positioned just right.

The only time I ever saw Papa run the horses was coming back to the rig with an empty wagon he had just unloaded. He would come pell mell because he was afraid my wagon would get too full and grain would start sliding out of the grain box before he could get the empty wagon in place. In later years he used a big truck, but at first he only had two wagons, and it was nip and tuck to get back sometimes, because one wagon held more than another and it took longer to unload back at the granary than the other one.

Papa had a tiny grain elevator with an engine that helped unload the wheat into the granary, which was pretty far from the wheat field where the threshing was going on. He had to start the engine, watch the grain unload, shovel it in, keep track of his team, watch how high his bin was getting not to overfill it, and get back to the rig before the other wagon filled up. It took skill and timing.

Sometimes Eino Jutila (the rig owner) would help me out a bit the first year or two I worked alone. He supervised everything that went on around the rig. I think he wanted to see what kind of yield we were getting, too.

Flying ants were a nuisance and a real disaster to me. If it were windless, they would come in swarms, get in my eyes, down my neck, up my nose, in my mouth — terrible. Even a small wind would help so much. Mosquitoes were never a problem at that season — the hot dry weather would have pretty much settled the daytime ones. The only ones that persisted came out at night, and by that time we were safely home.

Even though we loved to eat with the threshers, they never talked. Never said anything besides "Pass the bread." They took a full hour off at lunch — horses had to have a full hour rest at noon. Afterwards they would leave the table and go outside for their smokes. Papa never allowed smoking inside the house or anywhere near the barn, especially the hayloft. For good reason.

Anyhow, about the smokes. First the men had to roll them, which is quite a trick. They would select a little rectangular piece of cigarette paper from a wad they kept in their overall pockets; next, undo the strings of a little muslin bag holding the tobacco, then shake the smelly brown stuff onto the center of the paper. With one hand holding the paper and tobacco, with the other they put the tobacco bag up to their mouth and with their teeth, pulled the strings together, and replaced the bag into their overalls. They rolled the cigarette one-handed, and left the last quarter inch or so. That quarter inch they licked like a stamp and then rolled it over to make it stick. Then it was a cigarette.

These weren't Marlboro men dreamed up by Madison Avenue. These were the real thing: North Dakota threshers, come to help the Pearsons prove that they were indeed living the *best* life there was, on the *best* farm in the *best* of all counties in the *best* of all states in the *best* of all countries, the U.S. of A.

20

Tell me, pretty maiden,
Are there any more at home like you?
There are a few, kind sir,
Simple maids, and pretty too...
 High school operetta

Despite strenuous work in the fields, the five sisters were
ever aware of their gender; they strove for femininity with a
determination worthy of Scarlett O'Hara, a fervor propelled,
surely, by the programmed Virginia DNA of their great-grandmother Delilah Wingfield. Great care was taken by each of them,
even in the blistering summer sun, to wrap up in long-sleeved
shirts buttoned to the throat, wide straw hats with kerchiefs tied
under chins, gloves and a liberal application of lemon cold cream,
lest a latent freckle pop out or — ugliest threat of all — the
blazing sun hit the back of the neck and one become (shudder) a
red neck!

There were household potions, of course, for almost every
ailment, but the really important remedy to know was something
to remove any evidence of having worked in the sun. Should
some hapless Pearson girl be foolish enough to expose her fair
skin, a poultice of cheesecloth laced with buttermilk and un-
cooked rolled oats helped bleach her out quickly. Rolled oats
soaked in water also provided healing for chapped hands in the
winter. So did tallow, or mutton fat, the source of our modern
and expensive lanolin emollients as well as other beauty products.

In the rare instances where a real sunburn needed attention, out came the vinegar bottle to help relieve the pain. Unfortunately, it also helped tan the skin, and the miscreant was
tsked-tsked severely by her sisters for carelessness, and went
around smelling like a pickle for a few hours, woefully checking

to see how reprehensibly brown she was turning.

On those rare but welcome days of rain, the girls dropped whatever they were doing and ran to place any handy receptacle — usually milk pails — beneath the rain spouts at every eave of the house to collect the precious drops. Not for drinking, mind you (the five wells on the farm handled that concern nicely), but for hair-washing. Rainwater contains no minerals to bind with soap, a marriage which tends to make a muck that resists dissolution. The cherished rain leaves hair soft, silky, manageable, and significantly more beautiful. When rainwater was not available, which was most of the time, their final hair rinse had a bit of vinegar, if you were brunette or lemon juice if you were blonde.

It is hard for me to comprehend how Inda managed it, but somehow she was able to have all five daughters in white dresses for Sunday School on a weekly basis, dust storms and twisters notwithstanding. To keep up with the washing for that family of seven, even after the advent of the Maytag, must have been a nightmare, but even the *thought* of washing in hard well-water and ironing *five* white dresses each week using the heavy old black flat irons leaves me exhausted.

Inda had a special technique for softening water. She had a large oval copper boiler that she filled with water and heated on top of the range. When it was boiling, she added a can of lye (sodium hydroxide — *very* caustic) which reacted chemically with the minerals that make water hard. Pretty soon whitish particles would rise to the top; these she skimmed off, and magically the water became cooperatively soft, even to the point of eagerly allowing the soap to whip into suds.

That copper boiler, incidentally, met an unfortunate demise. It's Flora's story:

After the laundry was done, Mama would take the copper boiler outside beside the back steps, upend it, let it drain out, lean it up against the house, bottom-side up. A good place for it, you would think. Unfortunately, one day somebody had left a sharp garden hoe right beside it. The villain of the family came by and without any malice whatever, saw the hoe, saw the smooth bottom of the boiler and just had to connect the hoe — with vigor — onto the bottom of the boiler. That scientific experiment resulted in a huge gash in the boiler bottom. It must have been the urge to do some personal research on what would happen IF....

I don't remember getting punished for it, either. I do remember standing and watching, as an innocent bystander of course, when a traveling peddler came by. He had bought it, and was taking it away to re-cycle for its copper content, but first demolished it with a big sledge hammer so it wouldn't take up so much room in his wagon. I watched that demolition with properly detached scientific interest. I don't know that I ever admitted I was the culprit, but I'm sure they must have known. You see what I mean about my being the family criminal. No remorse, either.

When it came time for ironing, Inda placed a board padded by an old quilt and a used sheet across the backs of two chairs. This make-do contrivance offered, sadly, no open end to receive any tube-shaped piece of clothing, calling forth ingenuity and patience on the part of the ironer.

Black two-pound flatirons, which I use as book-ends today, were brought to just less than scorching heat on the kitchen range, and tested for the right degree of hotness with a drop of spittle. Then a white dress was unrolled from its starchy dampness in the big clothes basket and the task begun. As one iron cooled down, it would be replaced on the range, and its twin substituted to iron the next dress.

Elsie once recorded an incident that would rend the heart of any family laundress. Her story was really about Charlie and his cars, but included a white dress anecdote.

It seems that the family's first automobile was a 1909 Autocar that Charlie got second hand in 1910 or 1911 from a man in Iowa, acquired without spending a cent. There had been an ad in the *Emmons County Republican* (now the *Emmons County Record)* offering a used car in trade for a used Hart Parr engine or tractor. In the same paper was an ad offering for sale a Hart Parr engine that needed fixing. Charlie knew all about Hart Parr engines. He had used one for several fall seasons for threshing — the local farmers had joined together to get the equipment, and Charlie was the one who operated it and kept it running — and well it should run perfectly for he worked long, long tiring hours on that equipment. Once after a repair session he came home and slept soundly for a continuous 24 hours. Since he had never done such a thing, Inda became alarmed and finally woke him.

In any event, he traded some mechanical object he was willing to part with in exchange for the ailing Hart Parr engine, made its necessary repairs, and shipped it to Iowa. In turn the Autocar was shipped to Charlie, though not until after the spring thaw and the roads had dried, because all roads were wagon roads and cars were "put up" in the winter.

Thus did he parlay his first and much envied automobile without an outlay of a cent of cash, his absolutely most favorite way of doing deals. Soon curious neighbors came to admire and inevitably hint for a "little spin" in the horseless carriage, gladly given, but he never offered to let anyone else drive it. A few years later he allowed Inda's baby sister, (the girls' Aunt Faye) to drive one of his later acquisitions. Somewhere along the line Faye had learned a few auto repair skills, so none of the girls, less mechanically inclined, begrudged her this privilege.

The only other driver of a Charlie-car in anyone's memory was Aunt Laura's husband, Uncle Arnold, reputed by some in the family to be "crazy as a bed bug" anyway, who helped himself to a solo drive when the Pearson entourage was visiting in Bismarck. He climbed into the driver's seat, managed to get the car started and sailed off with the confidence born of inexperience. Unfortunately, he didn't know how to stop.

"Whoa," he shouted helplessly. "WHOA, DAMMIT I SAID WHOA." Car and driver shot around and around and around the block, Charlie chasing after them yelling instructions, to no avail. Uncle Arnold and the car that didn't know the meaning of WHOA kept on going until the auto finally ran out of gas.

Oh, but that first car, the Autocar, was a handsome thing. Shiny bright red, topless, with a wood frame, it seated five: two in a divided front seat and three in the rear. Handsome black leather seats, they were. She (why are cars always "she"?) had a gasoline capacity of 10 gallons and boasted two cylinders with horsepower of twelve to fourteen. The rear seating was actually two seats, divided by a third flat seat that lifted up for a rear entrance; the hinged door between the seats swung out. The older girls felt it was appropriate for the baby to have that least comfortable seat.

No royal princesses ever felt more grand than the

Pearson girls of Fairview Farms, circa 1911 — Lucille, Elsie, and the then-baby, Agnes, as they rode to church in royal splendor on sunny Sundays. Sunny or not, they had to be prepared to stop for Charlie to fix a flat tire with patches and boots. That too has a tale.

Tires in those days contained a separate rubber inner tube filled with air, providing passengers with a relatively bumpless ride. If the car ran over a nail or any other sharp object, it could pierce the tough casing all the way through to the inner tube, thereby letting the air escape and the tire go flat. Then the driver had to get out, jack up the car, remove the tire and affix rubber patches to the inner tube with a special adhesive to make it air-tight once more, and then pump up the tube again with a hand pump.

If the outer tire was damaged, it was treated to a "boot." This consisted of a part of another outer tire, a piece about 12 inches or so in length, laid inside the ailing original tire. When the inner tube was replaced in the outer case and all pumped up, the pressure of the tightly-fitting inner tube would keep the boot from wandering. All of this was an objectionable routine guaranteed to rile the driver and unnerve the passengers.

One memorable Sunday, the Autocar was waxed to a high sheen and sitting at the front door. Charlie had driven her up from our multi-purposed granary, the center of which doubled as the garage, and she was parked, awaiting her regal passengers.

(On both sides of the center aisle of the granary were the high grain bins. The center aisle was open on both the west and east sides for parking Charlie's latest auto. On the grain-bin sides, horses pulling a 3-tier grain wagon could walk in through one slightly ramped side, stand still while Charlie shoveled grain from the bin into the wagon, and then walk on out the other ramped side, ready for the long haul to Kintyre.)

On that fateful Sunday morning, after parking the new car in the front yard, Charlie dashed into the house to change from his work clothes as Inda brought the three girls out, all gussied up in their white Sunday best.

"Now stay in the car," she told them. "Papa and I just have to finish dressing, and then we'll be off to church."

The three daughters sat primly in their accustomed seats, the older girls no doubt mentally rehearsing their memorized Sunday School texts. They were soon startled from their private reveries to hear a loud *splat* followed by an enormous bellow of rage, chagrin, and an all-out yelp of distress from Agnes, who had somehow managed to topple from her royal perch out of the back-hinged door and into a waiting mud puddle. She emerged the very image of an outraged chocolate-covered kewpie doll. Elsie didn't relate whether they got to church at all that day.

There must be something about white dresses that invites disaster. Charline's tale of woe concerns the day she put a sheet of fly paper on one of the dining room chairs, promptly forgot she'd done so, and plopped spanking clean white-dressed self firmly into the center of the sticky, gooey mess, full of already-dead and/or dying flies. Lucille had the onerous task of getting the mess off both Charline and the dress, but how she did it is left veiled in lost memory — probably with a solution of bleach for the dress, or an ammonia or vinegar solution to de-glue Charline, though kerosene was an often-used solvent.

There was no magical *409* in those days, although by the nineteen thirties there was *Bon Ami* (pronounced *Bonn Am I* by North Dakotans). This sturdy competitor to *Old Dutch Cleanser*, used for cleaning up sinks and bath-tubs, was more appealing to me because of the fluffy yellow baby chicken on the container with the slogan "hasn't scratched yet." *Bon Ami* seems to be enjoying a renaissance, though *Old Dutch Cleanser* is now only a page in cleanser history. *Borax,* with a 20 mule team parading around the face of its black and white box with red trim touting its power, was also a popular cleanser still seen today in some supermarket shelves, especially in rural areas.

I don't know how early my mother delved into the magic of make-up. Before leaving home for Ellendale Normal School, I suspect, for she fell in love with the movies and all their glitz at an early age, although she didn't didn't actually get to see very many. Nevertheless she devoured movie magazines with the avidity of a philosopher in search of the True Meaning of Life.

Wild red berries such as chokecherries could sometimes serve to color the lips — how else could you attain the "bee-stung" lips of Clara Bow if there were no lipstick available to you? Burnt ends of matches could darken lackluster eyebrows, and an egg-white facial made even a smooth complexion more perfect. When the girls took a mud-pack facial, it was real mud. The best was a kind of thick, black clay coming from the Missouri River bottom. This was spread over face and neck and left on until dried, when it was peeled or broken off, leaving a pink, tingling skin.

About ten years later in 1929, while awaiting my imminent birth, my mother Lucille took a beauty school course in Minnesota, where she and my father then lived. My father was teaching; Lucille had also been teaching, but pregnant ladies did not appear in school once they began to "show." Not one to waste time knitting booties, she hit upon the idea of attending a local beauty school, though she never practiced hairdressing professionally, nor ever intended to, so far as I know.

Her younger sisters were the recipients of 'Cille's newly acquired skills as a hairdresser and a few years later, so was I. Deep waves were the fashion of the hour, thus the photos of all the girls during this period show them with very professionally smart "finger waves" made by the pressure of Lucille's fingers, held in place with a slimy sort of gel until dried and combed out.

Not too much later tin clamps or possibly they were aluminum, came into vogue that served virtually the same purpose. These double-pronged pinch clips ranged from two to five inches long and were placed strategically on one's head, held in place with mean little metal teeth. These rows of metal produced layers of firm ridges on the hair, and were much less attractive to today's eye than the finger waves.

Some ladies preferred the look of the new fangled kinky permanent waves achieved by sitting for hours under a huge electric head-piece from which dangled the curlers to which every hair of your head was attached in fifty or sixty white-padded rollers. My mother's horror stories about the clients who came to the beauty school for free hairdos, serving as guinea pigs, who went away with their tresses literally fried to death, was enough to discourage any of the Pearsons from trying this approach to chic hairdos, at least until a few years later when some of the perils of the process had been removed. Flora remembers being terrified of those dreadful monsters because just suppose a fire broke out in the building and there she would be, imprisoned by every hair in her head attached to that dangerous iron helmet.

My own narrow escapes were from the Marcel iron,

which my mother favored, particularly with the advent of
Shirley Temple. A Marcel iron, named for its French inventor
Marcel Grateau, looked like today's plastic-handled, gas-car-
tridge-driven, cordless curling irons, except it was black metal,
and was held over a gas flame until hot enough to curl hair —
and sometimes burned it, causing an aroma not unlike scorched
chicken feathers. This smell I knew very well from being
around when Inda singed the last hairs of a chicken headed for
the skillet. She placed a burning newspaper rolled up next to
the almost-nude body, after the basic plucking had been done, to
make it perfectly free of any offensive fine feathers. Pee-yoo!

The memory of the tedium of standing by our little gas
stove as my mother did her best to help me win the Shirley
Temple look-alike contests is still with me. Her efforts were not
entirely in vain. I got an honorable mention once and my
picture was in *Photoplay*, circa 1936.

There was never time for handicrafts per se in the
Pearson household, but Inda taught all of the girls to sew. By
the time I knew her, Lucille had abdicated the sewing machine
forever, but descriptions of her prior handiwork were handed
down to me by various of her sisters, and Flora commented once
specifically about the confirmation dress she made for her. "It
had a bright sky-blue skirt attached to a white bodice, and then
a sleeveless overblouse made of the same blue fabric. She even
found me a yellow artificial flower to wear on my left shoulder
that morning."

My mother would never have called her creation anything so pedestrian as a "dress." She believed in "frocks," and
the late-twenties-early-thirties photographs of her in light-
hearted chiffon would lead you to believe that she had never
seen the backside of a plow horse.

There was something about sending away for clothes
from the catalogue that made them infinitely more attractive to
the girls than anything their mother could make for them, or
indeed that they made themselves. This was true even though
the catalogue clothes never fit quite so well nor endured quite so
long as those they produced themselves. Perhaps the very fact
that the clothes Inda made lasted (seemingly) forever, and could
be handed down at least twice and sometimes three times to the
next younger sister was reason enough to loathe them. *How*

could Edna St. Vincent Millay write, "No I don't mind wearing other people's things...because if they are things I like, I always feel myself into them until I forget that they actually 'belong' to anybody at all."

Flora relates that her first sewing project was a pair of bloomers with narrow elastic bands at the waist and knees.

Bloomers, being an insurer of modesty, were worn over the girls' union suits — the kind with a back button-up flap on the rear. We always wore dresses to school — never pants. Once my mother tried to get us to wear overalls to school because it was so terribly cold, but do you think we would?? No! But we did wear long underwear (union suits) that came down to the ankle. These were topped by a pair of heavy black stockings with elastic garters pinned to the union suit waist on a reinforced band. Lumpy and bumpy of course, but resistant to the winter cold on the legs.

These union suit monstrosities were favored by protective mothers well into my own childhood, and I remember that the struggle to re-button that back-flap was sometimes more trouble than it was worth. The omission of rebuttoning, however, occasioned even more bulkiness than normal, with the flap bunching down into a little lump inside the bloomers that made sitting in a classroom an experience devoutly not to be wished. Oh for a bit of velcro!

When I was old enough to enjoy the humor of the situation, Lucille regaled me with what she touted as her life's most embarrassing moment: the elastic on her bloomers snapped at a dance one night in the early twenties, and fell to the dance floor. She might well have been performing the *Charleston* I imagined, or some other risqué jazz-dance of the twenties like the *Black Bottom*, or at any rate, one that required rigorous movement on the part of the dancer.

"Mo-o—ther!," I howled, in youthful shock — "What on earth did you DO??"

"I calmly stepped out of them, and danced away as though I had no connection whatsoever with that unspeakable garment."

"Didn't anyone notice?"

"Of course — but no one knew whose bloomers they

were. I pretended to be just as shocked as everyone else, as the whole crowd just danced around them. They went forever unclaimed."

"Everyone remembers things differently," Flora remarked dryly when I repeated this story to her quite recently. "And you must remember that Lucille had a flair for the... well... she had a dramatic imagination."

The way Flora remembers the same story is that it happened to a friend of Lucille's, and the item in question wasn't bloomers (long since abandoned by their crowd in favor of a slim little item called "step-ins" or a "teddy"). The garment lost on the dance floor was a petticoat or slip, but when it fell to the floor, the lady in question danced merrily out of it, her dance partner none the wiser.

Until they were into their teens, the sisters rarely had shoes that might be considered even remotely feminine. Those they wore to school were black, ankle-high and had to be buttoned with a button-hook. Flat, with no heels, they were only a hair's breadth more feminine than the lace-up clodhoppers they tromped around in doing chores. Flora writes ...

When the big Sears and Montgomery Ward catalogues came they were longingly examined by all of us girls, and the outdated ones were ours to cut out our paper dolls from — all the models in their fashionable clothes. When I became shoe conscious I spotted the very most desirable pair in the whole world in the Sears catalogue. Black cuban-heeled satin pumps! No shoe laces! No buttons! Pointy toes!

One evening as my mother was starting up the cream separator, grasping the heavy handle and pull-pushing it, at first very slowly and then with gradually increasing speed, and waiting until the ever-rising pitch, or tone, would indicate the proper time to open the faucet to let milk flow from the big container at the top, I was importuning her to order for me these glamorous pumps:

"Satin pumps, Mama! Real Skinner's satin! It says so right here! And Skinner's is the very best kind of satin!!" — this spoken with an authority which had no knowledge whatever of ANY kind of shoe satin.

What a good thing it was that the person who had assembled the separator parts that day (ME) had not as it sometimes happened, forgotten to put the important float in place — that float which prevented a flash flood of milk all over the floor the moment the spigot was opened to start the separating.

With no flood under her feet, Mama finally agreed to the horrendous price of <u>three dollars and ninety eight cents</u>! She put the yearning foot on a blank sheet of paper on the floor, traced an outline, compared outline to chart in catalogue, determined correct size, and then ordered — two sizes large, of course. (I might still grow.)

At the school program later I clop-clopped about in those elegant black pumps, cautiously not stepping right out of them, peril in every step. No shoes since have been less comfortable, nor more beautiful.

21

Maud Muller on a summer's day
Raked the meadow, sweet with hay...
John Greenleaf Whittier

Come with me now to our haymeadow, the pride of
Fairview Farms. It has never once failed — not even in all the
drought years of the thirties. People came from long distances
to buy hay from my grandfather during the depression, and like
Joseph in Egypt, he always had enough to let others from
parched lands share our bounty. Some folks around here grow
alfalfa to feed their stock, though we never have to because of
the haymeadow. I think the purple flowers in other people's
fields are wonderful. My aunts say alfalfa makes good tea, too.

Right now it is July or perhaps August and the haying
has started. It is hot, hot, *hot,* but we will not mind, for the
meadow is fed by at least five free-flowing, cooling springs —
some sluggish, some spurting. It isn't so hot at the slough as it
is up at the house, and the mosquitoes aren't out yet — at least,
not this early in the day.

One of the springs, which I am not allowed to go near if I
am alone, is very, very deep. Some people even say it's bottom-
less. One of my aunts once told me that long, long ago some
neighbors tried sinking 50 barrels into it. They all went down,
straight down and never came up. No bottom was found!

At some places down at the slough there is just a thin
layer of earth and roots that cover the swampy muck, and if you
jump you can feel the ground quiver and undulate beneath you
as if you were jumping on firm Jell-o. Sometimes our mules,
with their sharp, tiny little hooves, break through the layer of
soil and sink down up to their bellies and Grandpa has to pull
them out. Well, actually the horses do the pulling with ropes
tied around the mules' harnesses.

There is also a long, leisurely creek flowing through our slough, with tiger lilies growing all around it. You will love our creek. It has ducks and snails and frogs and minnows and turtles and water snakes, and clams and periwinkle snails with pointy tipped-shells, and leeches and — best of all, *cattails*! We can cut some of those and take them home with us and put them in vases. After a while, though, they dry out, swell up and shed — just like real cats.

The creek pushes out into a small bay area which we call the swimming hole. On the south bank there grows a willow tree which leans far out over the water, producing the only shade in the meadow. The shade, alas, is over the water. The Pearsons always "noon" at this spot where filling water buckets for the horses is not hard.

You and I are too young to help with the actual haying, but we will at least be counted on to carry food to the hayers. On our way, for it is a goodly hike of about a mile though it feels like more, we might stop to watch a small brown prairie chicken, startled out of her nest by our unwelcome presence. She will try to distract us from her babies clustered near where we have inadvertently trod. She will drag one wing low, skimming the rustling grass, coming quite close to us, pretending she is wounded and trying to make us think we can easily catch her. We can't, of course, for as soon as she has lured us toward her with her soft bird-moans, she will suddenly fly up out of our reach, and we none the wiser as to where her babies are now. We will laugh and plug along, lugging our load of edibles between us. We wouldn't have wanted to catch her anyhow.

Did you know that mother snakes will sometimes swallow their young if they think there is danger, and then later regurgitate them after the menace has passed? I've never seen one do it, but my Aunt Charline told me this is true. Maybe we will see one today — but it better not be a rattler.

We will for sure see plenty of jack rabbits as we walk along. They won't pay much attention to us, but they won't let us get too close to them, either. Their ears and their hind legs are much, much longer than a cottontail's, which is how you can tell the difference. They don't really run — they levitate. Maybe they're part kangaroo.

There will be quizzical gophers watching and a chorus of meadowlarks to serenade us as we wend our way. Who could not be happy when a meadowlark sings? The gophers can be one of two kinds: one is fat and slower than the other — he's a solid tan. The smaller kind is slimmer, called Richardson's Ground Squirrel. He will be striped.

Since you are a "townie" I'll explain to you that one should never, ever disturb the eggs in the nest of a prairie chicken, for if you do, she will not return to it. Someone in our family did once, after accidentally plowing up a nest. The unbroken eggs were taken back to the farm and placed under a brooding chicken hen. When they hatched, the little birds didn't live long because they refused to eat the chicken egg mash Grandma offered — and nobody had time to catch enough flies to keep them going for long.

The mash was held out to the babies with tweezers made from the tin strip left from opening a coffee can — another of Grandpa's make-do inventions. He first cuts away all but a small piece with his tinsnips, then bends and folds the remainder so it has a rounded handle at the top, and little pointed tips to pick up a particle to feed the birds by dropping the mash into their gaping maws.

Oops! We almost stepped on a killdeer's nest. Once my Uncle Harold (Charline's husband) was out plowing one day when he was a boy on his family's farm outside Bismarck, when he spotted a killdeer bird sitting on a nest. He stopped and moved it, just a few twigs and the eggs in it, to a spot on the already plowed area, covering the area first with more twigs and grass, so the bird might come back to it. The next round of the field he made, sure enough, there she was sitting on the eggs again. So you see, prairie chickens and killdeers are quite different in their nesting habits.

We are getting very close to the meadow now — smell the wild mint? Here, take a sprig and suck on it as we go. Want to hear about the old days when the girls were still here on the farm, and helped Grandpa with the haying? It wasn't such an easy job, let me tell you.

They would set out early, early in the morning, right after the milking was done and the stock fed, early enough to watch the mist rising from the valley, taking with them a two-quart tin filled with milk — a used Karo syrup can usually, with a tight lid. They all rode together to the meadow in the empty hay wagon, which would be filled with hay in two layers on the return trip that night. A large sling would be laid on the bottom of the hayrack first. Then when the wagon was half full with hay a second sling would be stretched across the hayrack and a second layer of hay pitched in.

When they got home, the top sling ends were fastened to the elevating apparatus on the barn's peak that protruded over the hayloft's big doors. A team of horses attached to the pulleys was driven away from the barn at a right angle, causing the second sling to pull together, and the first load to be hoisted up to the peak, swung into the hayloft and dumped into a high pile for storage. The second load sling got the same treatment.

If you like, tomorrow we can play in the hayloft and slide down the haystack, or swing by our knees on those slings that hang loose above the stack, or jump through the holes above the horses and down into their mangers where the girls pitch their meals of hay down to them from above in the hayloft. That is, if the horses living in that stall are out working, though placid Jane and gentle Maude wouldn't mind even if they were there, munching their lunch. Grandma would mind, though. She thinks it's dangerous.

As soon as the hayrack left the driveway in the early morning, my grandmother dashed out to chop off the head of a chicken, cleaned and fried it with unpeeled new potatoes in the same big pan brimming with butter. A little before noon she would have packed up the chicken and potatoes in an antique wide-mouthed pitcher, all covered with hand-painted pink roses. Also included would always be two big jars of coffee, well laced with cream and sugar, and fresh home-baked bread slathered molar-deep with fresh butter. Some days there would be cold boiled mutton instead of chicken; other days, salami (only we called it "summer sausage") — always a favorite. The smallest girl of the house would be entrusted to make the trip to the meadow at lunchtime, or if even she too were out there working, my grandmother would go herself.

In the early morning after arriving at the site my grandfather had chosen for mowing that day, one of the sisters would walk north the several block distance to Thompson's spring to leave the milk to cool. She would hang the tin pail (with its lid tightly closed) by a cord, and anchor it to a stick shoved into the soft ground, into the constantly bubbling action of Thompson's spring — his being far colder than any of ours.

Oh, but that is a fast-flowing *i c y c-o-l-d* watercress-rimmed marvel of nature. By noon that milk would be so cold it made their teeth ache, a welcome treat for the "nooning," their mid-day break.

All of the machinery for mowing would already be in place, for it was left in the meadow all summer and brought home only after all 13 stacks were completed at the end of haying season. The bullrake and the stacker were moved from our farm to the meadow only by Charlie. Both were heavy and cumbersome and w-i-d-e — so moving them proved a difficult venture, and only Charlie could manage the maneuver. The stacker traveled on sled runners, and had to be dragged along by four horses, making a very effective road block while in transit.

First in the day's routine came the actual mowing of grass, which grew tall — two feet or more. Each day enough grass would be cut to make one 8 to 10-foot high haystack, about 12 feet square, though the stacks varied slightly because of several natural barriers/boundaries, which determined the actual size of each. By the end of the haying season every year there would be 13 perfectly formed haystacks smelling of succulent savories like milkweed and mint, to which our sheep were particularly partial. Those 13 stacks were more than enough for our own livestock to feast on for the winter, plus plenty left over to sell.

Two of the girls drove the two horse-pulled mowers—each of these cumbersome contrivances had a long bar at the side with a sickle on it that sliced like huge, unwieldy scissors, cutting the grass down to a stubble of three or four inches. As the hayers began the day's mowing, grasshoppers came to life and sprang up to greet them, with a few bees now and then, but it was the flies and the flying ants that made the latter-day Maud Mullers miserable. In memory, those same Maud Mullers remember only the beauty of the scenes and scents of that lost era.

As the hay fell, it was left to lie in the hot sun to cure on top of the ground for the next 24 hours. After enough hay to make the next day's stack was cut, the raking of the previous day's cutting could begin. This was done with the dump rake, a machine that had two large wheels; its driver sat up on a high seat, steering the horses along as its widely-spaced teeth, curved in a semi-circle, accumulated and dragged the carpet of dried grass along the ground until its teeth were full. The driver —

some summers it was Inda — would cluck to the horses to get them trotting, for this work was not heavy, and they could speed along, ultimately accumulating all the rolls spread across maybe as much as a block of the mowed section.

By now it would be time for lunch; both hayers and horses were ready for their one-hour nooning. The meal-bringer should have been in sight by now, and as soon as she appeared, the hayers would unhitch the horses from their respective machines and bring them their water in buckets from the creek. Then they were tied to the hay wagon and given their oat bags from which they munched and crunched while the girls sought the only shade in the meadow — under or beside the haywagon, where they would crouch to eat their own lunch.

After dropping the lunch with the hayers, the lunch-bringer would then have to trudge north to Thompson's spring to retrieve the ice cold milk where one of the older girls had left it in the morning. Guided to that spring by Grandpa's pointing finger (like an Indian Scout) and his instructions to follow his finger and look for three tall bullrushes, trying to give her perspective of where they were in today's choice of haying area in relation to the spring. She would then dash off, almost always finding it with no trouble, plunge her hands into that cold, clear water, find the chilled refreshment, and march/plod back to the hayers. Her mission was to run, retrieve, and return before the other girls had unhitched and watered the horses. By now the sun was directly overhead, sending shimmering light that danced across the field and distorted the vision with wavy undulations. No sunglasses in those days, either.

When sated by Grandma's lavish spread, the girls turned on their backs in the stubbly cut grass and peered up into sky so blue it hurt, filled with fast-moving popcorn white clouds. They saw wonderful transitory pictures there, first sharply etched formations, then melting, and reforming into new magical kingdoms. Grandpa was near by, and they could hear him take a long drink of that icy milk, see him wipe his mouth with one swipe of his big hand, and emit his satisfied, drawn-out "Aaaaaaaaaaaah," as he settled back against the hay wagon, brought his straw hat down over his eyes and took a short snooze.

Soon it was time to be up and about again, and to begin stacking. Agnes was the bullrake specialist, sitting atop a seat on the end of a long wooden plank — like a teeter-totter — giving the driver the leverage with which to raise the ground-sliding scooping teeth when it was time to deposit the bunch onto the waiting teeth of the stacker.

Agnes and the bullrake would gather the big bunches of hay — as many as four or more and bring them into position where the new stack was to be started. This first bunch made the base. My grandfather would stand and indicate the border lines for the size and shape — usually square — that the stack should be, and the bullrake would drop its load precisely there. Then he would test the direction of the wind by picking up a few pieces of hay and let them flutter to the ground. Seeing which way they fell, he could then make the proper decision about where the stacker should be positioned — an iffy decision at best, because Dakota winds are notoriously fickle, shifting and vacillating capriciously.

The bullrake would drag, then drop several more bunches (four rolls equal a bunch) of hay into the outstretched teeth of the waiting stacker, to which a team of horses had been hitched. This was the machine that produced the lift to bring the hay above the stack and drop it down, building the stack higher and higher.

The bullrake then backed off to get its next load. Meanwhile Grandpa was standing in the middle of the stack, pitching the hay all around so it would be spread evenly as each avalanche of hay was dropped by the stacker. Thus was the stack pushed and prodded into the desired shape. His was the most strenuous, hottest, flying-ant ridden chore of the day.

He would call "WHOA" to the girl driving the stacker (usually Flora, who was an expert at this) which had been heading away from the stack at a right angle. The movement away from the stack by the horses and driver caused the hay-filled stacker teeth to lift from the ground, and his WHOA was the signal for her to stop the horses with a jerk so that the stacking arm with the teeth coming up with the load of hay on it would dump right over top of the stack — or the back or the middle, if the proportions were going askew. This called for precision teamwork between Grandpa and the driver plus instant obedience from the horses. Simultaneously Grandpa evenly distributed the layers of hay in the best possible formation to resist rainfall.

If the horse-power were coming from the mules, it could get problematic; mule reputation for independence of thought and action is not pure myth. One late afternoon during haying season it began to look like rain — so it wasn't too surprising for Inda to see our mules, Jack and Fritz, who had the stacker assignment that day, hove into sight. She was standing on the front veranda watching to see if the hayers would make it home before the rain started. What *was* surprising was that Jack and Fritz were walking alone, rather quickly, with no one behind them holding the reins. The two truants had just decided enough was enough. If it was going to rain, then it was time to go home.

Chasing right behind them, trotting as fast as a work-horse can trot, was Babe with Grandpa astride — Babe being one of the horses out on the day's assignment. Bringing up a far-distant rear and walking, was Agnes, helping along a very pale Flora.

What had happened was that the double-tree on the stacker — the bar to which horses are attached to something they are going to pull — had come loose and flipped backwards to hit Flora directly in the chest, knocking the breath completely out of her, though fortunately breaking no bones. Jack and Fritz seeing an advantage in this trouble, took the rest of the day off, though I understand there was some retribution in the barn not too much later in the afternoon. Charlie was not one to be sassed by a pair of mules.

That was no doubt one of the many times that my grandmother had occasion to remonstrate with my grandfather about letting the girls do heavy work in the fields which she strongly disapproved of. And that was also no doubt one of the times that he lapsed into Swedish with his gentling *Tust now, Gamla* (dear one) to calm her.

We've almost reached the haying fields, my townie friend, and we will be rewarded for bringing lunch to the hayers — they will invite us to eat with them. We will play by the creek until time to go home with Grandpa on the haywagon. He will be bringing home a load of fresh new hay to the barn and we can lie back in the middle of the hay, or sit up high, balancing on the edge of the wagon where he sits, driving Jane and Maude. Maybe he'll even let us hold their reins part of the way. Did you know that in Swedish a load of hay is called a *jag*?

22

All work and no play
Makes jack.
Anonymous quipster

My scholarly Jewish husband (who is as work-obsessed as he thinks I am) contends that my preference for gainful activity over what is generally considered "play" is a result of having been drenched at baptism in the waters of the "Protestant Work Ethic." He may be right. Certainly the Pearson heritage contributed to this tendency, but it was not *all* work at our farm.

The Pearson sisters have recorded tales of many outings, some of them productive but some of them occasioned just for recreation. I would rank trips with Charlie to Kintyre for shopping at Falgatter's General Store about tops in their estimate of fun, if the number of times Falgatter's is mentioned in various of their letters and reminiscences is any measure.

The master of this little domain, Myron Falgatter, was held up to the girls as a paragon of virtue: a self-made man. Short, stocky, pink-faced, energetic, affable — the Kintyre storekeeper was touted by Charlie, in great admiration, to have subsisted mostly on oatmeal and buttermilk while acquiring his college degree, simultaneously maintaining a full-time job. None other than the redoubtable Myron himself was the source of this tale of culinary deprivation and hard work.

Equally admired was Alice, Myron's wife, who was the girls' idea of perfect beauty and ideal graciousness. In my day she maintained a presence at the store along with Myron, but she is best remembered by the girls more for her beautiful garb, walking up Kintyre's dusty Main Street always wearing white gloves.

The chock-full Falgatter emporium (a shoe-horn could not have wedged in one more saleable article) was the epitome of *The Country Store*, as memorialized by an anonymous poet, to whom I cannot give proper credit since he/she is nameless, but surely he/she must at one time have visited Falgatter's:

> *Far out beyond the city's lights, away from din and roar,*
> *The cricket chirps of summer nights beneath the country store;*
> *The drygoods boxes ricked about afford a welcome seat*
> *For weary tillers of the ground, who here on evenings meet.*
>
> *Here everything from jam to tweed, from silks to ginghams bright,*
> *Is spread before the folk who need from early morn till night.*
>
> *Tea, sugar, coffee (browned or green), molasses, grindstones, tar,*
> *Suspenders, peanuts, navy beans, and homemade vinegar,*
> *Fine combs, wash ringers, rakes, false hair, paints, rice, and looking glasses,*
> *Side saddles, hominy, crockery ware, and seeds for garden grasses.*
>
> *Lawn mowers, candies, books to read, corn planter, household goods,*
> *Tobacco, salt, and clover seed, horsewhips and knitted hoods,*
> *Canned goods, shoe blacking, lime and nails, straw hats and carpet slippers,*
> *Prunes, buttons, codfish, bridal veils, cranberries, clocks and clippers*
> *Umbrella, candles, scythes and hats, caps, boots and shoes and bacon,*
> *Thread, nutmeg, pins and Rough on Rats, for cash or produce taken;*
>
> *Birdseed, face powder, matches, files, ink, onions and many more,*
> *Are found in heaps and stacks and piles within the country store.*

Charlie would usually allow himself to be persuaded that he needed one or two of the girls to ride with him in the Model T on his weekly shopping foray to gather necessary staples, and the little group would chug happily off with Inda's list of requirements in hand. Sometimes, though, the sisters had to stay home, as Flora wrote in one of her "remember when" letters to Agnes....

We were not always sweetness and light, were we? Now I am looking at us in the harvest season. The grainfield east of the house has been bindered — the bundles are lying in a row. You and I know who are going to gather them up into shocks — BUT — Papa is "going to town." Kintyre means grocery store, which means a treat of candy in a white sack arrayed with thin stripes of purple and green. WE WANT TO GO TOO! Papa says, "No, you stay home and shock." Glumly we go out to the field. Papa says, "What kind of candy shall I bring you?" Achingly, I want to say "a Baby Ruth," that new delight. But we sullenly and coldly refuse his offer. Did it give us some sort of satisfaction to rebuff his conciliatory gesture? I do not remember now, do you? the outcome of our petulance. Did we capitulate when he came home with (I don't doubt) a treat anyway?

Fruit was expensive but Charlie and Inda both felt it was not an extravagance; it was a necessity. There was always a wooden crate of apricots, prunes, dried apples or figs in the Pearson pantry, but the wily shopper Charlie found ways to keep costs down. One ploy was to keep his eye on the stalk of bananas that always hung from the ceiling of Myron's store. When they began to get beyond yellow and almost turning brown, he would say, "Those bananas are getting pretty ripe, Myron. I'll give you a quarter for the whole thing." And Myron, Scotsman though he was, would usually accept. Each thought he had gotten the better deal.

That stalk was then hung in our kitchen. Of an evening, taking turns at plying the crank on the separator until the job was done, the girls would have their reward: a bowl of sliced bananas doused in THICK cream. Charline's memories of those bananas is that they were not only brown, they were BLACK. Inda would coax her to eat the overripe fruit by saying that her father wouldn't even *consider* eating a banana unless it was ALL black. As far as Charline was concerned, that meant they were rotten!

Flora told Connie and Carla in the kitchen interview about Charlie's one-time shopping come-uppance.

My dad always tried to get the best of any deal. One time, though, and I think this must have been during the First World War, he got set back on his heels and he deserved it. He wanted some item that was in short supply because of the war. He always shopped at Myron Falgatter's, but this time his preferred grocer was out of the item in question, so he went across the street east to Gust Scheeler's grocery. My dad spotted the item and tried to buy it. Gust Scheeler speared him with his black, black eyes, and said, "I'm saving that for my regular customers." And my dad for once in his life didn't get what he went after.

When she was quite small, Inda and Charlie took
Charline with them for an after-supper trip to Kintyre. There in
Falgatter's store sat a lovely little wooden rocking chair, just her
size. She fell in love with it on sight. Myron saw the sparkle in
her eye and cannily suggested that she sit in it, which she
happily did, rocking ecstatically the whole time her parents did
their shopping.

*When the folks were ready to leave and looked around for
me, I was pretty slow to rise, and when I saw Mr. Falgatter wink
at me, I just didn't get up and out of that wonderful rocker. It
went home with us, with my mother holding it over her head all
the way because there was no room to carry it anywhere else in
that tiny Model T Ford. It must have been a good year for crops.*

When Flora wrote the sisters a Round Robin sometime
in the mid forties the sad news that Falgatter's had been sold,
they were stunned. No one ever thought that that beloved store
would ever come to an end. (The Round Robin was a letter first
initiated by Agnes, which the girls wrote and circulated all
during the thirties through the seventies. One sister would
start the letter, send it to the next, who would add her bit and
send it on, each adding her contribution and sending it on until
it had completely made the circle. The last to receive it was the
first who had sent it, so she would remove her first letter, write
a new letter and send on the remainder. Thereafter the enve-
lope each sister received would contain four letters, thus keeping the Robin going in perpetual motion, each ultimately getting
to read all of the contributions of her sisters, in a never-ending
circuit. Each would have her own letter back at the end, to keep
for her own files — a convenient diary.)

High on the girls' list of "fun things" besides Falgatter's,
was the annual day of Going to the River (the Missouri) for
bullberry picking — some people called them buffalo berries —
which occurred in the fall after the first frost. Off they went,
sitting up high in the Model T, riding the 30 or 35 miles past
mostly prairie. The girls were always delighted to go because it
meant they got to skip a day of school, even though it seemed
their timing was such that they were always spotted by their
classmates at recess as they passed the school, eliciting unintel-
ligible, but obviously rude jibes from jealous friends as they
sailed by at 25 miles an hour. Charline writes...

When we got to somewhere near the river, Papa always had to find a farmer who would give us permission to pick the berries on his property and permission to open the gates. We were welcome to all the berries we could pick, and it did not matter to the farmer if we chopped branches off the bushes, as no farmer wanted the thorny things. The river changed its bed so frequently, they would be floated away before another year had gone by anyway. Some of the time we were not to pick any of the wild grapes, if they were owned by a farmer who made wine from them. We didn't make wine, though wild grapes made good jelly too and we would have liked to pick them, but we didn't if the farmer said no.

Armed with the permission, we would drive on down a steep hill to the river bottom proper and Papa would spot a likely site to stop and where we could make a little fire for our coffee. Sometimes we picked berries first, but usually we ate first so the berries didn't have to sit in the sun.

After we'd eaten our picnic, Papa would get out a big tarp and cut branches from the bushes; by his beating on a branch, the berries would fall off onto the tarp, loosened by that first frost. Those that did not fall were for me and my sisters to pick off carefully and slowly, avoiding the long, mean-barbed thorns that surrounded the berries.

We'd head home after all the pails and boxes we'd brought were filled. We girls would keep a few in a pail or sack to eat while homeward bound, tart though they were. When we got there, Mama would start right in to make some jelly that night, tired as she must have been. We picked so many, though, some would have to wait for the next day. The mash left from the berries she fed to the chickens in small lots because it tended to make the yolks of the eggs too orange. The pigs got some of the treat, too.

Charlie was not an outwardly demonstrative father. The only time Flora remembers him ever touching her was one evening at about age six, as she came out from her weekly bath, flushed, damp, clothed in her snug cotton union suit. As she scuttled past him, he reached out and easily spanned her wee waist with his large hands. He'd known she was tiny, but he didn't know she was *that* tiny!

Nor did he ever pick us up and croon like Inda did if you

fell down. "Come over here, little girl, and I'll pick you up," he'd say. Sobbing, we'd get up and go over to him, but by that time we didn't need to be picked up. Instead, we might be offered a lemon drop, a sure cure for tears. On the few occasions when we fell down and really bruised a knee or had an injury he would quickly rub the bruise. We might have thought it was just a ruse to get us to forget the bruise, but we had to admit that rubbing did help the pain.

His affection took form in his own Charlie way, for instance, building a kiddy car. Short as he was of any leisure time, one Sunday after Charline had once too often noisily scooted around the dining room on a hunk of wood left over from some stray piece of carpentry, he marched out to his shop, and two hours later produced a wonderful new wooden scooter, the wheels of which came from the remnants of Charline's baby buggy. There was room for both Charline and Flora to scoot if they both sat carefully, but since the wheels came from HER baby buggy, Charline always considered the new toy hers.

One of his most memorable inspirations was an incredible swing that gave delight not only to his own daughters and their swarming swains, but to the myriad of youthful neighbors from near and far, who came to visit the farm over the years, not to visit the Pearsons, but to play on their swing!

Charlie envisioned no ordinary swing for the girls; it was to have ropes so long you could think you were flying up to the moon, or at least to the roof of the barn. No one is still around who remembers The Swing's genesis, but knowing Charlie, we know he made some kind of a deal in which he got "a good swap" in order to acquire two used, enormously tall telephone poles.

Exactly *how* he got the telephone poles into position, we can only imagine. He must have laid them on the ground, side-by-side, about 5 feet apart, fastening them securely together at one end with a sturdy wooden bar in which he had inserted two heavy metal rings attached to long, heavy farm rope.

Near the bases of the other two ends he would have had to dig two round, deep holes to receive and hold each pole upright. Then with a lot of mule power, the poles would be levitated into a vertical position, the bottom ends being guided into the open holes. Finally, once the poles were solidly upright, the holes would have been packed firmly with dirt around each base. The

seat was a wooden board, notched at each end to hold it in place
at the bottom loop of the rope.

The end result, of course, was a quintet of very happy
girls.

Then there was the advent of the binoculars — though
Charlie called them "field glasses." With them he was able to
share with the girls his love of the sky and its mysteries. Flora
says:

*On a cold clear, black night he would mount his treasured
field glasses on a fence post for stability, focus them on a certain
star, then call us to come and look to observe how quickly the
star moved out of the range of vision. He pointed out that it is
not the star which moved, but our own earth as it rotated on its
axis. And we became familiar with the landscape of the moon.
Never, though, did we ever catch sight of one of Lucille's "Semi-
Lunars." But I know they were real!*

Charlie's greatest coup, as far as I was concerned, was
the purchase for the girls of a small city bus, retired from the
Bismarck transportation system. He saw it advertised, drove to
Bismarck, hauled it back down to the farm, removed its wheels
and placed it on blocks out in our grove of trees, where it served
as a playhouse for every child who ever came to our farm.

For me it was sometimes a mail coach and I rode shot-
gun, sitting up high on its rooftop, scanning the horizon for
Indians or Billy the Kid. Once in a while, I was a gold miner,
finding the shimmery stuff hidden under strips of cloth on its
luggage racks (paste dried out, shone bright and sparkly and
one's imagination turned it to gold). Or on a lazy summer day, I
could pack a small picnic, go out to the woods with a book and
sit comfortably in one of the old leather seats, my secret hideaway reading room.

Even Inda's turkeys found the old bus an attraction, and
would use it as a nesting place. One time Charline and Flora
went out there to play, and disturbed a mother turkey on her
nest. Furious, she rose up and beat Charline hard with her
wings, so the girls had to give up their playhouse until the baby
turkeys had hatched.

In the winter, the girls did what they called "skating" on
the bigger of the two frozen ponds northeast of the house and
north of the barn, which they cleared of snow with shovels and

brooms to make the ice skatable. Only Inda and Charlie had
real skates, which clamped onto their shoes, but the ingenious
sisters made a game of running and sliding, seeing who could
skid the farthest from one run. That, to them, was "skating."

Winter games at home were the same ones they played
at school recess, such as *Fox and Geese* when there was a fresh
snow and if enough neighbors came over to play too. If not too
cold, there was always *Pom-Pom-Pull-Away, Prisoner's Base,* or
Run Sheepy Run. On pale moonlit nights the sisters would be
out in the front yard playing moon shadow-tag. Winner was the
one who could step on your shadow, making you IT.

> *RUN, Agnes, RUN!*
> *RUN, Elsie, RUN!*
> *RUN, Flora, RUN! Oh oh, too bad, Flora, you're IT*
> *again!*

Being the tiniest sometimes makes you want to slink off
alone into non-competitive moonlight contemplation — mourn-
ing the fact that tininess also makes you a never-chosen member of any athletic game at school.

In the summer you could wade in those same ponds you
slid across in the winter, provided the cows weren't taking up
the perimeter. They would get hot and thirsty, amble over to
the pond for a drink, then cast a curious eye at the youthful
waders, interloping on what the cows considered *their* territory.
The ponds were equally good for wading, or floating small blocks
of wood and pretending they were little boats. The wading part
was especially gratifying when you paraded around the slippery
edge, squishing your toes through the sensuously satisfying
mud.

Of an early summer evening, you could take one of
Inda's Mason jars and catch yourself a batch of fireflies (one of
Lucille's best talents), and watch them flicker noiselessly beside
you as you consumed the evening's offering of home-made ice-
cream.

Only very occasionally would the girls be allowed to go
down to the swimming hole in the creek that runs through the
hay meadow, partly because blood suckers lived in that swampy
marsh and invariably attached themselves to youthful legs,
making it less than desirable for swimming. Much better was to

be driven in a snazzy new car by one of the older girls' suitors to Lake Pursian north of Kintyre. In the early 20's Lucille, Elsie and Agnes wore swimming suits with stockings attached to the bottom of the legs but Flora and Charline were young enough to just wear whatever old clothes were available. One day, Otto Bauer, who was courting my mother, took the girls to the lake. Charline writes...

It was such a hot day the meadowlarks sat on the telephone lines with their feathers fluffed out for air (birds can't sweat). Of course we reveled that afternoon in the cool water, but did we get sunburned! I think the highlight of my day (was I four?) was seeing my very first water bug, who could walk on water! Or perhaps the best part was afterwards. Otto stopped and bought us all a bottle of NEHI pop at Kintyre on the way back. I always hesitated forever between strawberry and orange, but orange usually won out.

One unique outing was the 1928 Mandan Fair, which Charline wrote about in 1978, her memories so vivid I almost think I was there. The participation of Sioux Indians was what made it such a stand-out occasion.

Uncle Ed was there, too, though he didn't come with us; Aunt Laura rode over with us from Bismarck. Lucille and Otto may have been there, too. I'm not sure. Aunt Laura and Mama stayed together pretty much, and Papa alternated between going with them, and coming with Uncle Ed and me. Uncle Ed took me to see the Indian encampment and there were all the teepees set up just like the pictures. Women tended fires in front of them, raw beef hanging up outside to make jerky (covered black with flies!)
There was a wonderful Indian parade with one Chief riding on a horse with his war bonnet trailing from his head clear to the ground. It was an authentic bonnet and he had earned all those feathers. His face was so old and seamed.
All the Indians wore a combination of skin dresses/shirts and white man's clothing — quite an assortment. The women favored bright colors if they wore white men's garb — brilliant reds, blues, turquoise and greens. Many skin dresses were well trimmed with beads and feathers and other ornamentation.

Uncle Ed gave a couple of the Indian children nickels and they beamed at him.

There was a teepee race, too. The competing wagons — each loaded up with a folded teepee and poles — were driven by a brave, with his wife sitting inside the wagon. They had to drive to a particular spot; then the wife would set up the poles, cover them with the teepee cover; once up, she had to dismantle the lot, putting it all back in the wagon. The brave was sitting poised in the wagon, ready to lash the team into action. The first wagon back to the starting point won the race. One plump woman, about to get herself into the wagon, turned around to hoist herself in backwards. The brave lashed the horses a split second too soon and she landed on the ground. The brave never looked back but raced to the line. I don't remember if the lack of a woman in the wagon disqualified him or not!

Then an unexpected storm came up around 2:00 in the afternoon, and a cloud burst pelted us for about an hour. When it was over we took Aunt Laura home and she took off her shoes and hose to wade into her house from the curb where we left her off.

Papa and Mama were concerned about the farm and the roads so we didn't stay to visit or stop for anything to eat. We got along okay until about a mile and a half from home, though we had to drive terribly slowly after we hit the dirt roads. The gravel ended at Hazelton so we had 16 miles to negotiate the muck. It was slick where it was graded, so we crawled that last 16 miles, but suddenly the car slid off the road anyway, and we had to walk the rest of the way home in the mud.

We arrived after midnight to find the pantry floor inundated with water that had rained in. It had rained hard from the east, and it was wet under the upstairs windows and in the back porch, but the pantry was the most crucial of all. We got together a fast bucket brigade to rescue the bags of flour and sugar on the floor and saved what we could of them. The flour hardened of course.

While Mama and I cleaned up the pantry disaster, Papa went looking for the cows. He found them way out in the far eastern edge of the pasture. He brought them in, milked them and then we all had supper. Finally Papa went and pulled the car home (his brand new car!) with a team of horses. Finally we got to bed. That was a memorable day!

23

School days, school days
Dear old golden rule days
Readin' 'n writin' n' 'rithmetic
Taught to the tune of the hick'ry stick...
Gus Edwards and Will Cobb

There was nothing so revered in the house of Pearson as school and education. Under Inda's tutelage, all of the girls learned to read before they went to school. Inda's reverence for learning (after all, she'd been a schoolmarm) plus her own enlightened self-interest had a lot to do with the girls' proficiency. There was so little spare time for her to read aloud to each girl at whatever age and grade, it was only prudent to get them started early reading for themselves. Luckily for her — and for them — they were all precocious readers and entered school at second grade level.

Flora relates that though the much-touted *McGuffey's Eclectic Reader* was considered by many teachers (120,000,000 copies worth!) to be the best for young readers up to the sixth grade, she was taught by Inda from a green book entitled *The Rose Primer* and from a brown book with navy design, called *Brooks First Reader*. Her reading skills were honed in the winter months while the older girls were in school; mother and daughter hovered close to the big old range as they pored over the primers; then Flora read her daily assignments aloud as Inda went about her daily chores.

Books and learning were holy in that household, and it was Charlie's passionate intent, if not Inda's, who knew all too well the rigors of teaching in one-room schoolhouses, that all five daughters would follow in their mother's footsteps. They often heard him declare fervently that a school teacher was the *most* respected member of the community. After all, hadn't he married one?

Except for Flora, who quietly made her own as yet unannounced plans for her future career, they all followed his plan — for at least a while. Lucille, Elsie, Agnes and Charline each took a turn at teaching, though it was only Agnes who found her true vocation therein, much later in life in Colorado, not North Dakota.

My mother, never much given to explaining herself, once responded when I pressed for an answer as to why she stopped teaching, that she didn't mind teaching — it was having to deal with *parents* that drove her to another field. To my knowledge, she never ever again attended a PTA meeting after she stopped teaching, an inexplicable recalcitrance my grade school teachers found appalling. Nonetheless, her sisters give her full credit for their skills in English rhetoric. Agnes once told me Lucille was the best teacher she ever had, and Flora's expertise with the subjunctive mood, she says, came directly from my mother.

Lucille's distaste for teaching might also have stemmed from the fact that she and my father were teaching in Clearbrook, Minnesota, where the Depression hit the little community hard. There was no money to pay the teachers, but the school superintendent had planted a garden, and he invited all of his unpaid staff to come and help themselves to whatever was growing in his backyard vegetable garden. Unfortunately, the only crop that had done really well that summer was the rutabagas. After that experience it was no wonder that she was disenchanted with a no-pay career. Who could love a diet consisting solely of rutabagas — even if they were fried in butter.

The local teachers in the Tell District were scrutinized by Charlie and Inda to a fare-thee-well at least once a year and sometimes even more frequently. Being school treasurer for most of his daughters' pre-teen years, Charlie was in a good position to know who was who and what was what. Since the two schools in their community, Tell School, or # 3 School (sometimes called East School, but not by the Pearson girls) were equally far away — going on two miles unless you took the shortcut across the pasture — whichever school snagged the school marm deemed to be *the best* was where the Pearson girls were sent. Thus when a certain neighbor girl attained teacher status and was assigned to Tell, weighed and found wanting by the senior Pearsons, the girls were quickly shuttled from Tell to

East, and probably back to Tell the following year. Another unfortunate teacher may have been unacceptable partially because she was my rebellious and willful mother's most special chum, and was thought by the younger girls to be "wild and flashy." The two rebels went on *double dates* with local boys, an activity heartily disapproved by my grandfather.

Not all local talent was given the Pearson thumbs down, however. Young Peggy McAllister, who later married one of the Grunefelder boys, whose mother nursed Charline as a baby, met totally with their approval, and thus she was Charline's sixth grade teacher. Peggy was much admired and considered by the Pearsons to be "one of the best."

In one of her backward flights in time when writing to Agnes in 1994, Flora brought her in memory to the end of a school day at Tell.

From a sitting position facing the blackboard we make a 90° turn to face the aisle as we hear our teacher say "Turn. Stand. Pass." And this we do, grabbing lunch pails from the entry, and then head south down the slope. We reach the east-west road, turn left and up the slope until we have almost reached Levi Thompson's little white house. Shall we turn in? Well, yes, let's.

Short, rotund little Mrs. Thompson with her exquisitely tiny feet greets us happily, sets us at her table, reaches up high into a cupboard and brings out two slender little silver tea-spoons. She fills two white saucers with cooked and thickened prunes, and serves this treat to her receptive (and uninvited) guests. She laughs and titters and urges us to take more. She is enjoying us. We are made to feel we are valued guests, and we behave accordingly with adult decorum, daintily partaking of the proferred prunes with ladylike precision. The prunes do not, however, satisfy our afterschool hunger pangs.

Going on again east toward home we cut across our North 40, walk in the prairie grass, chase a gopher until he whisks down his hole, proceed toward our house, climb through the last fence barriers, walk past our big tree, "Old Shelter," through our yard and into the house. Home at last. Mama has baked bread, oh joy! We each take a thick slice, spread it with thick cream, thus fortified to endure the hour or so until supper is ready.

Another day, another year....this time we have been
attending Number 3 School. We walk homeward on the road
south with Nellie and Rhodie Johnson. Nellie volunteers to take
us into the house of her newly married sister Virginia, the oldest
of 13 siblings: Virginia, Ervin, Lily, Edwin, Nellie, Rhodie,
Arnold, Melvin, Darlene, Alice, Myron Peter, Sonny and Verner.
Virginia has just recently married that handsome Finnish man
with the coal black hair, Oscar Strom. Virginia is not at home,
but in we go anyway, look with awe at her wedding presents
which Nellie displays with vicarious pride. She shows us a nail
pounded part way into the window frame.

"That's where she hangs her wedding ring when she does
the dishes," says Nellie the tour guide.

(Our walks home from school with the Johnson kids were
not always so friendly and peaceful. How, when and why did we
go to war with the Johnson kids?)

Today we have brought to school our new rectangular
lunch pail the folks bought us, with the lid that is a hollow tank
container for our drinks. It is shaped like that famous battleship,
The Monitor, with its revolving turret on top. Mama has filled
that removable top with fresh milk before we left for school this
morning. At noon we drink the milk it held, but General Elsie
(our gentle sister Elsie could have done this??) in a secret strat-
egy has refilled this ship-shaped lunch pail. We have started
marching down the road together with the Johnson army, verbal
warfare escalating as usual. Suddenly Elsie implements her
well-planned coup, hurling her secret weapon from the lunch pail
— a deluge of cold water — at the enemy. Most of it hits Melvin
Johnson. The surprise ploy wins for us the battle. For today at
least.

Elsie is always pretty good at taunting Melvin. Fre-
quently she catches him and rubs his nose HARD with a circu-
lar, squashing motion of the palm of her hand. Not today,
though. The water assault has won the day for us and we are
free to trudge home, happy warriors unscathed by the Johnsons.

That Melvin was always into some kind of trouble.
Remember the day he hurtled head first, with arms outstretched
from the roof of the school's outdoor privy? Teacher ran out of
the schoolhouse to bind him up. She found no broken bones, but
severely burning, aching forearms. With no playground equip-
ment of any kind, how else is a boy to impress the girls and

express his pent-up steam but of course to climb the only climb-
able building around?

As the girls reached high school age, their days as
farmers were almost over. It was necessary for them to leave
home, one at a time. Lucille naturally went first. She was sent
to Ellendale, a town some 160 miles from the farm — too far to
come home for week-ends, ever. The trip to and fro at Christmas vacation, while anticipated with fervor by all the sisters
who attended school in Ellendale — Lucille, Elsie, Agnes and
Flora — was a major ordeal.

Returning to school, they first had to get from the farm
by car to Kintyre where they caught a Soo Railroad local to
Manango. There they had a long wait for a bus to take them
south to Ellendale. The long wait in the depot was a killer. Jam
packed into a tiny station with a large proportion of the
Ellendale student body, they had to endure the cold and no
indoor plumbing facilities. No wonder they didn't go home for
week-ends.

After Lucille's high school graduation, the following fall
she returned to Ellendale, where the State Normal and Industrial School was located. There she took a two-year course
which offered a teaching certificate, and earned the top score in
the annual State exam held in Linton. She then taught in
communities close to home, including a special summer session
at Goose Lake in 1921.

The summer session could have been held for one of two
reasons: either to make up for time lost from bad weather the
previous winter, or equally likely, the school district had run out
of money and could not pay the teacher cash, so she not too
surprisingly decamped. The school board might have offered
her a warrant, but it was uncashable until new tax money came
in. A teacher could legitimately leave before her contract
expired if this were the case, and usually did. Charlie frequently bought up such warrants from teachers and hung on to
them until the district obtained the tax money to cover them.
When he did that, the teacher stayed. Not too many of his
neighbors in the district were as passionate as Charlie about
education, and not so willing to make what usually amounted to
a long-term loan.

As Lucille was yet unmarried, four-year old Charline
also went to the Goose Lake summer session. Charlie believed

in chaperones, no matter how young. Flora remembers eighteen-year-old Lucille and four-year-old Charline flying off in the buggy, Charline's legs stuck straight out on the seat because she was too short for her legs to fold over the seat. About all Charline remembers of her days as a chaperone was that there was a sandbox at the Goose Lake school and Lucille let her play there to her heart's content with her first boyfriend — one Clarence Magrum, an older man of about five.

Sometime after 1924, after my mother and father were married, (they'd met at college earlier, each studying for teachers' certification) they both returned to Ellendale to finish their degrees, borrowing enough money from my grandparents to do so. My mother earned her baccalaureate degree in home economics (the only option for girls to study) and was valedictorian of her class; but her interest in home economics, like that in teaching, soon waned and she would, with Charlie-like determination ultimately be off to greener pastures. She did, however, always maintain her skill at baking bread, and never lost her enthusiasm for scrubbing floors, "because you can see what you've done." Other house cleaning held much less appeal for her, according to sisterly memories.

While Charlie and Inda footed a portion of their daughters' high school bills, it was their rule that college must be paid for by the girl themselves, the idea being that as one girl finished school and began paying back her loan from them, there would be money for the next girl's higher education. When it came time for Elsie and Agnes to go to high school (their choice was Bismarck) they worked for their room and board, like James Whitcomb Riley's *Little Orphant Annie,* doing household chores and baby sitting sometimes for their Aunt Laura (Inda's sister) and sometimes in other Bismarck homes. It was a bleak period in the lives of both of them; both expressed dismay at how little town children knew about *work*, or *keeping house*, or *respect for their elders* (namely themselves.) Later, they too would receive their 2-year course teaching certificates from the State Normal and Industrial School in Ellendale.

Agnes ultimately received her baccalaurate degree in Education from Denver University, specializing in skills to teach the deaf and blind children, including the mastering of Braille, but it was long after her son Gregory had received his medical degrees, and after her 22-year old daughter Gwen had died.

(Lovely Gwennie was a blonde college senior in 1963, about to
graduate with a June wedding planned thereafter. In about
March or April of that year she became afflicted with a trouble-
some cough; the cough proved to be a virulent lung cancer,
which ended her life on her birthday, October 4.)

Elsie began to teach almost immediately after receiving
her State certificate, like Lucille, starting at Goose Lake. Later
she taught in Napoleon. She had always had one wing around
little Charline from the time she was born, so it is not too
surprising that Charline elected to attend Goose Lake where
Elsie was her fifth grade teacher.

Inda's old horse Dolly was long gone, but Dolly the
Second, although well past horsely middle age was still able to
get around with some degree of friskiness, and so the two sisters
drove the 5-mile distance from our farm to Goose Lake School in
Dolly's buggy. Charline remembers one day they wished that
Dolly were not quite so competitive in her matronly years:

*Usually one of the big boys would harness her after
school for Elsie. All he had to do was put on the bridle as she
stayed in harness all day. The big boy who usually did this was
absent one day, and little Elmer Johnson* (not a Johnson of the
Pearson's close neighbor contingent) *all of ten years old and
about four feet high, volunteered to bridle Dolly for us. Elsie was
reluctant, but he assured her he could do it — he did his father's
all the time (he probably did.)*

*Anyhow, he brought the horse and buggy to the school
door and Elsie and I got in; he got on his own horse, his little
sister riding on the same horse behind him, and we all set off, as
we were all going in the same direction for about at least a mile.
Dolly seemed to want to race and Elsie had a hard time holding
her in.*

*"Whatever is wrong with this horse?" she gasped, pulling
and sawing on the reins, as Elmer and Ruthie dashed on past us
(if a plowhorse can be said to "dash"). Our hearts were pounding. Elsie was shouting, "Whoa, whoa, whoa," and I was holding
on to the side of the buggy, wondering if Dolly would turn down
the right road all on her own, because she certainly was paying
no attention to Elsie.*

*She finally slowed just enough to make the turn on two
wheels, and with Elsie still yelling "WHOA," she finally stopped.*

Elsie got out and found the bridle with the bit under Dolly's chin! Elmer had not gotten her mouth open or she'd spit the bit out while he was fastening the strap. But we knew he hadn't done it on purpose.

By the time Charline was ready for high school, Elsie was already teaching in Napoleon, then a bustling metropolis of 1,070, and the County Seat of Logan County. That, no doubt was when Elsie met my soon-to-be-uncle Leo, who was then the Logan County Superintendent of Schools.

For one year, Charline lived in a room there with Elsie and another teacher; the following year there was just Elsie and Charline. It was her sophomore year when Agnes, married and living in Wishek, came down with a severe case of tonsillitis or "quinsy" as it was called then. Elsie was needed to go down to Wishek to nurse Agnes; she was to leave on the Friday train and not return until late afternoon on Monday, thereby missing a day of teaching her class of second graders.

Charline, to her great amazement, mixed with pleasure and stark terror, was called upon by the Napoleon school board to try her fledgling wings as surrogate instructor for a day. To her untold relief it all turned out to be a breeze, and though she might not have realized it immediately, another Pearson teacher had been hatched. Of course, she says, Elsie had left explicit instructions on how to handle literally everything, and Charline followed her lesson plan to the letter. There was only one small unmanageable incident that has stayed with her even to today. Small Sammy Mitzman volunteered at the top of his lungs a very private family matter — exactly what, Charline does not recall. But Elsie commented afterwards that "Mrs. Mitzman would just *DIE* if she knew." History has not recorded whether Mrs. Mitzman ever learned of her son's blithe disinterment of the family skeletons.

After finishing high school in Napoleon, and graduating in a memorable pink taffeta evening dress topped by a short shoulder-cape held in place with a large pearl button, Charline went on to receive a teaching certificate from Wahpeton State School of Science. Soon she would be holding forth in a one-room schoolhouse just as her sisters had done before her. With mother and sisters on hand to pass along free advice plus all the school board piling on opinions and admonitions, Charline

sallied forth into her first career and soon found that experience
was her own best teacher, except for one thing Inda told her
that she took to heart: "Kindness to the children is the most
important thing in teaching — they need it badly, and some of
them do not find it at home."

One other piece of advice she found valid. At a pre-
school meeting the new teachers were warned not to allow
German to be spoken on the school ground (it was a German
community in which she was teaching). Charline did as she was
told, and was later glad she had listened, when she heard about
one poor novice teacher — who was of German extraction herself
which the kids discovered right away. They defiantly spoke
German all year despite her protestations. "Her students lost so
much of their English it set them back a year."

Teaching the three R's was only a fraction of what was
required of the country school teacher. Personal hygiene was an
issue ignored by the families of many of the students, and
Charline felt impelled to improve the methods in her school
room from the way things were done at her students' homes as
well as the way "teacher USED to do it." Her students were
accustomed to washing in the same basin — a before-lunch
ritual (contributing, no doubt to the ongoing problem of "The
Itch," an obnoxious skin parasite passed from child to child all
over the countryside). The problem of lice, equally obnoxious
and pervasive, had to be dealt with too — usually kerosene was
called on to rid a unhappy child of these unwelcome tormentors.

Charline's pre-lunch hand washing system was to have
the pupils hold out their hands over the basin while an older
student sparingly poured a little water and spritzed a dash of
liquid soap, watched them do a quick scrubbing of the hands,
poured a little more water to rinse off the soap, and passed them
on to the next student who was handing out paper towels.

Porting the water from an adjacent farm for the class to
drink as well as for the hand-wash was a privilege vied over by
the older students. It meant getting out of class 15 minutes
before lunch, and required a pair of students to pump and carry
the water back, probably exchanging a few pleasantries with the
farmer if he was around, though they had to be back within the
allotted 15 minutes, or not be allowed to go again.

Most of her students, ranging from the first graders
through the eighth-graders, liked school. Chattering at recess

and at noon made up the largest portion of their social life, for
after school they all had duties at home to help around the farm,
and woe betide the laggards. NO teacher EVER kept students
after school for discipline. Instead she cut short the lunch hour
or recess of problem kids, but even that Charline did rarely,
because "they needed their exercise, and to have some break
from sitting still the long day from 9 a.m to 4 p.m."

Although discipline did not appear to be a problem for
her, she had a few other challenges, such as, well, *smells*.
Brought up in Inda's antiseptic cleanliness, she found winters in
the tiny schoolhouse fetid to say the least.

*In the winter the boys added pairs of overalls in tiers to
keep out the cold. If they got a new pair they put them on over the
old dirty smelly ones. Then when they got home to the chores,
they whipped off the nice new ones. Can you imagine how
odiferous the building became after the stove warmed the room
up? Recess was as welcome to this teacher as to the kids. Many
times she would hold the door open, or open a window to air the
room, even if it were Dakota frigid outside.*

*At the school where I taught, the outhouse had been
incorporated into the building proper. And though it was supposed to be limed at proper intervals, by the time spring came,
the odor was quite penetrating even through two closed doors!*

*Country teachers were ever mindful of the weather and if
it looked like stormy weather, parents would stop by and pick up
their kids. Most of them had walked to school, as did I. Some
had as much as two and a half miles to get there. One of my
girls used the long walk as an excuse to rarely put in an appearance. Once students reached sixteen, they were no longer required to attend school.*

*On bad days one parent would sometimes take half the
school with him in his wagon if they were going his way at all.
Or sometimes on bad days my landlord, who was a member of
the School Board, would take all the class home, piling them up
on top of each other. He'd get them all in his car...teacher too!*

Some students broke her heart. One twelve-year-old boy
was severely retarded and she let him sit and read his primer
over and over and over again, day in and day out. He wore the
book out of course, but by the end of the year he had a 20-word
reading vocabulary.

A little eight-year old girl named Elena needed glasses. Even squinting hard, she couldn't see the blackboard from a front seat. Charline was unable to convince her parents of the problem, so she went to their home with Elena's reader to demonstrate how hard it was for her to read. No, they said. Elena was just dumb. "She is not dumb, she is SMART, and remembers everything she hears," Charline argued. But they remained unconvinced and adamant that Elena was dumb. Several years went by before she got glasses.

Being young and pretty had its own perils, but even those the youthful school marm was able to meet.

Once one of the boys (way past school age) from the farm across the road came over to school to "visit" the school during the day (and look the new young teacher over). The kids looked at me to see what I would do. I decided it was time for the singing session of the day. I then suggested a certain page in their song books and as they one by one found it in the book, gasps and giggles arose as the point sank in. The whole class sang lustily. The song was "Reuben and Rachel" and goes
"Reuben, Reuben, I've been thinking
What a grand world this would be
If the men were all transported
Far beyond the Northern Sea."

The young man went home. His name was Reuben.

Charline more than survived her first year out as a schoolmarm, and even met with the approval of the County School Superintendent, Leo Burnstad, who visited her school twice that year — once in the early fall to see how she was doing, and once in the spring to see if there were any problems or questions and to help her "pass" students on the border line. What she didn't know then was that in 1933 he would become her next brother-in-law.

Flora's graduation from high school in Ellendale is remembered by her as the "saddest day in my life." Her only wish then was to go on forever being a perpetual student, preferably at the University of Minnesota. Instead she reluctantly climbed into the back seat of the blue Model A Ford in which Inda and Charlie had driven to Ellendale to collect her, and she returned to the farm to face the Big Career Decision.

In 1929, Flora, whose native modesty sometimes shrouds the true story, had weighed the prospect of the burden of an educational loan. So thoroughly indoctrinated had she been by Charlie's daily preachment of NO DEBTS, why not, she reasoned, take up nursing instead of teaching? At that time in Bismarck, the Benedictine sisters of St. Alexius Hospital offered three years of first class nurses' training, plus room and board, with no expense to the trainee. Flora claims to this day this was one of the true motivations for her career in medicine. The other? A big nudge from Lucille, who may have secretly wished she had gone that route herself.

A few years later, having been the beneficiary of TLC from St. Alexius Hospital nurses after a surgery he had undergone, even Charlie began to see that nurses, too, have a place of some importance in this world!

It took courage for obedient Flora to come to her career decision, bravery on two fronts: first, knowing it would be a disppointment to Charlie who never let his displeasure go unnoticed; and second, the challenge of overcoming her inordinate fear of doctors. As she reminisced in her letters to Agnes,

Aside from the terror and fear of fire, highest on my list was "going to the doctor." Just stepping inside his building and smelling the Dr. Simon smell was enough to collapse me. When once he was called to our house where several sick ones languished, I saw him approach the victims with his sallow, yellowy face, wire-rimmed glasses, scratchy voice and some sort of doctor weapon in hand. Later I heard Mama calling to me so I could be examined. She called and called. I was not in my bed and I was not anywhere to be found. Long after I heard him take his departure. Long LONG after, I slowly unburied myself from the dirty clothes pile behind Mama's wardrobe in her bedroom. How wonderful to have a refuge when an invasion of terror occurs.

Either she overcame her doctorphobia, or it was less than her fear of debt. At any rate, she stood firm in her resolve and when it came time for her to leave for nurses' training, Charlie graciously supplied $50, because the nurses-in-training worked for their room, board and classes, but they had to supply such items as their own glass thermometers, hypodermic syringes

and needles which were expensive and somehow managed to get
themselves broken with expensive regularity.

*Try shaking down the thin line of mercury in an oral
thermometer; snap the wrist not just right and you have a
thermometer zooming up to the ceiling, and shattering into an
infinite number of glass splinters that defy the naked eye when
you try to clean them up.*

The $2.00 a month she received as a first year nursing
student (in addition to room and board) came nowhere near
covering the tyro's wrist-snapping thermometer fatalities. Even
the $3.00 as a second year student and $4.00 as a third year
student wouldn't have done it, but by that time she was no
longer a novice.

However she came to her career choice, it must have
been the right one, for she never suffered unemployment even in
the lowest days of the Depression, nor did she ever have to apply
or interview for a job her entire professional life. Somewhere
along the line she had parlayed herself a typewriter. Shortly
before her graduation, one of the doctors who owned a clinic in
Bismarck spotted her typing. Result? At graduation day, she
was one of the lucky few who already had a job. She was a
graduate R.N. who could *type*!

Book learning was never in short supply for the Pearson
girls. The Facts of Life, however, were a little more hard to
come by, for evidently Charlie and Inda felt that life on the farm
would teach them anything they needed to know about such
things — at least before marriage. Even what they could pick
up from observation was not totally free of parental editing.
Flora writes...

*Once several neighbor men brought a prancing, snorting,
huge stallion to our barn. Inda made certain that all the girls
were safely in the house and away from the windows facing the
barn, until the much calmer animal came out of the barn quite a
little while later, and quietly submitted to being led to the truck,
going home to his own turf again. I still feel deprived. P.S. We
named the colt Ted.*

Barnyard observation by itself, couldn't entirely fill the bill
anyhow. On one of her frequent stays at our farm, the girls'

young cousin Charlotte (Aunt Faye's baby) brought with her a playmate from Bismarck, to keep her from being lonely. The girls had already left home except for Charline who was a few years older than Charlotte, and not the right age playmate for her. The young visitor Charlotte brought with her was having her first exposure to farm life. Being a kind-hearted soul, she spent most of the two weeks of her visit wielding a broom in a vain attempt to pry the barnyard roosters from sitting on top of the hens. Inda probably didn't get too many baby chickens from her flock that fall.

How my mother came by her store of biological knowledge can only be deduced from the fact that with her early reading skills, she plowed through Inda's *Doctor's Book,* which graphically depicted in full color, a very pregnant person sliced down her center, and showing all her organs and contents. Lucille might then have passed along whatever she gleaned to her next little sister Elsie, who in turn most likely passed it on to Agnes, and so on down the line, although each probably had a go at the *Doctor's Book* herself — with Inda *in absentia*, of course. Whatever else they learned did not come from their parents, but each other.

One night under comforters out on the east room veranda, staring up at the stars, Elsie ventured to explain to Flora where babies came from. Impatiently, Flora said, "Yes, yes, I know all that. What I want to know is how they got in the mother's tummy in the first place." Thus ended that class. By the time Flora was in the second or third grade and a little more enlightened, she and neighbor pal Rhodie Johnson speculated on exactly HOW two humans could arrange contact of the necessary parts.

We drew a picture in which the participating parties were put in a horizontal position, arranging them head to toe, like a couple of old-style rigid clothespins shoved into each other from their split ends. We viewed our imagined technique and shook our heads. Another of adults' oddities, we decided.

When I was five the subject of "where babies come from" was much on my mind, and like the other Pearson girls, when curious about any subject persisted in questioning until I got a straight answer. Riding home in a taxi (I think my first such) I was hounding Lucille about this matter with such intensity and persistence that the taxi driver wearied of it, and as we exited his cab said to my mother, "Lady, I think you'd better tell this kid what she wants to know."

Apparently Lucille took his advice, as I cannot now remember a time when I didn't know where babies come from. Like all the other Pearson girls, I was a born teacher, and a year or two later demonstrated my fund of procreative knowledge to a younger and less enlightened playmate by pretending to extract a doll from between her thighs. Her outraged parents did not appreciate this classroom technique and I was banished from my friend Frankie Jo's for quite some time.

Actually, I guess I didn't know as much as I thought I did. The story of Charlotte's friend trying to defend the hens from the roosters has always amused me, but I must acknowledge that while I knew what the roosters were actually doing, I thought that it was the rooster's biting of the neck of his inamorata that made her eggs fertile.

Lucille had a horror of germs and uncleanness of any kind, and this spilled over to me and turned into terror. I lived for some time quite sure that I would die young of either leprosy or syphilis (which, never having heard pronounced, but only read, pronounced to myself "sy-flississ"). Lucille must have been a little less explicit about how these scourges were acquired than she was about the source of babies, but I was pretty sure it had something to do with strange toilet seats, on which I was not allowed to sit without four layers of toilet paper between me and it.

So far, I haven't died of either disease, and the other sisters seem to have acquired all the information they needed to have had happy married lives, but in no way thanks to the sex education of farm life in the early part of this century.

24

Boyibus kissibus sweet girlorum;
Girlibus likeibus, wantum some morum.
Fatherbus hearibus sweet kissorum —
Kickibus boyibus out of the doorum
Latin class nonsense

I suppose the sisters must each have had her share of
girlish heartbreak over some boy or other; certainly they were
the cause of a good deal of southeast North Dakota male melan-
choly themselves, and snapshots of unidentified suitors abound
in their various photograph albums. Details of their teen-age
crushes are sketchy at best, and my own memory contains only
the men they chose to marry, but there must have been a few
romantic flurries in what my mother might term "sparking"
days before their Mr. Rights were permanently installed, given
the abundance of song books scattered around the piano containing such daring lyrics as

Kiss me quick and go my darling,
Kiss me quick and go —
We'll cheat surprise
And prying eyes
Just kiss me quick and GO!

At some point along the line the girls were exposed to
the charms of the Burnstad boys, who lived in a neighboring
town some forty miles away from their homestead. Burnstad
was named for their Norwegian immigrant father, Christian Per
Burnstad, who like Olaf Pehrson had come to the new country in
search of land and freedom, both of which he found. He and his
bride, Victoria Day, produced a horse-riding contingent of four
girls: Iva, Lorna, Grace —who died at 18 in 1925 — and Helen,

plus seven rugged boys: Harold, Ralph, Mike, Pat, Ted (the ultimate Marlboro man), Leo, and Burdette. The girls all thought that affable, blond Ted, who later became a sheriff in Wyoming and married a beautiful girl (also named Grace) from Colorado, was more than special. Who would not fall for a man with the unselfconscious macho look of a real Dakota cowboy? Agnes, particularly, thought he was "pretty spiffy," but only Elsie married a Burnstad — my uncle Leo, who is described by Flora as "suave." The cheeks of the ordinarily unflappable Elsie reportedly pinked up whenever Leo came driving up to the front door, so the family knew there was serious courting going on.

I am told that my father was a "catch," being a Big Man On Campus at Ellendale Normal, noted for his rich baritone voice, his talent with saxophone and piano, his easy smile, good looks, and fashionably slicked-back shiny black hair, setting off oddly blue eyes with extraordinarily wide irises. The fact that he was a Lutheran preacher's son put him in good stead with my grandparents, and all in the family seemed pleased when a wedding date of April 24, 1924 was fixed. Otto Bauer was just a hair shorter than my mother, who had frequently expressed her admiration for tall men prior to the advent of Otto. That was about the only drawback to him that anyone could see.

Charline mentions Otto warmly in her "memory notes." I have always loved her description of a drive with him to Ellendale one fine spring morning, to fetch one of the other girls — Flora or Elsie. *We paced a duck flying companionably alongside Otto's new car, traveling at 45 miles an hour! Oh but that was a morning!*

Not too oddly, I suppose, given the divorce later, there are no photos extant of my parents' wedding, which took place at the farm with a total of twenty guests signing the small white wedding book remaining among her memorabilia.

Flora recounts as a twelve-year-old her horror when, during the preparation for the feast that was to follow the ceremony, her youthful misdeeds of many years were revealed...

Our large square kitchen table needed to be added to the large dining room table to accommodate all the guests. In order to bring it through the door from the kitchen it had to be tipped onto its side. Watching this maneuver I was shocked to see my criminal past come to light in front of everyone, for as that table

up-ended, out fell a shower of my years of hidden rejects from the convenient recess where I had stowed bread crusts, unwanted meat, carrots and every other vegetable I hadn't wanted.
(No wonder Flora stayed so tiny!)

Following the wedding festivities there was the traditional charivari — a word stemming quite appropriately from the Greek and French meaning "headache." Local folks pronounced it "shivaree," which entailed the shower of rice and a suitable number of tin cans tied to the automobile of the bride and groom, as they chugged and clanked down the country road, followed by other autos chasing behind for a few miles, a noisy but good-spirited send-off for the couple to begin married life.

My parents took their time about producing me, and Charline, who was only seven when they were married, yearned to be an aunt, the same way I ached to be one of the sisters. When Lucille died in 1964, Charline wrote me a long letter, giving me many insights into the closeness of the sisters, but in particular how Lucille dealt with Charline's anticipation of becoming an aunt:

Has anyone every told you how I pestered your parents for years before you were born, impatiently awaiting your arrival? Once Lucille came home after a long absence and brought me a darling little 2-inch doll in baby clothes cradled in a cardboard peanut shell. I was so sure it was an announcement of your impending arrival, I cried when informed you were not on the way. When you really were coming, she brought me a beautiful imitation pink flower with a tiny wee doll, not an inch long.

Agnes was the next to marry. She met my Uncle Oscar while teaching in Wishek, some 80 miles away. Oscar, like my Uncle Leo, was a Superintendent of Schools. Agnes and Elsie both, cheered on no doubt by Charlie, were drawn to men in the field of education. Agnes and Oscar Meyer, like Lucille and Otto Bauer were also feted with a wedding at home on July 3, 1932, with a larger assemblage of relatives and friends.

Elsie was the older, but married Logan County School Superintendent Leo Burnstad exactly a year and one month after Agnes married Oscar. Elsie had been teaching second grade in that Logan County town. Typical of both Elsie and Leo, never wanting to draw undue attention to themselves, they slipped off together (not unannounced, so it wasn't an elopement) and were married in a Lutheran parsonage in Herreid, South Dakota on August 3, 1933. They honeymooned in Waubay and other South Dakota points, according to an article the *Napoleon Homestead* printed two weeks later. The same newspaper commented that Elsie and Leo were the *second* school superintendent and second grade teacher to so wed, their immediate predecessors also having married each other. The paper also reported that the young couple would "reside in the Heisler house south of the court house."

The Heisler house was a trim little white cottage where I was a frequent visitor and where I developed my first full-scale crush on Leo's baby brother, Bud (Burdette) who stayed with them while attending high school in Napoleon. I was five. He was 16. No hope. Never mind — I soon fell in love again with a singing movie star, Dick Powell, long before June Allyson discovered him.

Flora took her time after nursing school about finding my Uncle Jake, though both were living in Bismarck. Her first contact with him was when her nursing school classmate and best chum Gert Wanzek and her soon-to-be-husband Ray Schaefer had arranged for a golf foursome with Jake and his current girlfriend Tina. At the last minute, Tina decided she would rather do something else than chase a golf ball all morning, so she drove away in Jake's maroon Ford.

Gert then called Flora to fill in — and Flora obliged. They were playing nine holes; just as they finished the eighth, and were coming in on the ninth over the top of a hill...

We could see Jake's car parked near the end of the course and Tina sitting in it. As we got nearer she was able to see that Jake was not alone. She became angry, jump-started the car into a dirt raising flurry and roared away in a cloud of dust and chagrin. Later Jake found his car down near his rooming house. That was the end of Miss Tina.

Not much later Jake and Flora had their first real date. I was wildly enthusiastic about their dates, because I was sometimes invited along, and remember well long walks over dusty golf courses, or trudging through prairie grass looking for pheasants, but most especially being taken on my first airplane ride at the age of six in 1936, for Jake was half-owner of a barnstorming bi-plane. And yes, he actually did barnstorm, though I never got to see his show. The word barnstorming, for those too young to think of it as anything but politicians making the rounds, was in those days meant to convey what daring young pilots did in making tours around rural areas where they gave flying exhibitions, did stunt flying, participated in airplane races, and most importantly, sold tickets for rides to curious rural families, which was the real business purpose behind the barnstorming.

What six-year-old in her right mind would not encourage her aunt to marry such a find as this flying ace!

Charline met my Uncle Harold after she had left the joys of teaching in one-room schoolhouses in the country and moved to Bismarck where she and Flora were roommates for a time. Earlier, she had taken a secretarial course at a business school in Wahpeton; under the good auspices of a former Emmons County neighbor named Matt Dahl (who had become a State official) she soon found a "first-rate" (Charlie's word) job in the Tax Department of the State Capitol. (My mother had already found a secretarial niche in the State Capitol building, the only prairie skyscraper in the country then and now.) Harold Falconer was a dashing young bachelor who also worked at the Capitol and was a dead ringer for John Wayne, though my Falconer cousins say they think he was more a Roy Rogers look-alike. Somewhere along the line Charline met Harold in that skyscraping prairie anomaly, and romantic sparks struck.

Paycheck raises at the Capitol were few and far between, and it was a day for celebration when anyone went from a hundred to a hundred and a quarter a month. I couldn't see what all the fuss was about when my mother's stipend went to a hundred and a quarter. What good was just a quarter? Ultimately I learned this meant $125 a month in secretarial jargon. Lucille would continue to brave the 20º and 30º below zero winter winds going to night school, walking the two miles from where we lived to white-haired Miss Digby's shorthand classes, honing the skills that would fulfill her dream and take her to Capitol Hill in Washington, DC, in late 1940.

Until that exodus, however, my mother shared a large

apartment with two room-mates, also State Capitol employees, located only two blocks from Flora and Charline's, so I was a frequent over-night visitor in my aunts' tiny basement studio apartment, underfoot a great deal of the time. One day at lunchtime, I was at their place (school was only three blocks away and everyone went home for lunch) and Charline was home also, waiting for her friend Harold to pick her up and drive her back to work. Anxiously, she pushed me towards an early return to school. I resisted.

"Why so early?" I whined. Finally she explained:

"If you are here, Harold won't kiss me when he comes." That was the first clue I had that Harold was going to be my Uncle Harold.

Flora married Jake, almost as quietly as Elsie married Leo, in a ceremony performed in Bismarck on September 12, 1940, to which only Charline as maid of honor and Harold as best man were invited. Not too much later, Harold left for a new career in California at Douglas Aircraft, but he and Charline had an "understanding." Less than a year later, in March of 1941 just before World War II broke out, Charline drove west with Harold's parents and sister Marion, to marry her love. On March 12, the bride was attired in a navy blue dress with white trimming and matching accessories, and carrying a bouquet of sweet peas, according to the newspaper account. The wedding took place in Los Angeles, sadly away from her home and family. Her life now would forever be in California.

The girls were really gone now. Charlie and Inda were alone at the farm.

25

To everything there is a season...
a time to be born and a time to die.
Ecclesiastes 3: 1

The beginning of the end of Charlie's homesteading was September 28, 1940. It was the day Inda died, appropriately enough with her boots on, metaphorically speaking. She was lying on a cot moved into the kitchen, propped up on pillows (having been told by the doctor to stay in bed), supervising the work of a neighbor's young daughter, who was helping with household chores during Inda's most recent attack of phlebitis. That day it became a terminal embolism.

Charlie was with her at the last. She had asked for a cup of coffee — one of the farm's sure-fire panaceas for whatever ailed you. This time, not only did it not work, but Charlie, in panic, badly burned his hands. In his desire to speed the heating of the coffee, he had set the pot directly on the coals in the range and when he picked it up, bare-handed, the fire had done its work all too well. At the time, he hardly noticed his pain, for Inda was gasping deeply; they both sensed that she was dying.

Charlie the resourceful, Charlie the confident, begged her for some word of comfort for himself, some guidance to him for how he should survive without her. But she was already leaving and could give him none. His lifetime partner and beloved wife died, if not in his arms, very close to them.

Inda was buried where once the church that Olaf built stood guard over the Swedish cemetery. The church building was now long gone (moved to Kintyre) and only the monuments of other graves were there to oversee her remains. Charlie ordered a marble monument, but more meaningfully, planted two pine trees, one for Inda and one for himself. For several years the feeding and watering of the trees seemed to be almost

an obsession with him, but it was a nurturing that paid off.
Those two lone pine trees stand tall and proud today, 57 years
later, defying the elements as they keep a lonely vigil over that
wind-swept prairie graveyard.

Other than the obsession about the trees, Charlie gave
no outward evidence of the depth of his loss, nor that his lifelong
commitment to the homestead was reaching its final days, but
the emptiness of a house that had once rung with the laughter
of five girls, and then held only Inda's calm voice, now gone too,
was more than he could bear.

Swallowing his pride in self-reliance, he brought in first
one young couple who didn't last long, and then another, to help
him run the farm. The final blow came less than two years later
when the pregnant wife of the second couple died, like Inda,
from a heart condition, leaving her husband and Charlie both in
a state of shock, the will to go on farming drained from both of
them.

Sometime shortly thereafter, Charlie made the decision
to sell the farm. "Selling out," the phrase was, as the neighbors
put it. Actually, it was an inevitable step to the next chapter of
his life, a decision the girls could hardly not approve, since none
was in a position to help him maintain the homestead.

By then my mother had achieved what she had set out to
become: an executive assistant for a congressman on Capitol
Hill in Washington; Elsie, married to my Uncle Leo Burnstad,
also wound up in the nation's capitol. Leo was occupied with
something secret for the erstwhile Atomic Energy Commission;
Elsie had found a career as an analyst with the Veterans
Adminstration.

Agnes and my Uncle Oscar Meyer took root in Denver
where Oscar became the Deputy Regional Director for the
western region of the U.S. Post Office; Agnes ultimately ful-
filled Charlie's ambition for his daughters. She returned to
teaching, but of a very special sort. She took intensive graduate
classes, including Braille, in order to teach blind and deaf
children. As expected of a Pearson girl, her grades were at the
top of the class. Perhaps more important, she was acutely
aware of the needs of her special students: she always made a
point of wearing a rustling taffeta slip for the blind children to
hear, and faint, flowery fragrances the deaf could enjoy.

Newly married Flora and my uncle Jake Johnson maintained their residence in Bismarck. (As fate would have it, Flora returned from their honeymoon to hear of her mother's death the day before). Flora was pursuing her nursing career, and Jake, who had left his father's farm to enlist in the U.S. Army where he became a master mechanic, greatly talented at taming things mechanical, never returned to farming. He was for several years the Foreman/Superintendent of the Highway Equipment shops in Bismarck, but eventually owned and operated the *Dakota Autoparts* there.

Charline's husband, Harold Falconer (also a Dakota farmer's son) left the land to put his mathematical aptitude to work at Douglas Aircraft in Long Beach, California. After producing three children, Charline would later once again put her secretarial expertise to work at a school in Long Beach.

No, the girls would not be coming back to help run the farm. Nor would Charlie have wanted them to abandon the paths they had chosen. Charlie's decision was the one he had to make.

Besides the death of his helper's wife (Faye Roberts was her name), Charlie was feeling aches from a broken leg sustained one winter many years earlier from the well-placed kick of a frisky colt, and the onset of what would prove to be an almost crippling arthritis. His preventive action taken twenty years earlier of having all his teeth pulled — in one day, mind you — the popular prescription touted in the thirties because it was believed that hidden tooth infections could be the source of arthritis, hadn't proved out. Having *all* of them pulled in one day, however, was his idea, not the method advised by any dentist. The family remembers that he drove 60 miles to Bismarck one day in the pick-up truck, and returned home that night, toothless and very pale. He ate only tomato soup for some time.

The girls had mixed emotions. They wanted a less arduous life for Charlie, each urging him to make his home with her after the sale was over, but knowing that their birthplace was leaving family hands left them all with an ache in their hearts.

The transfer of the property took place quietly, from Charlie to our Finnish neighbors, the Stroms. Few, if any, of the other neighbors were aware of it.

Only Flora and Jake lived close enough to attend the

auction of the livestock, the farm machinery and the household furnishings of the Pearson girls' childhood. The sale was held on a brisk, sunny Friday in October, 1944. It was to begin at 1 o'clock sharp, Mountain War Time. "Maria Swedish Aid" (the Ladies Aid Society of Maria Lutheran Church) would serve dinner — meaning lunch — according to the flyer sent out all across the southeast and central part of the state.

The flyer touted seven head of horses with harness, 100 head of sheep, 23 head of cattle (13 good milk cows, Jerseys, Red Polls, Shorthorns and three coming yearling heifers from the best cows; a Shorthorn bull — three years old — one spring calf, four fall calves and a heifer, one-and-a- half years old.) Also going, going, *gone* would be the Deering binder, the Moline corn planter, a bullrake, two Deering mowers, two wagons with hay racks, all of Charlie's blacksmith tools — his forge, his post drill, his vise, his anvil and all his carpenter tools, his Model T coupe, the McCormick separator, and the Maytag washer (with gas motor).

Household articles were to go too — dressers, beds, tables, all fraught with the pain of parting; treasures from the side closets in the east bedroom: old schoolbooks, the *National Geographics* collected over 20 years, Charlie's glass negatives, his pictorial history of the girls and uncounted numbers of the area's immigrants who'd made their way to his doorstep to sit for a photograph to send home to relatives across the sea.

Perhaps the most painful to let go were Inda's sewing machine, the big old rocker with the leather seat we'd all been comforted in ... and the Kimball piano.

Once that anguished day was over, and the entire proceeds divided equally among his five daughters (he preferred to watch them enjoy the money rather than to leave it in a will — and after all, hadn't they earned it?), Charlie attacked life with his usual gusto. Retire? No siree! He headed to Bismarck and found himself a job. He signed on as a guard at the State Penitentiary located just outside of Bismarck. "The Pen" he called it.

Those were the days before guards were trained to maintain an adversarial, punitive attitude toward prisoners, or if they were so trained, it didn't jibe with my grandfather's sense of how to treat another human being. Gregarious Charlie soon made friends of his charges, most of whom he felt "shouldn't be there." He would bring home to Flora, her girls and to me, trinkets like plastic rings and bracelets the inmates made from melted down toothbrushes, as well as wooden picture frames for photographs they had given him as tokens of their friendship. He in turn importuned my mother by letter for extra Congressional campaign give-away calendars so the inmates could keep track of the days. No inmate would go without a calendar if he could do anything about it.

He continued his early rising and lengthy daily walks all during his years as a guard. He thought nothing of walking the several miles from the Pen on the outskirts of Bismarck to Flora's home, disdaining ride offers of friendly motorists along the way. One morning he arrived at Flora's doorstep at 6:30 a.m. with the intention of using her phone immediately to respond to an ad he'd read in the *Bismarck Tribune* classifieds the day before. Flora remonstrated, and finally convinced him that even if the sun was up, 6:30 was a little too early in the morning to telephone town people. As far as Charlie was concerned, it was the shank of the day.

Finally, seven years later, when the arthritis became too much for him, he reluctantly retired from his latter-day career, and made his primary home with Flora and Jake, though he allowed himself to be persuaded to visit the other far-flung Pearson girls on an occasional basis. He toured the West, took the healing waters at Thermopolis, Wyoming, picnicked in the shadows of Colorado's highest mountains, took his first airplane ride piloted by grandson Gregory, viewed the historical buildings and documents in Washington, DC, hiked through Civil War terrain and visited Inda's grandmother's "plantation" in Boones Mill, Virginia.

But come September, no matter where he was visiting, it was time to go "home." Home meant Flora's and Jake's 4-plex apartment in Bismarck, where he could count on Flora to cook like Inda, and Jake to take him pheasant hunting, and occasionally ask him to do a repair or two or give mechanical advice out at Jake's "Shop."

Charlie would hint broadly that the best pheasants were to be found in Emmons County, and of course if they dropped by the old homestead, the Stroms would undoubtedly load them up with fresh eggs, butter and heavy cream to bring home. Jake never said no. He, too, loved those nippy fall days when the two of them quietly made their way into a grassy field of prairie tranquility, hoping for signs of one of those gaudy rooster pheasants, with their brilliantly plumed bodies, but sometimes having to settle for the trill of a cheerful meadowlark.

Toward the end, Charlie's arthritis kept him from being able to climb the Johnson's steep flight of stairs any longer. And so it was that he died peacefully in his sleep on April 24, 1960 at the age of 84 1/2, at a Baptist home in Bismarck, thus complying approximately with Agnes's pronouncement of our family's dying habits. (Agnes herself achieved 85 years, one month, three weeks and 3 days.)

While living at the Baptist Home he had focused his attention on religious matters — sharing his simple and literal spiritual beliefs with his compatriots, and converting at least one Baptist we know of to his own customized version of Luther's teachings.

Although not significantly ill, by everything he said and wrote everyone knew that he believed it was time to go — and he never wanted to be late. He had had no fear of death, but seemed rather to be looking forward to the next chapter, hands lying folded across his chest, as if he had been ready and was just waiting.

Among the memorabilia he left, the girls found a page from his childhood autograph book, somehow salvaged from the fateful day of the auction, and later translated for them from the Swedish in which it was written:

> *Tell, No. Dak.*
> *Nov. 1 1896*
>
> *Dear Karl (Charles):*
>
> *Do your best on this earth as you travel the road of life. Later I will meet you in Heaven where the flowers are always blooming and there will be peace and happiness.*
> *Your Mother*
> *Karna Pehrson*

If Karna's description of Heaven proved correct, there would be for Charlie fields of wild prairie roses with their faint, spicy aroma, acres of spiked goldenrod and seas of orange tiger lilies. Delicately striped in bengal black, they would be hiding coyly in wind-swept meadow grass, but oh, dear Walt Whitman, we so hoped, as you put it, that there would be lilacs and star and bird twined with the chant of his soul.

Smell the lilacs for us, Charlie.

Epilogue

Deep in my heart is a song—
Here on the range I belong
Drifting along
With the tumbling tumbleweeds
"Tumbling Weeds"
—Bob Nolan

The farm is gone now. Well, maybe not gone, really, but terribly different. Agnes wrote me tersely, "Never go back." Flora later wrote why.

She hadn't been back herself for many, many years, but on impulse one Sunday morning in the nineties, she and our cousin Charlotte (the daughter of Inda's baby sister Faye) and Charlotte's husband Bob Barchenger, made the trip from Bismarck to the old homestead.

Eight years before my sojourn at the farm Charlotte had also been left in Inda and Charlie's care at a critical time in her mother's life. Little "Ludie" was too young in 1927 to know that her father was dying from cancer, Aunt Faye too distraught and emotionally burdened to care for both her ailing husband and three-year-old daughter.

The whole family counted on Inda and Charlie to nurture their youngsters in times of crisis — everything from orphan lambs to small girls like Charlotte and me — and sometimes small boys like cousin Charles (Uncle Marshall and Aunt Esther's younger son) whom they sent to the farm to visit all one summer when they thought their older son Jack was dying. At any rate, Charlotte too, became an almost-Pearson girl, cosseted and protected by the other five, as I was. She, too, remembers the long vigils at the roadside mailbox, sometimes in the heat and dry wind with only an occasional meadowlark, grasshopper or prairie gopher for company. She shared the same hope I had — would there be a letter from Mother, containing perhaps a dime or a stick of gum?

Flora wrote about that drive back with the Barchengers:

I had long wanted to make this trip, but was not brave enough to venture out by myself. We all happily skipped church, had a Spanish Rice brunch at my table and then left for Emmons County. We took the River Road going down, and I got to see again some of the many places Jake and I used to roam, and the hills we climbed. (River Road follows the Missouri on the east side.)

Oh Kay, our Native Americans wisely say, "You can never step in the same river twice." I thought of that as we approached the farm and saw nothing as it once was.

As we came along the highway and looked south for the farm, something looked very wrong, and then we saw that our big barn was gone. It gave us an empty feeling — no big red sturdy barn with its two huge cupolas — one wearing a golden sheep weathervane atop its ridgepole, and the other a golden prancing horse that swung on a pivot, always pointing with an arrow the direction the wind was coming from — how could OUR BARN have weathered away and shambled to the ground in the short time since I was a child! Such shocking things must be turned away from and disbelieved!

That barn is really still there, I know, filled with fragrant hay-slough hay on the second floor, where sparrows chirp on the sling rails, and old Silver beds down her numerous batches of kittens.

Such change — and we all resist it, don't we? The house has been altered — many windows removed, the old back stoop gone and replaced by a new garage. There is dark gray siding now, our familiar eggshell paint is gone. The grove of trees that sheltered us so many years is now scraggly and sparse, done in by too many years of bad drought. The northwest and southwest "turning in" roads have been replaced by one dissecting line in the center, and the airy yard of my childhood is filled with sheds and farm equipment. A large sign warns BEWARE OF DOG and a shaggy white barker came bounding out to the road as we drove slowly past. And drive PAST we did.

The lovely pasture hills to the west are still there, so that much I still have.

But I do go back, Flora. And you are right. The big red
barn is still there.

I never know what will trigger my trips to the farm. The
last time it was a two-inch ad in the *New York Times*.

OWN YOUR OWN
NORTH DAKOTA TUMBLEWEED
Original or sprayed gold
Send check or money order to:
Tumbleweed, Box 141 (Rural Rte. 1)
Carrington, North Dakota 58421

What an extraordinary idea, thought I to myself, wondering why on earth someone in North Dakota would think
Manhattan cliffies would want a tumbleweed, plain or gilded.

"Why, *I* would," I realized — though not sprayed gold. I
clipped the ad with the intention of sometime sending it off as a
mailbox stuffer for the amusement of some appropriate corre-
spondent and thought no more about it.

In the wee hours of that same night I woke, my heart
pounding hard and loud with excitement. I am having sharp
flashes of total recall, so sharp it seems intense reality, not
memory. I am at the farm. I am wearing my favorite seer-
sucker playsuit with brown squares centered with yellow and
white, a silver-colored buckle at the midriff. I have exhausted
all of my usual efforts at solitary self-entertainment.

A few mud pies sit baking on the steps of the back stoop
in Mason jar lids, decorated with dainty orange wild flowers.
Grandpa is nowhere to be seen, so I can't follow him to the shop
and watch the bellows fire up the forge. I am tired of my
clothespin dolls, and the hollyhocks have gone to seed so I can't
make doll faces from their undersides. I've already collected the
eggs from the chicken coop at Grandma's behest right after the
rooster woke me.

It is Saturday morning, so the girls *might*, just *might* be
coming down from Bismarck for the day. Grandma must think
so too. She has chopped off the heads of three chickens, now
jumping headless about the back porch steps in their final death
throes. I know that I will help pull out the loosened feathers
after Grandma has scalded them with a full tea kettle of boiling

water. I hate the smell of those wet feathers, but the fried chicken with pan gravy makes it worth the disagreeable odor.

Now it is about 10:30 and I am already planted at the end of the front drive, peering vainly to see if there is a cloud of dust on the road beyond the Norwegian Lutheran church where Tickle Hill makes its big dip, and where, if you are riding in the car, an obliging uncle will speed up just before he reaches it so that when you glide down, your stomach drops, just like a roller coaster.

It's really too early, but they MIGHT come early, though eleven or twelve noon is more realistic...but is it, is it, *is it*? Yes! It is a cloud of dust! But no, a side-paneled truck is turning down the other road to that Finnish family....why doesn't their name surface? The Stroms. Yes, that's it, the Stroms, where Grandma says they take baths in a little house where you sit with hot rocks and pour water on them and you get clean from steam and sweating.

But oh yes, yes, there's another cloud of dust and it's coming our way. They're coming, Grandma! *THE GIRLS ARE COMING!*

Index